3 8002 01777 686 7

Muslim Women of Power

D1615158

Also available from Continuum:

In Search of Jesus, Clinton Bennett
In Search of Muhammad, Clinton Bennett
In Search of the Sacred, Clinton Bennett
Interpreting the Qur'an, Clinton Bennett
Muslims and Modernity, Clinton Bennett
Studying Islam, Clinton Bennett
Understanding Christian–Muslim Relations, Clinton Bennett

Muslim Women of Power

Gender, Politics and Culture in Islam

Clinton Bennett

continuum

Continuum International Publishing Group

The Tower Building
11 York Road
London SE1 7NX

80 Maiden Lane
Suite 704
New York NY 10038

www.continuumbooks.com

© Clinton Bennett 2010

All rights reserved. No part of this publication may be reproduced or transmitted in any form or by any means, electronic or mechanical, including photocopying, recording, or any information storage or retrieval system, without prior permission in writing from the publishers.

British Library Cataloguing-in-Publication Data
A catalogue record for this book is available from the British Library.

ISBN: HB: 978-0-8264-3638-2
        PB: 978-0-8264-0087-1

Library of Congress Cataloging-in-Publication Data

Bennett, Clinton.
  Muslim women of power : gender, politics, and culture in Islam / Clinton Bennett.
     p. cm.
  Includes bibliographical references and index.
  ISBN-13: 978-0-8264-3638-2
  ISBN-10: 0-8264-3638-2
  ISBN-13: 978-0-8264-0087-1 (pbk.)
  ISBN-10: 0-8264-0087-6 (pbk.)
  1. Women politicians—Islamic countrie˙ –Case studies. 2. Muslim women—
Case studies. 3. W   I.   C   Title.

Coventry
City Council

CEN*

2010007106

3 8002 01777 686 7	
Askews & Holts	Oct-2012
909.09767	£22.99

In memory of

Ratna-Gorva Ma Sushila Sarker, 1942–2009

Contents

Maps, Images and Boxes

Boxes

Abbreviations

AKP	*Adalet ve Kalkinma Partisi* (Justice and Development Party – Turkey)
AL	Awami League (Bangladesh)
ANAP	*Anavatan Partisi* (Motherland Party – Turkey)
AP	*Adalet Partisi* (Justice Party – Turkey)
BAKSAL	*Bangladesh Krishôk Sromik Aoami Lig* (Bangladesh Peasants, Workers and Peoples League)
BNP	Bangladesh Nationalist Party
CHP	*Cumhuriyet Halk Partisi* (Republican People's Party – Turkey)
CIA	Central Intelligence Agency (USA)
DP	*Demokrat Parti* (Democratic Party – Turkey)
DPD	*Dewan Perwakilan Daerah* (Regional Representative Council – Indonesia)
DPR	*Dewan Perwakilan Rakyat* (People's Representative Council – Indonesia)
DYP	*Doğru Yol Partisi* (True Path Party – Turkey)
EU	European Union
GDP	Gross Domestic Product
GEM	Gender Empowerment Measure
HDR	*Human Development Report*
IDEA	Institute for Democracy and Electoral Assistance
IOJ	*Islami Okiya Jote* (Islamic Unity Front – Bangladesh)
ISI	Inter-Services Intelligence (Pakistan)
JI	*Jamaat-e-Islami* (Pakistan; Bangladesh)
ML	Muslim League (India, Pakistan)
MPR	*Majelis Permusyawaratan Rakyat* (People's Consultative Assembly – Indonesia)
MSP	*Milli Selâmet Partisi* (National Salvation Party – Turkey)

NGO	Non-governmental Organization
NU	*Nahdatul Ulama* (renaissance of scholars – Indonesia)
NWE	*New World Encyclopedia*
PBB	*Partai Bulan Bintang* (Crescent Star Party – Indonesia)
PDI	*Partai Demokrasi Indonesia (*Indonesian Democratic Party)
PDI-P	*Partai Demokrasi Indonesia Perjuangan* (Indonesian Democratic Party-Struggle)
PKB	*Partai Kebangkitan Bangsa (*National Awakening Party – Indonesia)
PKI	*Partai Komunis Indonesia* (Indonesian Communist Party)
PNI	*Partai Nasional Indonesia* (Indonesian Nationalist Party)
PPK	*Partiya Karkerên* (Kurdistan Workers Party – Turkey)
PPP	Pakistan People's Party
UN	United Nations
USA	United States of America

Acknowledgements and Preface

My interest in gender and Islam dates back to 1992, when I took up my first academic post. That year, I read Leila Ahmed's *Women and Gender in Islam* and started including her scholarship in my teaching. Later, I added the work of Fatima Mernissi and other women Muslim writers. In *Muslims and Modernity* (2005), discussing "Muslim Voices on Gender in Islam," I specifically referred to the five women who have led – one is currently leading – government in four Muslim countries. Later, I found myself working on entries for each of these women as History and Biography editor for the online *New World Encyclopedia*. As I scrutinized existing literature, I realized that, despite what is available, there is a deficit of material on what all five represent: the phenomenon of *Muslim women of power*. What follows, strictly speaking, does not focus exclusively on the five but uses their careers to explore a range of interlinked themes in Islamic Studies, namely culture, gender and politics. The political contexts, colonial legacies, search for identity and religion/state dynamics of each country are also essential background to considering the women's rise to power and issues that confronted their governments.

   This book combines three areas that have dominated my research. I have used anthropology to balance literary analysis with living voices, exploring practice as well as precept and text. The relationship between culture and Islam occupied my thinking for many years. I have had the opportunity to compare Islam in various contexts, including Bangladesh, Indonesia, Morocco, Turkey and Egypt. My thinking was influenced at an early stage by Clifford Geertz's comparative study of Islam in Morocco and Indonesia. Political thought and movements, and different views of how Muslim states should be governed, were a major concern of my 2005 book. In writing this current book, I was primarily motivated by the apparent paradox that four Muslim states have had women leaders while the popular perception is that Islam oppresses women. Even allowing for special circumstances, such as four of the five women's ties with slain male leaders, these states have impressive – though imperfect – gender empowerment records. Some more prosperous democracies lag behind. The record of the four Muslim states raises issues about whether Muslim states elsewhere – in the Arab world, for example, where gender empowerment is less advanced – might learn from their experience. Discussion about what helps and hinders gender equality in the following pages places the five women in a broader, global context.

I owe a debt to the Royal Anthropological Institute, of which I am a Fellow, for access to the resources of ATHENS, constantly utilized while writing this book. Through ATHENS, I consulted the *Encyclopædia Britannica* online (Academic Edition) for biographical entries on each of the five women. I remain an admirer of *Britannica* for consistent, reliable, concise information. I bought a hard-copy set when I was 16 years old, which I regularly consulted throughout my undergraduate studies. Having shipped it once from Australia to England, I sent it back to Australia in 1979 instead of taking it with me to Bangladesh because I knew that the weather damages books. My mission housing lacked air conditioning!

I also owe a debt to the *New World Encyclopedia* for stimulating this book. The *Encyclopedia* currently uses the Creative Commons Attribution-Share Alike 3.0 Unported License. Some articles are original. However, most were initially copied, within terms of the License, from Wikipedia, then edited and revised. Wiki is certainly a very convenient source but articles are neither consistent nor always accurate. As well as hopefully correcting errors and achieving stylistic conformity, NWE aims to add "value," suggesting moral significance that readers might take away from each entry promoting happiness, prosperity and peace. Knowledge can be organized to serve specific purposes, malign or positive. Regarding claims to neutrality as suspect, the *New World Encyclopedia* tries to use knowledge to nurture wholesome living and a healthy planet for all. As well as editing entries in NWE on each of the women, I worked on a range of articles relevant to this book. These include "Mustafa Kemal Atatürk," "Bangladesh," "Partition of Bengal (1905)," "Partition of Bengal (1947)," "Ottoman Empire," "Hossain Muhammad Ershad," "Muhammad Zia-ul-Haq," "Muhammad Jinnah," "Zulfikar Ali Bhutto," "Sayyid Abul A'la Mawdudi," "Young Turk Revolution," "Sukarno" and "Suharto." No NWE articles are directly quoted in this book. I draw on research carried out for the project.

Referencing their work indicates indebtedness to other writers, although several merit specific acknowledgement. In addition to Leila Ahmed and Fatima Mernissi on Islam and gender, I want to express appreciation for Aminah Wadud's work on the Qur'an. On women in Bangladesh, Indonesia

and Turkey, Elora Shehabuddin and Taj I. Hashmi, Susan Blackburn and
Yeşim Arat respectively proved invaluable. I enjoyed electronic communi-
cation with Ali Riaz, who clarified a point with reference to the Bangladesh
context. On Pakistan, I am especially indebted to the writing of Benazir
herself, whose assassination took place while I was researching this book.

Staff at the SUNY New Paltz's Sojourner Truth Library, not least those
who handle inter-library loan requests, more than deserve appreciation.
With Internet sources, I try to use material likely to prove durable, such as
online journals or newspapers. Access dates indicate availability when last
checked. However, there is no guarantee that material will endure. Qur'an
references follow Ali (2001), referenced by chapter and verse. *Hadith*, if cited
outside a quotation, are when possible traced to Khan's translation of
Bukhārī (1987) using the conventional Book and hadith number reference
format. Popular *hadith*, following common practice, may be left unsourced.
Diacriticals are used when possible, especially in personal names. I have
followed a convention throughout of referring to Benazir Bhutto, Khaleda
Zia, Sheikh Hasina and Megawati Sukarnoputri by their *given names*,
which is consistent with cultural practice. Tansu Çiller is referred to by her
family name, following Turkish practice since 1934, when surnames became
compulsory. Before then, a woman was referred to by her name and the
honorific *hanim* (lady). Generally speaking, family names are rarely used
in Muslim contexts. In Indonesia, many people have a single name. Maps
reproduced in this book are all in the public domain. The map of "Dinia"
was downloaded with permission from Tom Shelley's website. Others were
taken from Wikepedia and from the University of Texas Library. I am
grateful to the university for providing this service. All images but one,
Çiller's, were downloaded from English Wikipedia. Çiller's is from the
Kurdish version. All are in the public domain.

As with my earlier writing, I am interested in perceptions, how presuppositions predetermine what we see. I want to challenge stereotypes that,
at least as I see reality, lack foundation in fact. Aware that my presuppositions also shape how and what I see, I am open about the commitment that
colors my work. It will be clear from what follows that I do not think Islam
opposes women's political empowerment or leadership, at least when interpreted as I suggest. Construed as many Muslims increasingly do, Islam does
not hinder but encourages gender equality. If we read the Qur'an predis-
posed to find sanction for male superiority, we find this. Yet the lenses we
wear do not always distort what we see, depending on their specifications.
They may help us to see more clearly, which is why I wear spectacles. My
lens is a type of humanism, asking what promotes the common good, the
health and wholeness of the world? Gender justice as a humanitarian

imperative provides the lens through which I attempt to look at the material presented and discussed in this book. The State University of New York's motto is "to learn, to search, to serve." Writing this book led to my learning more about the issues discussed. The research was a quest for greater clarity. My aim is to serve the cause of truth, promoting better interreligious understanding.

On a personal note, as an ordained minister, my theism is public knowledge. On the one hand, belief or otherwise in God is irrelevant for examining Islam, gender and politics. On the other hand, as stated above, my convictions shape what I write, so I will be clear about my belief that God communicates through all religions, not exclusively through mine. Incidentally, God speaks to us through some who deny God, such as Karl Marx, Sigmund Freud and Richard Dawkins, although they would not thank me for saying so. They tell me that religion can retard maturity and hold us back. That is especially true when we confuse religion with vested interests and traditional interpretations. I believe that God speaks to us through scriptures, through inspired women and men, through nature and also through the collective conscience of humanity. This has authored such documents as the Universal Declaration of Human Rights and the Millennium Declaration. It has achieved consensus or close to consensus on other moral and ethical standards, including those voiced through the Convention on the Elimination of All Forms of Discrimination against Women. I do not view Islam as incompatible with human rights, gender equality or democracy, or as somehow inherently and inevitably at enmity with the non-Muslim world. I believe that Islam, correctly interpreted, embraces religious diversity; that Muslims are encouraged to make common cause with others to achieve a truly just, sustainable and peaceful world. Personally, I would like to see Turkey within the European Union.

The Qur'an says, "We created you from a single pair of a male and female, and made you into nations and tribes that ye may know each other," to which Ali (2001) adds the gloss, "not that ye may despise each other" (49:13). Farid Esack has developed an Islamic theology of liberation that sees all who share commitment to end oppression as "*m*uslim." Some identify formally with the Muslim community, some do not, but all qualify as *Mu'minun*, believers, who "enjoin what is right and refrain from what is wrong, and hasten in emulation in all good works" (3:114). Farid, whom I have known for many years, merits my gratitude. His work greatly impacts my thinking. I most recently saw him at the American Academy of Religion meeting in Montreal, November 2009, where I thanked him for his writing. It was also at an AAR meeting, Chicago 2008, that I met Leila Ahmed, seizing the opportunity to express appreciation for her academic work as well. A few people suggested, while I was researching this book, that a woman should write it. My view is that women's empowerment concerns women and men. I happen to be male. Actually, I try to be human first. I think the world would be a sad place if men cannot write about women's issues as well as about men's and vice versa. Similarly, as a non-Muslim scholar of Islam, I think it would be regrettable were I to be told that I had no business studying, teaching or writing about Islam; that only Muslims should.

As always, I am grateful to many people at Continuum. I want to record gratitude to Rebecca Vaughan-Williams, my previous commissioning editor, Kirsty Schaper, my current editor and Tom Crick, Assistant Humanities Editor. For diligent, careful work during production stage, thanks are due to Nick Fawcett and the Free Range project management team. My wife, Rekha Sarker Bennett, aided this project in numerous ways. I draw on her experiences, as referenced in the text. For example, she was present in Bangladesh when I was not during the last election. She also undertook fieldwork in Jordan and Bangladesh researching her master's dissertation in Development Practice, which focused on women's empowerment. I accompanied her during some of the Bangladesh fieldwork, engaging in research of my own, but I have not had the chance, yet, to visit Jordan, which I regret.

I have written elsewhere about the aim of passing over into another culture, worldview or religion, so that we become as comfortable there as we are within our own. Debate about whether outsiders can ever fully appreciate or comprehend another culture or religion can result in pessimism about the possibility of genuine cross-cultural understanding. On the one hand, every man and woman knows that, at a certain level, however intimate we are with someone of the opposite sex, at times we think them a mystery! This, though, can be equally true for people of the same gender. Perhaps this ought to be so, since we have a right to privacy in the deepest recess of our being. On the other hand, I am personally persuaded that enough can be understood across cultures and genders to enable us all to affirm membership of one human family.

I actually experienced greater cultural shock during a summer internship in a new town housing development in England than I did in Bangladesh. Perhaps I was more prepared for the second than for the first, having failed to anticipate that my class, education, accent and background would make me feel like a fish out of water, although I had not left England. However, I learned to swim in that water. I bonded with the community, leading a successful children's program that attracted media interest. By shedding arrogance, conceit, even ideas of personal superiority, we realize that those we thought "different" are human, just like us. Circumstances, contexts, conditions, cultures – not to mention languages – vary. However, people are not really that different at all. If we assume difference, we encounter this. Assuming sameness, this is what we find. If sameness is too radical for us, accepting similarity could be a step in the right direction. Next, we try to see what they see, looking through their eyes. We try to walk in their shoes. We think, feel, imagine and intuit our way beneath their skin. It might be true that outsiders never totally penetrate the fullness of insider experience. Yet I think that enough distance can be covered to effectively blur if not destroy the outsider–insider distinction, or polarity. Strangers become friends. If not, world peace might elude us, as might better cross-community relations in our neighborhoods and nations.

I believe that cross-cultural, cross-racial, cross-faith and cross-gender insight, empathy and understanding is possible, or I would not have written this book. I would stop teaching Religious Studies. I would abandon my dream of human solidarity, of a world where no one lacks shelter, food, meaningful employment, access to education and healthcare. Those who predict a clash of civilizations want one, to further their interests and agendas.

While finishing this book, Rekha's mother, Sushila, passed away, which directed my thoughts to memories of her hospitality in Bangladesh, where she made me feel at home. Like Hasina, one of the five women of power discussed here, my mother-in-law loved the soil, the flowers, the plants, the rivers, the fish, the colors, sounds and aromas of her native land. She loved its music and culture. Though I speak good Bengali, I did not spend much time learning words for flora and fauna, so she took great delight telling me names of everything in sight on the family property, in the water-tanks, streams and fields. She was a strong, independent, autonomous Bengali woman, powerful in her own right. Her family revolved around her. I dedicate this to her memory. Sushila was awarded the *Ratna-Gorva Ma* (mother of jewels) title for raising five children who graduated from College. About thirty women are acknowledged annually with this state-recognized honor, sponsored by the Azad Group of Companies.

Clinton Bennett PhD
Philosophy Dept
State University of New York at New Paltz, New York
February 2010

Introduction

Five Women, Four Countries

The Women

Five women have served as leaders of four Muslim countries, namely Benazir Bhutto, Khaleda Zia, Tansu Çiller, Sheikh Hasina and Megawati Sukarnoputri, in chronological order of their first or only period in office.

Five Muslim Women Leaders

Benazir Bhutto: Prime Minister of Pakistan 1988–90, 1993–6; Opposition Leader 1990–3, 1997–9.
Khaleda Zia: Prime Minister of Bangladesh 1991–5, 2001–6; Opposition Leader 1996–2006 and from 2009.
Tansu Çiller: Prime Minister of Turkey 1993–6; deputy Prime Minister and Foreign Minister 1996–7.
Sheikh Hasina: Prime Minister of Bangladesh 1996–2001 and since 2009; Opposition Leader 1986–7, 1991–6, 2001–6.
Megawati Sukarnoputri: Vice-President of Indonesia, 1999–2001; President 2001–4.

Bhutto, Hasina and Zia also led or lead their parliament's official opposition. Megawati, like Çiller, was first elected to parliament in 1991. She led her party in opposition, one of only two permitted to operate against the president's Golkar, overlapping Çiller's term as prime minister. The president, who had earlier ousted her father from power, removed Megawati as party chair in 1996 to prevent her from running in the next election. When he fell from power, she reorganized the party, winning the largest vote share in 1999. Çiller continued to head her party until 2002. Megawati ran unsuccessfully for the presidency when her term ended in 2004, losing in the second round. She tried again in 2009. However, she remained party leader.

The five women's careers have attracted praise and censure but overall their narratives represent an extraordinary record, one that challenges the widespread perception that Muslim women are oppressed. Muslim Bangladesh may be the only country so far where both prime minister and leader of the opposition are female, an example of women in high positions to a degree that no non-Muslim country has yet experienced. Four of the women belonged or belong to political families by birth or marriage, raising interesting questions about the extent to which this played a role, alongside skills and personal qualities, in their rise to power. To what degree did culture rather than Islam aid and abet their roles, or is it sustainable to distinguish Islam from culture? This study of the lives of the five women uses their careers to explore relevant issues, such as the role of culture, gender in Islam and the nature of the Islamic state.

The Countries

Two of the countries, Pakistan and Bangladesh, are officially Islamic. Turkey is a secular state. Indonesia's constitution enshrines belief in God as a principle, alongside democracy and social justice, but there is no state religion. None of the four have full-blown Islamic law. Their legal systems, based on codes inherited from colonial times, make accommodation for Islamic family law except in Turkey's case, where the Swiss Civil and Criminal Code was adopted. Taken together, the four states represent a huge proportion of the world's Muslims. Indonesia, the largest Muslim-majority state, has 15 percent of the global total. Pakistan is the second largest Muslim majority state, Bangladesh the third. India, which borders Pakistan and Bangladesh and shared their geo-political history until partition in 1947, actually has the third largest Muslim population. Turkey is the fifth largest Muslim-majority state, followed by Iran. Iran also has the largest Shi'a population. The largest Arab Muslim state, Egypt, is seventh. The Indian subcontinent has 30 percent of all Muslims, more than the Arab nations put together (20 percent). Approximately 60 percent of Muslims live in South Asia. All four of the states under scrutiny in this book are majority Sunni, although Pakistan and Turkey have substantial Shi'a minorities (roughly 15–20 percent).

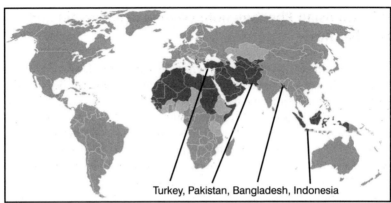

Turkey, Pakistan, Bangladesh, Indonesia

Map 1: The Muslim world (darker hue = Muslim majority).
Source: public domain.

The number of nations that have or have had women heads of state or government is increasing but remains quite small. Ireland has elected two women presidents in succession; New Zealand has had two women prime ministers, one of whom was elected, with one succeeding the other. Prime ministers are usually able to take up office during the life of a parliament without an election if a predecessor dies or steps aside. This was the case with Çiller. The way in which the five achieved office varies but all did so within a constitutional framework. One of the four countries – Bangladesh – has elected two women, both of whom have won power more than once, alternating in office for almost two decades. Sweden, so far, is the only country where women outnumber men in government, 60 percent as of 2007. On the Gender Empowerment Measure, Sweden is second to Norway, where women comprise 37.9 percent of parliament's members (*Human Development Report* 2007/2008, p. 330). This measure uses several indices to calculate the level of women's empowerment, including their economic status and participation in senior commercial and other non-political roles as well as in politics. It was 1999 when women first outnumbered men, by 11 to 9, in the Swedish cabinet. With 47.5 percent women members of parliament, Sweden is also number two using this scale. The credit for leading the world in terms of women in parliament goes to Rwanda, with 56.3 percent, an outstanding record regardless of regrettable circumstances that contributed to this achievement. Rwanda is unranked on the GEM scale of 93 states. Three of the four Muslim states that have or have had women leaders are located in South Asia, where the list of nations that have or have had women leaders is higher than for any other region.

A South Asian Phenomenon: Women's Leadership and Familial Ties?

In fact, South Asia led the way, when Sirimavo Bandaranaike of Sri Lanka, widow of an assassinated previous prime minister, became the world's first woman prime minister in 1960. She served from 1960–5, 1970–7 and 1994–2000, when her daughter was president (1994–2005), so here we have the first South Asian political dynasty. Bandaranaike followed in the footsteps of her dead husband; her son, Anura, has served as Speaker, foreign minister and opposition leader. India elected Indira Gandhi, daughter of Jawaharlal Nehru, as India's first woman prime minister, in 1966. She served from 1966–77, then from 1980–4, when she was assassinated. Her son, Rajiv Gandhi, succeeded her. Following his 1991 assassination, his widow, Sonia, became chair of the Congress Party, giving us another political dynasty. Rajiv's son, Rahul, is a member of parliament. Sympathy for the surviving relative of the slain leader also works for men. Benazir Bhutto's widower became president in 2008, very soon after her tragic assassination, despite corruption allegations that had dogged his and her careers.

The fathers of Indira, Hasina and Megawati each founded their respective states. Similarly, some representations of Zia, Khaleda's husband, depict him as Bangladesh's true founder, while Benazir's father is represented as the real pioneer of Pakistani democracy.

Familial Ties of the Five Muslim Women

Benazir Bhutto: daughter of Zulfikar Ali Bhutto, President of Pakistan 1971–3; Prime Minister 1973–7; executed 1979.

Tansu Çiller: not related to any other leader. Was a protégé of Süleyman Demirel, seven times Prime Minister of Turkey between 1966 and 1993; President 1993–2000.

Khaleda Zia: widow of Ziaur Rahman, President of Bangladesh 1976–81; assassinated.

Sheikh Hasina: daughter of Sheikh Mujibur Rahman, first President of Bangladesh 1971–2; Prime Minister of Bangladesh 1972–5; President January to August 1975; assassinated.

Megawati Sukarnoputri: daughter of Sukarno, first President of Indonesia, 1945–67; died 1970 under house arrest.

The third woman prime minister was Golda Meir of Israel, serving from 1969–74. Like the sixth woman prime minister and first European in the ranks, Margaret Thatcher, she was not related to any male politician. Meir and Thatcher were dubbed "iron ladies." Number five was an African, Elisabeth Domitien (Prime Minister of the Central African Republic from January 1975 to April 1976). When elected in 1988, Benazir Bhutto claimed the tenth position. Khaleda Zia was twelfth, Çiller sixteenth, Sheikh Hasina twenty-second. On the list of women heads of state rather than of government, Megawati was the thirty-first although this list includes a few who served for brief periods, including Captain-Regents of San Marino, a very much smaller state than Indonesia. Megawati was the first Muslim woman head of state of modern times. Before her, Cory Aquino, another widow of a slain male politician, became President of the Philippines in 1986, Asia's first female president. The Filipinos chose another woman, Gloria Macapagal-Arroyo, in 2001. India elected its first female president, Pratibha Patil, in 2007. Malaysia had a woman leader of the opposition, Wan Azizah, during 2008, but she stepped aside for her husband. Myanmar has a prominent opponent of the military government, Aung San Suu Kyi, winner of the 1991 Nobel Peace Prize. Nor does this list exhaust Asian female politicians. South Korea's Park Geun-hye, daughter of an assassinated president, led the Grand National Party from March 2004 to July 2006, and Japan's Makiko Tanaka, daughter of a former prime minister, was her country's first female foreign minister from April 2001 to January 2002. Incidentally, family ties are common among Japanese politicians. The paternal great-grandfather of the current PM, Yukio Hatoyama, was speaker of the House of Representatives from 1896–7; his paternal grandfather, Ichirō, was also prime minister and first president of the Liberal Democratic Party; while his father served as foreign minister.

Examining the G8's Record

Though several of the world's leading economic powers (members of the G8) – namely Canada, Great Britain, France and Germany – have had or currently have women leaders at the head of government, the rest – namely the United States, Japan, Italy and Russia – have not. Unelected hereditary heads of state such as Britain's Queen Elizabeth II are not included in this survey. The US has a woman Speaker of the House, the first female in that post, and a woman Secretary of State, the third.

Given the popular perception that Islam oppresses women or that women play subservient roles to men in Muslim societies, it is at the very least of interest that four Muslim countries have had women leaders while several of the economically most prosperous states, considered to be liberal democracies, have yet to choose a woman to head their governments. Benazir took office in 1988. It was in 2007 that the most senior woman leader thus far took office in the US, the 60th Speaker of the House, second in line to presidential succession. The first woman US Secretary of State – the highest ranking cabinet member, fourth in presidential succession – took office in December 1996. By then, Benazir had served two terms, Khaleda one, Hasina had taken up office, while Çiller, having ended her term, was Deputy and Turkey's first female foreign minister. In 2008, Pakistan elected a woman Speaker of the House, Fahmida Mirza. Britain also had a female Speaker. Of course, the only country in the world that lacks the female franchise is a Muslim one, Saudi Arabia, so nobody is arguing that the Muslim record is perfect. Kuwaiti women lacked the franchise until May 2005. When the allies liberated Kuwait from Iraqi occupation in 1990–1, supposedly in the name of freedom, Kuwaiti women could not vote. However, four women gained seats in the 2009 election. Massuma al-Mubarak, one of the four, had served in the 16-member cabinet from July 2006 to March 2007, upon which two women were appointed, also sitting in parliament *ex officio* (HDR, p. 333, note f). Oman first elected women in 2003, but these lost their seats in 2007.

The Islamic Context

Are there any particular reasons why the five Muslim women rose to power? This may be an impossible question to answer. However, the purpose of this book is to explore their lives and achievements, arguing that their careers raise issues of scholarly significance and interest. Given their contexts – four Muslim states – areas particularly worth exploring include whether or not Islam played a role in their rise to power, whether it played the same or different roles in each context, whether cultural factors outweigh Islamic, whether this distinction is valid, and whether their gender was or was not actually a major factor at all. There are similarities and differences *vis-à-vis* Islam's role across the four states. Islam's legal status has changed over time in at least two of the four. Arguably, Islam's actual relationship with the state differs in each. On the other hand, so-called Islamist parties dedicated to creating true Islamic states or to making society more authentically Islamic operate in each. All five women have had to deal with Islamism as a political factor. Research cited in this book suggests that Islam is of increasing political importance in all four states. All the women have, to various degrees, participated in or contributed to a process that has made Islamic discourse and discussion about Islam's role more acceptable in the public square. If this is the case, it could be argued that instead of representing an affront to Islam, these women have helped promote an Islamic agenda. In other words, instead of contradicting or compromising Islamic purity or their state's Islamic *bone fides*, their leadership led to a more, not less, Islamic society.

A conclusion that Islam did not impede their political careers could challenge the perception that women are second-class in Muslim societies. A conclusion or claim that culture outweighed religious factors would challenge the notion that Islam explains everything in Muslim society, inviting a revised understanding of the relationship between "Islam" and "culture." Interestingly, in addition to all four states having a Muslim majority, several other parallels exist. In different yet similar ways, all four fit the "imagined community" understanding of how nations begin. Proposed by Benedict Anderson (1983), this may be relevant in terms of identifying specifically feminine aspects of these women's political appeal. All four states can be described as post-colonial, imagined into being by their leaders and citizens who transformed an idea, the "idea of Turkey," the "idea of Pakistan" etc., into reality. Early leaders of each of the states, including Hasina and Megawati's fathers, were concerned with nurturing national identity and solidarity. Yet, while the geographical space occupied by each state obviously existed before they were founded, and some historical continuity exists between them and former geo-political entities, all four can also be understood as new. Is the fact that all are still relatively young of any special significance in understanding how and why women rose to power? Specifically referring to Indonesia, Anderson wrote, "until quite recently, the Javanese language had no word meaning the abstraction 'society'" (p. 6). He continued:

> The late President Sukarno always spoke with complete sincerity of the 350 years of colonialism that his 'Indonesia' had endured, although the very concept 'Indonesia' is a twentieth-century invention, and most of today's 'Indonesia' was only conquered by the Dutch between 1850 and 1910. (1991, p. 11, n4)

Indonesia' was 'imagined' in the early twentieth century. Pakistan, it could be argued, was imagined into reality as a home for India's Muslim population, with Islam as the glue to cement different people into a single nation. Pakistan has always had to deal with Islam's role in what was created as a state for Muslims. It has consistently faced the question, "as a state for Muslims, is it also a Muslim state?" Founding father Muhammad Ali Jinnah (1876–1948) told the people of Pakistan on the day he was elected president of the Constituent Assembly in 1947, "you are free to go to your temples, your are free to go to your mosques or to any other place of worship ... You may belong to any religion or caste or creed – that has nothing to do with the business of the state" (cited by Bhutto 1989, p. 314). One of his ministers was Hindu (Ahmed 1997, p. 182). Bangladesh, stressing a different heritage, was at first a secular state, perhaps with Turkey as a model after separating from Pakistan. However, with an 85 percent Muslim majority, the issue of Islam's status and role could not be ignored. Zia, Khaleda's husband, reformatted national identity. Pakistan and what is now Bangladesh were two provinces of the same state, from 1947 to 1971. Indonesia's pluralist heritage led to a stress on equal opportunities, rights and freedoms but once again the issue of Islam's status repeatedly surfaced. Turkey's founding father, Mustafa Kemal Atatürk (1881–1938) set out to create a modern, secular, European-style nation-state after the collapse of the Ottoman Empire. Although older than the other states, Turkey had a one-party system until 1950 so multi-party democracy did not begin until after Pakistan and Indonesia were founded. In his effort to distinguish Turks and Turkey from the Ottomans and their defeated, discredited empire, Atatürk separated Islam from the state. Islam was relegated to the private sphere. Yet over the years, Turks refused to sideline Islam, so Islamic options and solutions entered public discourse, represented today by Islamic political parties. Nor is Islamic discourse restricted to Islamist parties. One commentator says, with reference to Bangladesh, "political Islam" is no longer the "monopoly of the Jammat-i-Islami and other 'Islam-loving' political parties, nor is Islam any longer irrelevant to the day-to-day affairs of the government and its people" (Hashmi, p. 192). Similar remarks can be made *vis-à-vis* Islam's role in the other states. Turkey's secular constitution means that Islamist parties tend not to advocate an Islamic state or Islamic law but they are distinctly oriented toward Islam. One such party, the subsequently banned Welfare Party, governed from June 1996 to September 1997 in partnership with Çiller's True Path Party. Welfare's successor, the Justice and Development Party, took power in 2002. In Bangladesh, the *Jamaat-e-Islami* supported Khaleda in 2001, gaining two cabinet seats. Megawati, for her part, found herself caught after the Bali bombing

(October 12, 2002) between the secular left and the Islamist right. Riaz attributes her vice-president with militant sympathies (pp. 143, 174). According to Jones, determined to prove "the Islamists wrong" about a Muslim woman's inability to govern, Benazir "felt the need to present herself as a prime minister who could be trusted to protect and even advance the role of Islam in the Pakistani state" (Jones, p. 18). Hasina made common cause with the *Jamaat* in 1995, campaigning to introduce legislation for neutral caretaker governments to supervise future general elections, an idea that had actually originated with the *Jamaat* (Hashmi, p. 190). In the 1996 election, the *Jamaat* did not perform well, repeating this in 2009 when it lost seats gained in 2001. Three of the four parties that chose the five women support secular, pluralist policies but Khaleda's party identifies closely with Islam, although it is not Islamist. Again, however, it is not insignificant that a party with a specific Islamic identity happily chose a woman leader, who has twice gained power. Çiller moved her party in an Islamic direction.

The Women, National Security and the Role of the Military

The role of the military is an issue in all four states, where interventions in civilian and democratic rule have taken place. How, if at all, have these women dealt with the military? In Turkey, the military regards itself, with some constitutional recognition, as the guardian of Turkey's secular, democratic tradition. This is one reason why questioning secularism is off-limits. The Welfare Party government resigned in 1997 when the military expressed concern that the constitution was under threat. This has been called a postmodern coup. Previous interventions took place with the intention of strengthening democracy, thus the military-supervised transitions to civilian rule. Pakistan's former military leader, Pervez Musharaf (in power from 1999 to 2008), saw Turkey as a model, "an approximation" of what he and others would like "Pakistan to become …" with "one foot in Europe" and an army presiding "over a generally liberal and secular society" (Cohen, p. 275). In Pakistan and Bangladesh, the military have intervened to end alleged corruption of civilian politicians and to protect national stability but their militaries have had less or no commitment to democracy. At least, such a commitment has been ambiguous, although from 2006 to the end of 2008 the Bangladeshi military supported the caretaker government that eventually supervised the election, which Sheikh Hasina won. My wife, who was visiting Bangladesh at the time, shared the opinion of international observers that the election was free and fair.

Pakistan's military, the sixth largest in the world, does much more than defend the state. A powerful and wealthy landowner, it has numerous commercial interests and activities. Siddiqa (2007) describes how some of the largest corporations are controlled by the military. In both Bangladesh and Indonesia, presidents have granted the military representational privileges, blurring the armed services' role. Riaz and Kharleker see more disturbing parallels between three of the four states, asking whether Pakistan's "Talibanization" will be followed by that of Bangladesh, perhaps also by Indonesia's. Pakistan, Turkey and Indonesia currently deal with separatist movements. Bangladesh had to deal with tribal unrest and conflict in the Chittagong Hill Tracts bordering on Myanmar, where Hasina is credited with negotiating a peace accord. Not a few call Bangladesh a weak, even a failed state; thus stability and the ability to govern effectively is a major issue. Do the governments of these states control all territory under their legal jurisdiction? Undeniably, areas of Pakistan where the Taliban are in charge lie outside Islamabad's rule, while insurgency destabilizes the largest province, Baluchistan. Strong insurgencies make governance difficult in eastern Turkey (Kurdistan) and in seven regions of Indonesia: Aceh, Bali, East Java, Raiu, South Moluccas, Sulawesi and West Papua. Bangladesh is geographically small yet I recall how daily life really did not change at all following Zia's assassination in 1981. A new president in Dhaka had little or no impact on village communities, whose concerns were for clean water and a flood-free year.

The Family-tie Issue in Wider Context

As hinted above, some explain four of the five women's careers as merely continuing dynastic traditions. Is this an adequate or plausible explanation? This issue does not easily go away, so is revisited here in a broader context. As noted, other South Asian women leaders had or have family ties to slain male politicians. Given the patriarchal nature of these societies – all four of the Muslim states are habitually described as patriarchal – the fact that women have succeeded men as leaders demands examination. It appears to defy cultural norms. It could be, as Thompson surmises, pure coincidence that South Asia has produced so many women leaders who happen to be related to dead male predecessors. He does attempt some speculation but says that the question "why Asia?" cannot be answered. It nonetheless remains of interest that "dynastic female leadership" has been prominent in a region widely described as "patriarchal" (Thompson 2004, p. 38). There may be nothing here of particular interest. Indeed, given that around the world it is not uncommon for members of the same family to enter politics, too much attention may be given to this aspect. After all, the United States has seen sons follow fathers into the White House. Gabon, Syria and North Korea have sitting presidents who *immediately* succeeded their fathers, unlike Adams and Bush. Cuba saw a brother hand over to a brother. None of these four govern genuine democratic states. One woman, Christina Fernárdez de Kirchner, succeeded her husband as President of Argentina in December 2007, a political first. A much longer list, including four members of the Churchill family in Great Britain, could be drawn up of successive generations of the same family who entered political life. In the case of the US Kennedy family, three siblings entered politics, one serving in his brother's cabinet. In fact, a large percentage of women elected or appointed to the US Congress were related to dead male predecessors. Senators are usually appointed following a death in office – then must seek election to retain their seat. By 2009, 46 women had directly succeeded their husbands, 38 in the House of Representatives and 8 in the Senate. Eight succeeded fathers; three followed husbands but not in direct succession; ten were married to fellow legislators. It was not until 1993 that *three women* sat at the *same time* in the Senate, while at the time of writing only 2 percent of all people elected to Congress since 1789 were women. There were periods during which no woman sat in the Senate, 1922–31, 1945–7, 1973–8. The number, though, of women with family ties has dropped: between 1997 and 2006, only 9 percent were widows of former Congressmen (data taken from the website, *Women in Congress*). The first woman to take her seat in the British House of Commons, Lady Astor, succeeded her husband, who moved to the Lords. She served from 1919 until 1945. In her maiden speech, she asked members not to look at her as a "fanatic or lunatic" but as the spokeswoman for "hundreds of women and children throughout the country who could not speak for themselves" (*House of Commons Factsheet M4*, p. 4).

The achievements of women who gain high office should not be explained away solely on the grounds that they were or are related to male leaders. Is Hilary Clinton's career as a former senator and current Secretary of State to be explained away simply because her husband was president? Can her abilities and achievements be reduced to her choice of a spouse? Perhaps Bill Clinton owes some of his success to his wife's political acumen? Nor should democracies prohibit anyone from participating in politics because a relative, alive or dead, holds or held elected office. This would rob us of several members of the Kennedy family, three Churchill generations in Britain, two US presidents and countless other people around the globe.

The four women who followed a dead relative into politics all rose to power within democratic, constitutional frameworks. They did not seize power illegally. In the South Asian context, does the fact that these women *were chosen as leaders* have anything to do with their countries' specific political contexts. All – and here Turkey can be included – were undergoing types of democratic reform or restoration. Do women have specific roles in these struggles? The "Dynasties and Political Top Female Leaders in Asia" project, funded by the German Science Foundation, 2003–6, led by Claudia Derichs and Mark Thompson, explored this question. It saw some correlation between women leaders and democratic reform. Is this sustainable? Çiller's gender may have played a part in Turkey's post-1983 context. Following military intervention, a new generation of politicians entered government, supposedly untainted by past affiliations. Unrelated to any other politician, Çiller entered politics as the protégé of a former prime minister (later president), although he remained neutral when she stood as party leader against three male contenders and won (1993). She is the only one of the five women in this book who did not win a general election as party leader before assuming office, becoming prime minister during the life of the 1991–5 parliament. Megawati was indirectly elected president by the upper and lower houses of parliament, not by the general public. However, her party had won the largest share of seats in the 1999 election. She oversaw a change to direct presidential elections. Others won office through the ballot box, gaining an absolute majority or the largest block of seats. With reference to Benazir, Hasina and Megawati, much is made of a desire to restore their father's legacies. Yet again, this is not unusual. Winston Churchill believed in destiny, setting out to vindicate his father's reputation (Addison, pp. 5, 73). George W. Bush's "decision to run for governor of Texas and president, and his decision to invade Iraq, were driven in part by his need to live up to his father's expectations and desire to vindicate his father's legacy" (Maranto, Lansford and Johnson, p. 38).

Are Women Naturally More Pro-democracy than Men?

None of the male relatives of the four women leaders left unambiguous democratic legacies, while some argue that the women themselves have questionable records *vis-à-vis* their commitment to democracy, tending to further dynastic or personal interests. Park Geun-hye's slain father took power in a military coup and has been described as "authoritarian." She justifies this as having been necessary to "save the country through industrialization" from which "democratization" followed (Burnell, p. 41).

Similar arguments defend the authoritarian actions of Hasina's father, Sheikh Mujib, and of Megawati's father, Sukarno. What others call "one-party" or "no-party" rule becomes consensus and nation building, as under "guided democracy" in Indonesia (Katz, p. 88).

Çiller may be an exception, lacking a dynasty, but her record has been described as problematic *vis-à-vis* democracy. She "emerged on the Turkish political scene at a time when there was a general yearning for new political leaders who would depart from past leadership styles," which, as a woman, people thought she might deliver. However, once in power, her administration was not "renowned for its concerns for democracy" and she "built a huge financial fortune for herself" (Cizre, p. 213) resorting "to political patronage and nepotism" (Heper, p. 225). Critics depict her as a self-interested opportunist with an insatiable lust for power. Some accuse Tony Blair of having no "underlying convictions" except a belief that he was destined to lead his nation. Yet he won three consecutive victories and stayed in office longer than any previous Labour prime minister (Gray, p. 95). Perhaps the lesson here is that we should not ascribe better virtues to women than to men, or expect different behavior merely because of anyone's gender. No few male politicians have appointed cronies to office and accumulated personal fortunes. The latter is not necessarily illegal, depending on how the politicians in question conducted their private business in relation to their public office. On the other hand, the volume in which Cizre and Heper were published, Heper and Sayari (2002), is far from neutral toward Çiller. If she did weaken Turkish democracy, this might challenge the notion that women are inherently pro-democracy, men more inclined toward autocracy. In Britain, Margaret Thatcher often seemed less compassionate, more aggressive, than her Labour opponent, Neil Kinnock. She even took lessons on how to soften her public persona (Evans, p. 16).

Corruption allegations against four of the five women have been dropped or dismissed. Megawati was criticized for failing to tackle corruption rather than for being personally involved, although allegations swirl around her husband's business dealings. He is currently Speaker of the People's Consultative Assembly. Unfortunately, accusations of corruption are rampant in all four countries, a tactic used to discredit opponents or to justify removal from office. It is difficult to separate innocence from guilt.

The question remains: did these women's rise to power, to some degree, rest on the popular perception that they had a distinctive role to play in restoring or establishing democracy? Unfortunately, women leaders do appear to feel a need to exhibit or develop supposedly male qualities in order to be taken seriously, especially when national defense and security issues are at stake. Thus the term, "iron lady." Coined for Golda Meir, the label has subsequently been used for Thatcher, Çiller and Hasina. On the other hand, feuding between Khaleda Zia and Sheikh Hasina gave us "the battling Begums." Their disagreements have been belittled as hormonal and emotional, not serious political debate. Yet, from several visits to the Stranger's Gallery and from watching parliamentary broadcasts, I recall many men in the House of Commons screaming hysterically at each other, so I would suggest that depictions of the "warring Begums" reflect gender bias.

Clarifying the Agenda

What follows in succeeding chapters uses the biographies of the five women to explore the issues identified above, namely:

- What role did Islam play?
- What role did culture play?
- What role did dynastic ties play?
- Did gender play a significant role in their rise to power?
- Did gender play any role in their exercise of power?
- Is there any particular relationship between their gender and strengthening democracy in the four states?
- Does the post-colonial context have any bearing on their careers?
- Did these five women promote women's issues and rights?

The last question is inevitably posed during discussions of women in politics. On the one hand, lack of female legislators means that legislatures do not mirror their constituencies. Bodies representing diversity may govern pluralistic societies best. Pakistan (60 out of 338 since 2002) and Bangladesh (45 out of 300 since 2004) have reserved seats for women and, in the former, for minorities, which is one strategy to ensure diversity. Such a policy attracts controversy because it creates a separate category of legislators, who may enjoy less prestige than those – women or men – elected to open seats. Britain's Labour Government introduced female-only shortlists between 1993–7, resulting in a record number of women gaining seats (120) in 1997. This practice was abandoned when a tribunal ruled that it breached the 1975 Sex Discrimination Act (*House of Commons Factsheet M4*, pp. 5–6). There were 43 women MPs in 1990, when Thatcher left office. Yet whether a legislator is male or female, they represent the needs and concerns of all constituents, male and female, black and white, party supporter and political opponents.

Legislators also take their own interests in causes and policy areas with them, staking out claims to expertise. These interests may have earned them votes, though sometimes they emerge after an election. There is a general expectation that women may prioritize women's issues, and that a Muslim might voice an opinion when Islam is involved. On the other hand, women and minorities may have other priorities, equally valid. They may not want to be seen as one-cause politicians. A member from the majority can have a reputation for promoting equal rights and social justice, while a member from a minority community may focus on healthcare reform. A man can promote women's concerns, while a woman might adopt education as her issue. Tony Blair, with a 35 percent female cabinet, did more for women in politics than Thatcher, who appointed *one female* to her cabinet (*House of Commons Factsheet M4*, p. 5). The automatic assumption that women in politics will choose to promote women's issues may need to be critiqued.

A strong argument for taking steps to ensure that women are elected is that violence against women, still rampant, has no "parallel" in most men's experience. Men may be less inclined to tackle issues surrounding women's reproductive health. Women may best take the lead in dealing with these and other areas through education and the legislative process (Chowdhury *et al.*, p. 11).

Relevant Research and Literature

There is less literature than there should be specifically on the five women. Of the five, more is available on Benazir – the first to gain office – whose writing was also a valuable source. Her compelling narrative as "daughter of destiny" has unexplored aspects, as does her thinking on Islam and democracy, set out in her posthumously published *Reconciliation: Islam, Democracy and the West* (2008). The "daughter of destiny" self-image is found in the careers of Sheikh Hasina and Megawati. The later women were influenced by Benazir's achievements. Muslims in Indonesia found it harder to claim that a woman leader was contrary to Islam because women had already led Turkey, Pakistan and Bangladesh (Blackburn, p. 107). Benazir's election stimulated a great deal of scholarship on Islam and gender, not least several groundbreaking books by the Moroccan scholar, Fatima Mernissi, and work by the Egyptian, Leila Ahmed, who now teaches at Harvard. The latter, on which this book draws, included a close scrutiny of relevant *hadith* and of how Qur'anic verses are interpreted. This in turn stimulated more reflection on gender in Islam, resulting in the contributions of Aminah

Wadud and other Muslim women. Moghissi, though, dismisses the possibility of an Islamic feminism as an oxymoron. The problem for women, she
argues, is Islam per se, not men's wrong interpretation or practice.
Bangladesh's controversial feminist, Taslima Nasrin (or Tasleema Nasreen),
who fled a "death threat" in 1994, agrees.

The status of women and the role of Islam attract field research in all four
contexts, which supplements textual analysis. This research, a major source
for what follows, includes studies of women's participation in Islamist
parties in Turkey (Arat 2005) and Bangladesh (Shehabuddin), while
Blackburn touches on this phenomenon in Indonesia. She refers to new
Muslim women's organizations and says that what they tell us about
"changes within Islam on gender issues" and about how Muslim women
"have developed a more independent voice deserves further investigation"
(p. 225). Several studies of the political contexts draw parallels between
some or all four states, suggesting, as indicated above, that links exist
other than the possible accident that all had women leaders. The statistic
of 18.5 percent as the global average for women in parliament obscures the
fact that some women, like their male colleagues, have very limited roles.
A privileged elite, elected or unelected, usually all male, may control
government. The fourth UN World Conference on women at Beijing in
1995 set 30 percent as the goal.

The Four States, Arab Space and Other Contexts: A Comparison

Percentages of Women in Parliament (Lower House or Unicameral) as of September 30, 2009: Some Comparative Data

Iraq (Arab) 25.5 percent (70 out of 275)
Pakistan (South Asian) 22.5 percent (76 out of 338) (60 reserved
    seats)*
United Arab Emirates (Arab) 22.5 percent (9 out of 40) (20 elected,
    20 appointed, no legislative role) (one woman was elected, seven
    were appointed)
Iraq (Arab) 25.5 percent (70 out of 275) (constitutional provision for
    25 percent women members)
Bangladesh (South Asian) 18.6 percent (64 out of 345) (45 reserved
    seats for women)**
Indonesia (South Asian) 18.2 percent (102 out of 560)***
Israel (Middle East Jewish majority) (17.5 percent)

United States (North America) 16.8 percent (73 out of 475; counting
the Senate, 17 percent)
Morocco (Arab League member) 10.5 percent (34 out of 325) (30
reserved seats)
Syria (Arab) 12.4 percent
Turkey (Euro-Asia) 9.1 percent (50 out of 549)****
Kuwait (Arab) 7.7 percent (5 out of 65)
Jordan (Arab) 6.4 percent (7 out of 110) (6 reserved seats for women)
Lebanon (Arab – 40 percent Christian) 3.1 percent (4 out of 128)
Iran (Middle East/non-Arab) 2.8 percent (8 out of 290) (reserved
seats for minorities not for women)
Bahrain (Arab) 2.5 percent (1 out of 40)
Egypt (Arab) 1.8 percent (8 out of 442) (dropped reserved seats)
Yemen (Arab) 0.3 percent (1 out of 301)
Oman (Arab) 0 percent (0 out of 80) (note: two women won seats in
2003 but lost in 2007)
Saudi Arabia 0 percent – has no female franchise

* Pakistan was unicameral until 1973, when it created a Senate.
Legislation must pass both houses. President elected by votes in
central and provincial assemblies, reconciling differences.
** Bangladesh is unicameral. President elected by the Assembly.
***Indonesia has two houses. One is the legislative chamber. The
second chamber, of which the legislators are also members, met once
every five years until 1999, then annually. It sets policy and exercises
constitutional oversight. Until 2004, it elected the president and
vice-president, who are now directly elected.
**** Turkey was unicameral from 1923–61. It had a Senate from
1961–82. It is now unicameral. The Assembly elects the president.

Note: global average is 18.5 percent.

Source: The Inter-parliamentary Union (the *World Development Report* uses
the same data in calculating the Gender Empowerment Measure;
http://www.ipu.org/wmn-e/classif.htm).

Can lessons from non-Arab Muslim experience of women leaders be translated into Arab space? The Arab world *gave Islam* to Turkey, to the Indian
subcontinent and to Indonesia. Perhaps the evangelized can reflect positive
aspects of Islam, of how Islam took root in their cultures and societies, back

to the historical center? My argument is that Islam in the four nations was an important factor, so lessons can be applied to other Muslim states. My conclusions tend to support the claim that Islam is the dominant influence in Muslim societies. Combined with certain other factors, Islam empowers women, so it can empower women in Arab space too. No one is claiming that democracy is as secure in the four states under scrutiny as it could be, even in Turkey. Turkey was the first of the four to enfranchise women but lagged behind in the number of women elected to parliament. In comparison, only Iraq among Arab states can be said to compete with all five, trumping them with a higher percentage of women in parliament. A complexity would be analyzing the role of outside intervention in Iraq following the 2003 invasion. The United Arab Emirates matches Pakistan. The small assembly, however, is half elected and half appointed, with a limited, advisory role. Syria trumps Turkey but has a one-party system, with almost all power vested in the president, one of three current presidents in the world who succeeded his father. The status of elected bodies varies, while political systems differ.

On the GEM, Egypt is one place below Turkey. At 88, Morocco outranks Turkey. The Arab state that tops the scale is the United Arab Emirates, at 29. The rest are much lower. Oman is 80, one above the highest of the four, followed by Qatar at 84. The rulers of these Arab states, who have promoted gender equality, are also moving toward greater democratization, so credit should be given where credit is due. The same applies to King Abdullah II of Jordan. Knowing that constitutional monarchs have managed to survive in such states as Norway and Sweden, at the very top of the GEM ranking, they may be less paranoid about losing *all their privileges*. Non-hereditary heads of other Arab states, whose rule more or less lasts for life, have less impressive democratic records. Mernissi describes what she calls "one of the miracles of the century – 'reigns' of Arab presidents as long as those of kings" (1992, p. 64).

Factors that hindered representation in Turkey and Indonesia, it will be argued, had more to do with the *dominant political ideology* than with Islam or culture. Indeed, as the oldest of the four states and as the one that can be described as unambiguously secular, Islam could be said to be the *least influential* in Turkey, where women's empowerment has made *less progress*. With the highest Gross Domestic Product of the four (17th in the world), Turkey shows that national prosperity does not automatically empower women. Indeed, several nations with high GDP rankings score much lower on the Gender Empowerment Measure. Prosperity alone does not result in women's empowerment. Saudi Arabia, a G20 member, ranks 23rd on the World Bank's list of Development Indicators (2009), one higher than

Norway, one lower than Sweden. The latter tops the GEM, on which Saudi Arabia is almost bottom. India is below Pakistan on the Gender Empowerment scale (it is not among the 93) but is 12th in GDP ranking. The comparative weakness of democracy and strength of patriarchal systems in the Arab world may have more to do with non-Islamic than Islamic factors. The fact that rulers such as the kings of Morocco and Jordan, who are good Muslims, support gender equality and implement relevant policies to promote this suggests that Islam is not a hindrance.

There is a large body of literature discussing the particular issue of women and politics in Arab space. Sabbagh (2009) is an excellent overview. The Arab region is ranked second lowest in the world on the Gender Empowerment Measure, after sub-Saharan Africa, lowest in terms of percentage of women in parliament (Sabbagh, p. 52). Jordan has reserved seats for women (and also for minorities). Six of the seven women elected in 2007 occupy reserved seats, one an open seat. Morocco, moving toward becoming a constitutional monarchy, with a strong women's movement, has 10.5 percent. Egypt dropped its quota of 30 reserved seats (established in 1979) in 1983 and female representation fell. The president, who appoints ten deputies, included five women in 2005. Four were elected to open seats. The four Muslim states compare favorably, too, with Israel, commonly regarded as the Middle East's most stable democracy. With the world's 41st highest GDP, it has 17.5 percent of women in parliament. On the GEM, though, it ranks higher than the four, at 28.

Comparison of the four states, all of which are low on the human development scale, with the United States, which is toward the top, highlights what the former have achieved. The records on women's leadership of four Muslim states, typically described as patriarchal, which are said to oppress women, hold their own compared with the USA, universally recognized as a leading democracy. Few, too, would call the US patriarchal. Women in US politics are also going from strength to strength. As they obtain senior posts, more follow. This appears to be a general lesson. Men as well as women realize that a woman can be as capable as a man, and then elect more women. No one, male or female, however, makes a competent politician *solely because of gender*.

Indonesia and Turkey are behind Pakistan and Bangladesh in the percentage of women in parliament. This improved, though, following their experience of having women leaders. Indonesia, having introduced legislation in 2003 to encourage parties to field 30 percent female candidates, is now a percentile point ahead of the USA. Both are a little below the global average of 18.5 percent, which Bangladesh scrapes past. Only Turkey, of the four, is below the US. Several other G8 members are below

Bangladesh: France (18.2 percent) is still close to the global average; Japan at 11.3 percent is lower but outranks Turkey. On the Gender Empowerment Measure, however, the US is ranked 15th (one below the United Kingdom). The four are much lower, toward but *not at the bottom*. Bangladesh leads at 81. Pakistan is 82nd and Turkey 90th. Indonesia is unranked. All four are placed within the medium range (*Human Development Report* 2007/2008, pp. 330–2). Due to data availability, the measure ranks 93 out of the UN's 192 member states but gives some statistics for 177 of them. On this score, Bangladesh marginally outperforms the others. Egypt and Saudi Arabia make the GEM scale at positions 91 and 92 respectively, followed by the Yemen. With Turkey, India is a G20 member. On the World Bank's GDP ranking, at 19, Indonesia is ahead of Pakistan (47) and Bangladesh (61). These, however, make the GEM's 93, while Indonesia does not. Rwanda, with the highest number of women in parliament, ranks 143rd out of the 186 nations listed on the GDP scale. This places Rwanda toward the bottom of all African states. Most though not all states lower on the list are small islands. Another African state with an even lower GDP, Losotho (159th), has the 40th highest score on the "women in parliament scale." Again, factors specific to context require scrutiny.

Scope of the Inquiry

Statistics in this Introduction naturally flow into the opening segment of Chapter 1, which discusses factors that help and hinder women's empowerment – this is not only about calculating percentages on indices. Chapter 1 then turns to Muslim views on women's participation in politics and on women's status, discussing some contested scripture verses and other texts. The next five chapters explore the women's careers against the background of specific geo-political contexts. Every detail of each nation's history cannot be explored. Rather, an overview is sketched to establish context, highlighting events or issues relevant to the women's careers. The questions listed above are used to structure each chapter. Inevitably, there is some overlap – two of the women are from the same country (Bangladesh), which used to be part of another of the four (Pakistan). However, a conscious effort is made to cross-reference rather than repeat. No attempt is made to do anything like justice to every policy the women pursued, to every stage of their political journeys. Nor are all criticisms considered, positive or negative. The focus is on issues identified in this introduction. Nonetheless, since this book is partly biographical, it aims to offer adequate vignettes of their lives.

The book identifies popular perceptions that women could play unique roles in their particular political contexts. It tends to agree with Derichs and Thompson that this *was a fact*or in these women's rise to power. Begum (2006) describes what she calls a "generalization" reached by "literature on female leadership" that "women capture leadership positions when there is a crisis ... usually created by the death of leaders or the onset of the democratization process" (p. 270). However, this book will also suggest that there can never be any certainly that a woman *simply because she is a woman* will meet any specific expectations. The same is true for men, *simply because they are men.* A man may prove more compassionate than a woman. A woman's foreign policy may be tougher, more hawkish, than a man's. Megawati's male predecessor did more to promote women's issues than she did (Blackburn, pp. 107, 227). Khaleda's husband is remembered for empowering women. Çiller showed little interest in women's issues. Women may try hard *not to be seen* privileging women's concerns above others, although critics are often interested in whether women leaders try "to reduce gender difference," one of the questions explored by the Derichs-Thompson project. Hasina likes to be addressed as "sir," not as "madam," which she thinks has "dubious connotations." She famously declared that she would "boot the madam," that is, Khaleda, "out of power" (Thompson 2004, p. 48). How women leaders choose to dress, the image and symbols they cultivate, are also of interest, as are images of them created by "the gendered media" or by "the rival political party" (Begum, p. 271). Hasina and Khaleda lead *rival parties*, the Awami League (AL) and the Bangladesh Nationalist Party (BNP) in the *same country*, so presumably appeal differently to their supporters. Both were involved in the struggle to restore democracy, so differences in their political philosophy and perhaps in how they view democracy require discussion. Hasina is regarded as pluralist and secular, Khaleda as more Islam-centered. Khaleda is seen as more protective of Bangladesh's national interests, Hasina as pro-India, thus she is accused of potentially comprising Bangladeshi sovereignty. Khaleda may prefer a presidential style; Hasina is said to value consensus, a term she uses in speeches. The AL is internally the more democratic (Molla, p. 233; Hossain 2004, p. 213). Non-Muslim Bangladeshis identify with Awami as a party for everyone, regarding the BNP as a party for Muslims.

The issues identified above take us to the frontier of scholarship of Islamic societies, where politics, textual analysis, ethnography and post-colonial studies converge. The book does not definitively answer most, if any, of the questions it asks. What follows intends to stimulate further reflection on the issues by shining some light into these areas. It uses five women's careers as lenses to examine significant topics. Evaluating their careers is not central to this enquiry. They have supporters and critics. All five have held high office, so have secured a place in history. It is difficult for this writer to be completely neutral with reference to the two Bangladeshi leaders, since my wife's family favors one rather than the other. Nonetheless, in offering any evaluation, I attempt to be objective, supporting comments with facts or opinions from informed sources.

After opening remarks setting each chapter's parameters, the literature and research used in writing this book is surveyed. A final chapter sums up what can be offered by way of concluding remarks. These include the contention that Islam *did not hinder* these women's rise to power. Indeed, a major contention of this book is that *no incompatibility exists between Islam and women exercising political leadership*. These women actually helped make Islamic voices *heard* in the public square. However, the claim that Islamist parties are becoming too influential, that those with very different political goals out-manipulated these women, is misplaced. Rather, these women may be steering people away from the type of Islam represented by the term "Islamist." Islam in these contexts is taking a different direction, one that women at the village level are also shaping. Culture did play a role, probably positively. Although Islam is deeply embedded in each national context and culture, factors specific to Turkey and South Asia may have aided these women's political empowerment. Arab Muslim states have yet to produce a senior woman politician, so the specific cultural contexts of these four non-Arab Muslim states may be conducive to *liberating, pro-female interpretations of Islam*.

Of course, there may be as many interpretations of Islam as there are Muslims, yet an argument can be made that Islam and women's rights are natural allies. Culture and Islam are intimately related, yet it is also true that the culture with which Islam is intimate varies from context to context. Muslim societies cannot be reduced to their "Islamic" aspects. South Asian and Turkish Islam are not identical in all aspects with Arab Islam. However, the temptation of some to reject South Asian and Turkish Islam as somehow less pure, less legitimate, thus *permitting the anomaly of women leaders*, will be critiqued. Elevating Arab Islam, 20 percent of the world's Muslims, over Asian Islam (at least 60 percent) as "better" is unfair and problematic. Writers often remark on the distinctive nature of South Asian Islam as *inherently tolerant and open*. Sufi influence impacts here, as it does in Turkey, which can be described as Euro-Asian. In contrast, the Saudi regime is antagonistic to Sufism. Could it be argued that South Asian and Euro-Asian Muslims, lacking that pride of race that *can color Arab Islam*, recovered neglected aspects of their faith, maybe because they are at a *distance from the Islamic center*? Istanbul under the Ottomans, of course, claimed *to be* the Islamic center, although this never had wholehearted Arab support. To de-center Islam, on the one hand, denying that it serves as a metanarrative, agrees with postmodern skepticism that any such narratives exist. A preference for *local narratives* flies in the face of Muslim self-belief in *Islam as a unifying tradition*, in what has been called a "master-signifier" (Sayyid, p. 48). Preference for an interpretation of Islam as a *gender-equal tradition* could be dismissed from a postmodern perspective as one among many possible interpretations, with a *gender-biased* interpretation equally valid. Or, challenging the view that any reading can claim equal legitimacy, can we affirm that a reading that conforms to *international standards of human rights* is in fact the correct one? Gender-biased interpretations are not what God, who gifted us rights as humans, intended.

Dynastic ties played a role in four of the women's selection as party leader. On the one hand, without dynastic ties, they probably would not have entered politics. On the other hand, it is absurd and untenable to explain their careers away *solely as surrogates for dead male relatives*. Çiller's lack of a dead male relative has not exempted her from the charge that her mentor's early support made her political debut possible. Talent, apparently, is not part of the equation. Of the four with familial ties, Khaleda Zia draws less attention to this in her speeches.

It is difficult to assess whether the five women's achievements support the claim that *women and democracy make good partners*, since their legacies are ambiguous. On the one hand, their commitment to democracy, with some reservations, is impeccable. On the other hand, their *conduct in office has not always matched the highest standards*. Then again, in politics, *whose conduct does*? How many politicians are there who never, ever engage in opportunism, or in self-promotion? This might describe most politicians. Why single women out? At this point, *women are being held more accountable than men*. We actually have great expectations for them, wanting them to succeed where men fail. I personally hope that women leaders will be more reluctant to fight wars, more inclined to resolve disputes peacefully. Others share some blame for what blemishes the records of such women. Even a prime minister or a president works within existing systems. They do not govern alone, or begin with a *tabula rasa*.

There is no doubt, though, that *all five of our subjects advanced women's rights*. The evidence here is strong, even when women's issues were not among their major concerns. They did use the gender card to play on images of sister, daughter and mother of each and every citizen. As four of the five bore the tragic loss not only of the nation's former leader or founding father, but also of their relative, so they assumed the suffering of the nation in its struggle against adversity, poverty and other problems. Çiller used the Turkish concept of "sister" as "honorable" and "untouchable" to create distance between her own image and the "partisan, aggressive, self-centered, self-interested, fractious, unscrupulous, and constantly wrangling imagery of male politicians prevalent in society" (Cizre, p. 207). Post-colonial factors helped shape the agendas they had to deal with such as separatism and national unity. Did their gender, rather than non-gender-related aspects of their leadership, have any special impact here?

Dealing with separatism, especially with armed insurgency, is always difficult and daunting. The notion that women are more inclined toward peace, non-violent resolution of conflict and reconciliation could be a factor. This might be why Hasina was able to conclude the Chittagong Hill Tracts accord. She has received several peace awards. On the other hand, Çiller was tough in dealing with Kurdish insurgency, while Megawati was accused of being too soft in responding to terrorism, even of avoiding action. Thatcher reacted decisively when Argentina invaded the Falklands. Was she acting as she thought a man would, to prove that gender was no handicap; that she could be trusted to protect British interests? Women in power may *not yet be truly free to be women* in a world that men and notions of masculinity still dominate. They may also be accused of using feminine guile to manipulate men! Men, of course, never manipulate women!

Finally

The content of this book draws on personal observations, conversations and informal fieldwork. I have spent time in Turkey, Bangladesh and Indonesia, three of the four states, as well as in Arab space. My wife has sometimes traveled where I have not, so I draw on her experience too. For longer than I like to remember, I have been a close watcher of events in Bangladesh and Pakistan especially. I have also paid a lot of attention to Indonesia and to Turkey over several years, as I have to gender, politics and culture in Islam. Engagement with the four contexts and with these issues impacts what I write. The following, while not ethnography as such, was anthropologically molded and shaped. Much of the published research consulted used formal fieldwork and qualitative social science methodologies.

Chapter 1

Women Leaders: The Debate

Establishing Parameters

This discussion looks at the thinking on gender that informs opposition to and support for Muslim women's participation in politics. Specifics of responses with respect to particular women are revisited in subsequent chapters. The issue of women's leadership is inextricably linked with broader discussion about women's rights and status in Islam. Attention is also given to the wider issue of women's participation in politics. The chapter first summarizes literature and research used in researching this topic. No claim is made to exhaust available material. It should be seen as a representative selection. Next, we survey women's representation in parliament and government around the world, identifying issues raised by those who champion women in politics. This survey, building on material contained in the Introduction, situates the five women's careers in a wider context that draws attention to their achievements. Then, the chapter discusses Muslim opinion on the issues of gender, women's rights and whether women can lead men as well as women. Three positions are identified. One opposes Muslim women holding high political office as *contrary to Islam*. This is the *equal but different view*; women and men are equal but duties and rights vary. Political leadership is a male duty, *from which females are excluded* and *for which they are naturally ill suited*. Yet some compromise may be possible. The leading conservative scholar, Mawdudi, lifted objection to a woman seeking high office, endorsing Muhammad Jinnah's sister, Fatima, in her unsuccessful 1965 bid for the Pakistani presidency, risking his reputation in the process (Shehabuddin, p. 60). He said that a woman could lead *in special circumstances*. This ambiguity may explain why, in Bangladesh, his party has supported and withdrawn support from women leaders. The second position says that

Islam does not discourage or prohibit women's participation in politics or from exercising leadership. This discussion visits *hadith* and Qur'anic verses cited in support of position one, offers alternative interpretations, or questions the authenticity of some *hadith.* Men as well as women advocate this approach. Benazir's election stimulated scholarship, on Islam and gender, which owes a debt to her achievement. The third position agrees with the first, that *Islam hinders gender equality,* dismissing the second view that, *correctly interpreted,* Islam is *female friendly.* However, unlike position one, position three rejects Islam itself, advocating that *all religious influences on society* should be opposed, eliminated, relegated to history. The chapter supports the view that an interpretation of *Islam as gender equal* is legitimate, since it aligns Islam with what God reveals through other mechanisms, such as human rights. This draws on the thinking of Iranian scholar Abdulkarim Soroush, who suggests that Muslims can properly utilize internationally accepted human-rights standards as criteria when interpreting scripture and primary documents. "The norms and principles of rationality and humanity are all applicable to religious jurisprudence," he says (2000, p. 149). Soroush, with whose work Benazir was familiar, reminds us that while scripture may be divine and infallible, our reading of it is human and very fallible (p. 31).

Those who regard *religion in general and Islam in particular as dangerous* will remain unconvinced but for religious people this may be the most attractive option, one that, as another Muslim, Bassam Tibi, says, *anchors Muslims within humanity* (1998, p. 206). Before arguing in favor of position two, I aim to discuss all arguments objectively. Postmodern thought presents some difficulty when defending a single position. However, it also healthily liberates us to declare personal commitments and beliefs. Students should not have to engage in textual archeology to identify what influences our writing. I believe that openness about our commitments is academically honest but that we must also give alternative perspectives serious thought. The temptation, which can never be fully resisted, to permeate our work with bias must be confronted. We all take baggage with us to our research; we all look at the world through colored lenses. These lenses may or may not distort what we see but by declaring presuppositions we protect ourselves from the worst excesses of seeing only what we want to see. Some people's lenses result in seeing others as irreconcilably different, as less civilized, less intelligent, less moral. Yet lenses and even shades when sunlight is bright can also help us see more clearly. My lens is a type of humanism, always asking what promotes the common good, the health and wholeness of the world?

Reviewing the Literature

On women's participation in politics globally and on comparing the four Muslim states with other contexts, I draw mainly on material in Nelson and Chowdhury's *Women and Politics Worldwide* (1994) and on the International Institute for Democracy and Electoral Assistance's handbook, *Women in Parliament: Beyond Numbers.* Julie Ballington and Azza Karam edited the 2009 edition. Nelson and Chowdhury have case studies on Bangladesh and Turkey. Especially useful chapters in Ballington and Karam include the case study on Indonesia, chapters on "Reserved Seats in South Asia," Sabbargh on the Arab states, and material on contexts where quotas have been used, such as the Nordic states. The case studies are also sources for subsequent chapters. Krook (2009) is about reserved seats and quotas. The Nordic countries, the United Kingdom, Pakistan and India are discussed. Thompson's work on female leadership and democratic trends in Asia sheds contextual light on four of the women's careers. His work, though, is cited more in subsequent chapters. His 2004 chapter on women leaders in Asia is available as an article in *Pacific Affairs* (2002–3), with slight differences. In comparing and contrasting the four Muslim states with the Arab world, Keddie (2007) was an important source, containing case studies, historical background and analysis of current developments. On women and Islam, I analyze the work of of Abul A'la Mawdudi (1903–79) for position one, Leila Ahmed, Fatima Mernissi and Aminah Wadud for position two. Mernissi's work on *hadith* criticism and Wadud's on Qur'anic verses supplement Ahmed's focus on theological and historical aspects. Although I mainly use Hashmi (2000) later in this book, his chapter "Women in Islam: A Reappraisal" is an excellent summation of relevant discussion and different interpretations. He uses much of the same literature as I, and I concur with his view that "man-made law and pre-Islamic customs and traditions, not Islamic teachings, are responsible for the promotion of misogyny and subjection of women in Muslim societies" (p. 8).

This chapter also refers to some male Muslim contributors on gender, including M. M. Ṭāhā and his protégé, Al-Na'im. For convenience, where possible, references are to extracts in Kurzman's volumes *Modern Islam* and *Liberal Islam*. Position three draws on Moghissi, Nasrin and Afshari. As in the Introduction, when identifying factors that aid or hinder women's political participation I refer to the United Nations *Human Development Report* for the Gender Empowerment Measure and to World Bank data on Gross Domestic Products.

Women in Politics Worldwide

Ballington (2009) argues that women's representation in parliament is a human right. Women comprise half the world's population and half the workforce yet a billion women live in poverty around the world (p. 24). Chowdhury *et al.* take the view that women's participation in politics is necessary for the adequate representation of women's issues. Men falsely universalize their experience, thus women's voices need to be heard on the "particularity of their experience" (p. 11). Of course, women in parliament represent men too, just as men represent women and all represent political supporters and opponents. On the one hand, I think some men do good jobs representing women's interests. On the other, a parliament with men and women and members of minority communities reflecting social diversity will ensure that all voices and concerns are heard. If the statistic that 70 percent of women in the world suffer violence from men is accurate (Ban-ki Moon, UN Secretary-General, launching his campaign to end violence against women, November 2009) Chowdhury *et al.* may be right that women cannot rely on men to ensure their "safety and security" (p. 11). A male legislator might be guilty of harming a woman. Men may be less likely to advocate or protect "abortion and reproductive rights" or to provide "maternal and child-care programs" without which access to employment and other opportunities, including political, are difficult (p. 11).

Equal participation of women and men in public life is a cornerstone of the Convention on the Elimination of all forms of Discrimination against Women, adopted by the UN General Assembly in 1979, now ratified by 179 countries. Former UN Secretary-General Kofi Annan drew a link between achieving peace in many parts of the world and gender equality. In 1995, the percentage of women in parliaments globally was 11.3. In 2005, it was 16 percent and worldwide "women hold more elected offices than ever before" (Ballington, p. 25). Most progress has been made in the Nordic Countries, least in the Pacific and the Arab world. Positive change is attributable to "sustained mobilization, institutional engineering" and "party political commitment" (p. 26). Where less progress has occurred, obstacles are both *attitudinal and socio-economic* and *political and institutional* (p. 27). It is generally agreed that where opportunities exist for women in employment and education, where societies are freer, government is transparent and democracy healthy, women are more likely to enter politics.

However, even in prosperous, free, democratic societies, institutional obstacles exist. Political parties may be reluctant to choose women for safe seats. The institution of parliament may resemble a men's club, with late-night sittings and no child-care provision. Chowdhury *et al.* suggest that "patriarchy and fraternalism" dominate politics, what "in Great Britain is called the 'chaps' mentality of parliament" which alienates women (p. 16). Shvedova calls this the "masculine model of politics" which is often *confrontational and competitive*, not collaborative and concerned with consensus making (pp. 35–6). *Women in Parliament: Beyond Numbers* suggests that where some special measure, such as reserved seats or quotas to increase women's participation, is adopted, progress occurs. Turkey, which has no special provision in place, lags behind the other three Muslim states that do. Reserved seats and quotas attract controversy. Arguments against quotas, says Dahlerup, return "again and again with each election cycle" (p. 152). They are criticized as "undemocratic," contravening the "principle of equal opportunity for all, since women are given preference" (p. 143). Women occupying reserved seats can be seen as second class compared to open seat holders, "regarded as representing only women" (Rai, p. 181).

In Pakistan and Bangladesh, seats are allotted proportionately based on the size of parliamentary parties, then those already elected to open seats vote for candidates to fill the reserved seats. When "female legislators" speak out on women's issues, men remind them that they, not women, elected them (Krook, p. 66). In Bangladesh, reserved seats represent larger constituencies than open seats (Chowdhury 1994, p. 98). In 2000, a national commission in Pakistan called for implementation of the Beijing recommendation that women and men vote directly to fill reserved seats (Krook, pp. 83–4). Arguments for special measures center on the need to "compensate for actual barriers" that prevent women from gaining their fair share of political seats (Dahlerup, p. 144). Dahlerup identifies two concepts of equality. The first grants women the vote, then assumes that equality will follow; that the "rest was up to individual women" (p. 144). The second focuses on "equality of result," arguing that the removal of formal barriers is not enough while other obstacles remain, thus "compensatory measures must be introduced as a means to reach equality by result" (p. 145).

Shvedova suggests that lack of women in the parliaments of some European countries violates their human rights (p. 34). The main argument in favor, though, is that both reserved seats and quotas work, resulting in an increase of women in parliament. In Pakistan and Bangladesh, when reserved seats were dropped, the number of women elected to open seats also fell. When they were restored, the number of women elected to open seats also rose. When Egypt dropped reserved seats, the number of women in parliament fell dramatically. Comparison of Pakistan and India serves to highlight the success of the reserved seat system. The difference between reserved seats and quotas is that the former require legislation, setting a certain number of seats aside for women, while the latter may be created either by legislation or voluntarily by political parties (Dahlerup, p. 141). They set a "minimum percentage of candidates for election" but, of course, these may or may not succeed (p. 142). Bangladesh and Pakistan chose the "reserved seat" policy, while the Nordic countries and the British Labour Party chose party quotas. Indonesia opted for a law in 2003 that encourages but does not require political parties to meet quotas. This did not result in a dramatic increase of women in parliament in the 2004 election, although the percentage did rise from 8.8 in 1999 to 11.3 in 2004 (Parawansa, p. 82). Parties did not have much time to change practice between the passing of the 2003 law and the 2004 election. The 2009 election, however, saw an increase to 18.2 percent, higher than the USA. India chose reserved seats for women at local but not at national level (Krook, p. 57). As a result, Pakistan now has 22.5 percent women in parliament, India 10.7 percent.

The fact that Turkey is below India and lacks any special measure underscores that some form of official commitment is one of the most important factors in ensuring women's representation in parliament, more important perhaps than economic prosperity or even educational achievement. India has a higher GDP and a longer history of democratic stability than Pakistan. Yet it serves as an example of how, even when such factors as national prosperity and a healthy democracy are in place, lack of other factors hinders progress. Chowdhury *et al.* observe that "in the decades before independence, women constituted 10 percent of those jailed" in India "for anti-British activities," while in independent India at the time of writing, women had never held "more than 8 per cent" of seats in the lower house of parliament" (p. 15). Few if any would argue that quotas and reserved seats should be permanent measures. They may, however, be necessary to "kick start women to gain entry to politics" (Dahlerup, p. 143). Following her election as India's first woman president in 2007, Pratibha Devisingh Patil declared that 30 reserved seats for women would be introduced at national level.

I drew attention in my Introduction to the fact that, compared with Pakistan and Bangladesh, the USA and Japan, though higher on the Gender Empowerment Measure and among the wealthiest countries in the world, score lower on the percentage of women in parliament scale. Japan, a prosperous state, is widely regarded as a stable democracy, but is lower on the women in parliament scale (GEM 54th; women in parliament 97th; 11.3 percent). Evidence of the Nordic countries supports the claim that where women have access to employment and education they are more likely to also enjoy opportunities in the political arena. These nations are among the most prosperous, with high scores for transparency, human rights and freedom.

Again, however, progress can be made where these are less evident. Rwanda, with the highest number of women in parliament, has one of the lowest GDPs in the world (143th). Reserved seats (24 out of 80) and the unusually large number of households headed by women following the genocide of 1994 contributed to this extraordinary achievement. South Africa, with Africa's highest GDP, is also 3rd from the top on the percentage of women in parliament scale. On the one hand, South Africa faces many challenges related to wealth distribution and equal opportunities for blacks and whites. On the other, it has committed itself to gender equality. Farid Esack, the Muslim scholar-activist, was a gender commissioner in the Mandela administration. If prosperity and strong democratic institutions alone were sufficient, the USA and Japan would top all gender-equality measures. On this basis, Turkey and Indonesia would outperform Pakistan and Bangladesh, but in fact the reverse is true. Turkey has the 17th highest GDP, Indonesia the 19th, Pakistan the 47th, Bangladesh the 61st. Pakistan and Bangladesh have special measures in place. Indonesia, having more recently adopted a measure, is 3rd. So far, two political parties in Turkey have quotas but these have not been honored in practice, reflected in the low number of women in parliament (9.1 percent). Yet progress has occurred. When Çiller was in office, there were 8 women (1.5 percent). Turkey ought to be higher too, given an impressive female literacy rate of 79.6 percent compared with Pakistan's 36 percent and Bangladesh's 31.8. Turkey has a rather impressive legacy here: "in several key professions, including university teaching, there existed in 1970 a higher percentage of women in Turkey than in most Western countries" (Keddie, p. 83).

All publications stress that women's organizations play crucial roles lobbying for and advocating women's participation in politics. The women's movement has had a comparatively weak history in Turkey. It has been an elite movement in Indonesia. Bangladesh and Pakistan have had more non-elite involvement. Compared with such more prosperous countries as the USA and Japan, the four Muslim countries perform more than adequately *vis-à-vis* gender equality, thus the contention that Islam hinders gender equality is difficult to sustain. It would be as logical to say that Islam *helped* the four states and that *lack* of Islam as a major influence in the USA and Japan hinders progress there.

However, if *Islam does not hinder progress* in these four states, what can be said of the Arab world, where less progress has taken place? Here, the literature agrees with my assessment that *non-Islamic factors and not Islam* are mainly to blame. Writers also point out the popularity of what I describe as "position number one." I am not claiming that Islam never hinders progress toward gender equality; rather, that interpretations of Islam which do so are not the only option. Sabbagh identifies tribal traditions, weak civil societies and other non-Islamic factors as hindrances (p. 55). Keddie writes, "many of the features of women's status often attributed to Islam turn out to have been borrowed from prior civilizations ... and from other religions" (p. 166). It could be, then, as Sabbagh surmises, that "non-Arab Muslim women have had better chances than their Arab Muslim sisters" (p. 55), for example due to healthier civil societies and stronger democracies.

The four nations to which subsequent chapters turn have seen episodes of military rule yet, despite setbacks along the way, have managed to develop democratic governance. This is less true for the Arab world. There are limited restraints on the power of the king in such countries as Kuwait, Saudi Arabia, and the United Arab Emirates. Morocco and Jordan are becoming constitutional monarchies, while democracy has yet to blossom in Syria, Egypt and elsewhere. I cited in my Introduction Mernissi's comment on the unparalleled length of presidential "reigns" (1992, p. 64). Sabbagh refers to the "freedom and democracy deficit" (p. 53) of many of the 22 states within the Arab League, commenting that though other regions have "moved towards democracy as their economies have developed ... the Arab region has not shown such a tendency, despite [noticeable] increases in most recent socioeconomic indicators" (p. 54). Saudi Arabia, where women do not vote and many restrictive practices exist, has the 23rd highest GDP. As I also noted in the Introduction, Sweden and Norway, which lead the world in gender equality, border the Saudis in terms of GDP, being ranked at 22 and 24 respectively.

Yet the picture in the Arab world is not entirely bleak. As a general rule, where democracy is taking root, women's participation in politics has increased. There is no doubt, on the one hand, that the Saudi government regards itself as an authentic Muslim regime. With the Qur'an as its constitution, regulations on women's dress and other aspects of their status and rights are derived from the officially sanctioned interpretation of Islam. On the other hand, rulers of the equally conservative United Arab Emirates have appointed seven women to their consultative assembly. Voters have elected another. One presumes that these Muslim rulers do not regard the appointment of women as un-Islamic. The rulers of several other Arab states have taken pro-gender equality steps. These rulers also see themselves as good Muslims. In fact, some exercise leadership within the Muslim world, which, as Guardian of the Sacred Cities, the Saudi monarch claims for himself.

The Jordanian royal house, descended from the family that ruled Mecca since the tenth century, traces itself to Muhammad. The present king's great-great-grandfather, Emir Hussein bin Ali of Mecca, adopted the title caliph when the Ottomans fell. Prince Ibn Saud drove him out of the Hejaz, then, inspired by the teaching of al-Wahhab (1703–92), set up his version of an Islamic state. Officially the *Muwahiddun*, or Unitarians, al-Wahhab's heirs are usually called Wahhabis. Jordan sponsors an interpretation of Islam that stresses pluralism and good relations with other religions. This represents an alternative to Saudi Islam. While Christians are prohibited from worshipping in Saudi Arabia, Jordan's cabinet almost always includes several Christians. The royal family sponsors an Institute for Interfaith Studies (established 1994). Just as a member of the royal house, Prince Hassan, uncle of the present king, takes a lead in promoting interreligious harmony, another member, Princess Basma (with whom my wife attended university and undertook a field trip to Jordan) has led on gender equality (Keddie, p. 135). The King of Jordan sponsors the Amman Interfaith Message (http://amman-message.com/index.php?option=com   _content& task=view&id=80&Itemid=54) and the Amman Message (http://amman-message.com/index.php?option=com_content&task=view&id=16&Itemid= 30), both of which affirm that Muslims and followers of other religions stand on "common ground."

The ruler of Qatar and his wife have strengthened democracy, although they point out the need to proceed gradually so that "core historical, cultural and religious values" are preserved (Sobhani, p. 21). Sheikh Hamad, as does King Abdullah II of Jordan, supports "an Islamic legal and political system that would allow room for religious pluralism" (Sobhani, p. 24). Unlike in Saudi Arabia, Christians can import Bibles for personal use (p. 25). Sheikh Hamad has also permitted the building of non-Islamic places of worship (p. 25). Yet the official interpretation of Islam in Qatar is Wahhabi. The 2003 constitution has 30 members of the consultative assembly elected, 15 appointed. It has more legislative powers. The emir is trying to fight corruption and improve transparency. Qatar is 84th on the Gender Empowerment Measure. There are no women in the assembly but 8 percent of senior officials and managers are women (HDR, p. 333). Switzerland (which did not grant women the franchise until 1971) and the UAE are also listed at 8 percent. Japan has 10 percent.

The present King of Morocco, where a women's movement has emerged, introduced reserved seats in 2002 and legislation that removes almost all gender-discriminatory laws "except that polygamy was not completely outlawed" (Keddie, p. 146). Descended from Muhammad, the king uses the title "commander of the faithful," traditionally reserved for caliphs. Women's groups, says Keddie, prompted the reserved seats provision (p. 147). Mernissi, who has not confined her work to the academy, impacts gender equality in her home country (Keddie, p. 145). As long ago as 1957, the then king publicly unveiled his oldest daughter. Hassan II appointed a prime minister in 1998 from the opposition, while reforms in 1992 and 1996 gave parliament greater authority. In 2000, the first female minister took office.

The unelected rulers of Morocco, Jordan and Qatar possess greater powers than constitutional monarchs in Europe but their states are moving towards authentic democracy. Unlike some advanced democracies, they have taken special measures to promote gender equality. It is unthinkable that these men, all of whom are very conscious of their Muslim identity and have some genuine claim to leadership within the Muslim world, think that either strengthening democracy or women's participation in politics is un-Islamic. We need to be sensitive, though, to the possibility that what emerges in Arab states may be different from democracy elsewhere. Why should one model fit all cultures and contexts? Neither Jordan (95th highest GDP) nor Morocco (59th highest) are as *prosperous* as Saudi Arabia but they are *more democratic* and have made *more progress* in gender equality. For comparison, Jordan has 84.7 percent and Morocco 39.6 percent female literacy. Saudi has 70.8, UAE 81.7 and Qatar 88.6. In 2003, female literacy in the UAE was higher than male literacy (76 percent) (Keddie, p. 159). Literacy statistics are available in the CIA *World Factbook* (https://www.cia.gov/library/publications/the-world-factbook/fields/ 2103.html). Certain cultural factors in South Asia undermine the view that patriarchy is the whole story there, though it is *more embedded* in the Arab world. Muslims who see Islam as trumping culture, who embrace interpretations of Islam that undermine anti-equality cultural factors, will empower women wherever they live, in or outside Arab space.

Position One: Muslim Women as Equal but Different

Although this position is typified in the influential writing of Mawdudi, it also represents Wahhabi ideas. Mawdudi differed from Wahhabis on how he believed an Islamic state should be organized, arguing in favor of a "theo-democracy," but his ideas on gender are very close to the Saudi form of Islam. He was awarded the prestigious King Faisal Prize for his contribution to Islam in 1976. I refer to Mawdudi's ideas about political organization in Chapter 2. With Sayyid Qutb (1906–66), Mawdudi is widely regarded as one of the twentieth century's most influential Muslim thinkers. His view on most issues can be taken to represent the "right," although not always the extreme "right." Mawdudi's ideas on gender resurface in subsequent chapters of this book. Many writers stand in his debt, including Gamal A. Badawi in Ahmad (1999). The editor, Khurshid Ahmad, who held political office in Pakistan, was a Mawdudi protégé.

Mawdudi's *Purdah and the Status of Women in Islam* was first published in 1939 (2nd edn, 1972). He begins with a survey of women's status in different civilizations and how women in pre-Islamic Arabia and

until recently in the West lacked rights. He argues that the Western insis-
tence on "equality" is unnatural (Mawdudi, p. 12), castigating the West
for treating women as sex objects. He continues at some length,
condemning the excesses of Western sexual morality, which becomes a
platform for defending Muslim belief and practice. Mawdudi says that
due to Western criticism, Muslims compromise too quickly. Westerners
said that Islam disfavored art, so Muslims quickly insisted that they had
patronized art for centuries (Mawdudi, p. 20). They condemned
polygamy, so Muslims said that this was not really permitted except in
extraordinary circumstances. Mawdudi disagreed. He stated categorically
that Qur'an 4:3 unambiguously gives men permission to marry up to four
wives and argued that the Islamic credentials of Muslims who dispute this
are suspect. He calls this "conditional polygamy" because the husband
must treat all wives equally. In fact, says Mawdudi, the West ought to
abandon prostitution and adultery in favor of polygamy. Sexual
immorality is so rampant in France that "loss in physical strength" results
(p. 51). Mawdudi establishes the idea that polygamy is morally superior
to the lack of sexual morals in the West, building on the idea that Islam
is the "natural religion" *(din-al-fitra)*. The West treats women and men
as if they were physically, biologically, psychologically and emotionally
the same, forcing all to act like men. Islam recognizes man as naturally
stronger than woman, so God raised men a "rank" above women for the
latter's protection and maintenance, distinguishing their roles. Men are
suited to lead, women to nurture. Consequently, their rights are *similar*
but *different* (Qur'an 2:228).

Mawdudi asserts equality but says that equality does not imply *same
rights*. Rights follow responsibility, not vice versa. In his discourse on
human rights, Mawdudi insisted that the West's preoccupation with
these compromises God's rights, which take priority. Human duty, not
rights, is central. Since men are always responsible for the maintenance
of women (Qur'an 4:34) men require a greater share in inheritance
(Qur'an 4:11). Even a husband, however, lacks any claim on a wife's
wealth, whether from earnings, inheritance or the bridal price. She may
voluntarily contribute to household expenses but is not obliged to do so.
Mawdudi was emphatic that women should not lead men, so certain jobs
are closed, especially those requiring physical strength and emotional
stability. However, he supported Fatima Jinnah's presidential campaign,
believing that she had the best chance of fostering national unity. Arguing
that monthly menstruation makes women unstable, Mawdudi said that
this precludes them from judgeships, senior posts and – in normal circumstances – from high political office (Mawdudi 1972, p. 120).

Badawi cites the *hadith*, those who entrust their affairs to women will not prosper, and takes it as axiomatic that a woman cannot head a state. He says this has "nothing to do with the dignity of woman or her rights," everything to do with women's menstruation, which makes them unsuitable for leadership due to "excessive strain" and periods when "rationality" loses to "emotionality." Commenting that "in the most developed countries it is rare to find a woman" leader, he ascribes this in part to the "backwardness of various nations or to any constitutional limitations on woman's rights," but adds that it also reflects the "natural and indisputable differences between man and woman" (p. 143). Since he wrote, four Muslim countries have had women leaders, while many "developed countries" have yet to do so. Mawdudi saw women as less intellectually capable than men. He accepted women's right to work but prioritized their *domestic duties*, "bringing up children, looking after the domestic affairs and making home life sweet, pleasant and peaceful" (p. 121). Western women lose more than they gain. "Burdened with economic responsibility," they throw off their real responsibilities. Mawdudi did not think reform necessary in Muslim society with reference to gender relations. Instead, the West could learn a great deal by copying Islamic models. Veiling and segregation honor women. He takes references in the Qur'an to seclusion (33:53) and veiling (33:59) to apply to all Muslim women. Muslims on the right usually regard these as legally binding. Some countries, such as Saudi Arabia, Iran and territory under Taliban control, enforce seclusion (women must be accompanied by a male relative) and the veil. Mawdudi-inspired voices opposed the election of women leaders in Bangladesh and Indonesia as well as in Pakistan. However, they did not prevent their elections. In Indonesia, Islamist parties dropped opposition and conceded that a woman could be president (Blackburn, p. 107).

In Bangladesh, Mawdudi's party entered an alliance with Khaleda Zia while at the same time publishing a pamphlet *Female Leadership in the Sight of Islam* (1991) by M. Ruhul Amin, echoing Mawdudi's arguments against women leaders (Shehabuddin, pp. 167–8). Turning to Turkey, we do not find specific voices against Çiller's candidacy, but we do find support for Mawdudi-like attitudes and assumptions. Given Turkey's history and secular constitution, objections on purely religious ground are unlikely. In Bangladesh and Pakistan, which are officially "Islamic," and in Indonesia, which recognizes "religion" as a principle of national philosophy, politicians find it easier to stand on purely Islamic ground. The fact that no constitutional barriers to women becoming head of government or state existed in *any of these Muslim-majority countries* would seem to support the claim that Islam was not a major hindrance, although this did not prevent a ruling by some Pakistani *ulama* that Bhutto could be prime minister as the current president was a man (Thompson 2004, p. 47). Again, we see Muslims agreeing that a woman could lead, even though some Muslims could not accept a woman head of state. Incidentally, based on such Qur'anic verses as 16:97 and 33:35, no one questions that Muslim men and women are *spiritually equal*.

Position Two: Muslim Women and Men are Equal

The second position represents what can be called Islamic feminism, although it has male and female supporters. Much discussion focuses on particularly problematic Qur'anic and *hadith* verses. There is some common ground between supporters of this position and Mawdudi. For example, they agree with him that Islam vastly improved women's status compared with pre-Islamic Arabia. The right to work and to keep their earnings (4:32), to inherit (4:11), and to give evidence at court (2:282), for example, were either entirely absent in pre-Islamic Arab society, or easily abused. Similarly, women in pre-Islamic society may have lacked any right to divorce, whereas under Islam, while they need to petition a court – unlike men – the Qur'an nonetheless guaranteed them this right (4:128). Qur'anic verses guarantee women rights, even if as heirs and witnesses these are not the same as men's. Some explain the testimony requirement of two women for one man by saying that women in Muhammad's day were less used to public procedures, so could be easily intimidated. Classically, Islamic law has required two men as well as two women, on the basis that men as well as women can err (Hossain 2003, p. 112, n10). Fatima Mernissi and Leila Ahmed argue that the *ethical intent* of the Qur'an calls for *complete equality* (see Ahmed, p. 91). However, men were not prepared for this in the seventh century, so the Qur'an pointed in the *right direction* but did not *complete the process*. This responsibility falls to Muslim men and women today, guided by the *ethical spirit and intent*, not by *the letter of the Qur'an*. A similar argument applies to the *hudud* (extreme) penalties mentioned in the Qur'an, such as amputation for theft (5:38). An alternative penalty can be substituted, signaling the severity of the crime but without causing physical harm. Rejecting the view that the Qur'an (4:3) gives universal permission for men to marry up to four wives, supporters of position two point to the reference to caring for "widows and orphans," and note that 4:3 is dated after the defeat at Uhud (March 625), when many men died. Other verses depict the ideal as a lifelong partnership between one man and one woman (see 30:21; 42:49). Islam only permits polygamy in limited circumstances, similar to the context after Uhud. It idealizes monogamy. Ahmed argues that while women were creators of the texts in the formative period alongside men, contributing to the collection of *hadith*, Islam became increasingly patriarchal. As the empire expanded, women were categorized as either elite (wives and female relatives safely at home) or as objects for sexual satisfaction (women captured through conquest). As authoritative legal compendiums were compiled, men's assumptions about gender "and about women and the structures of power" were "inscribed into the texts the men wrote, in the form of prescriptive utterances about gender" (Ahmed 1992, p. 82). Non-elite women were turned into "sex objects" while elite women were part of *haram* space – sacred, protected, secluded: the *harem*.

Mernissi did a great deal of work looking at misogynistic *hadith*, such as "I looked into paradise and saw that the majority of its people were the poor, and I looked into the Fire, and found that the majority of its people were women" (Bukhārī and Khan, Book 76: *hadith* nos 16 and 51) and "the dog, the ass and women interrupt prayer if they pass in front" of a man while praying (Mernissi, p. 75). She discovered that Ayesha, the prophet's widow, contradicted many of these *hadith* in a collection edited by the famous exegete Imam Zarkashi (Mernissi 1998, p. 124). A number were attributed to a somewhat suspect narrator. All authentic *hadith* must be traced through a reliable chain of honest, pious transmitters (the *isnad*) to a close companion of Muhammad. Many woman-hating *hadith* are attributed to Abu Hurayra, who had a reputation for telling too many stories (p. 125). Despite being included in the "sound" collection of Bukhārī, he was suspected of lying.

Turning to a detailed study of what she calls the "conversation stopper" – the *hadith* that no people prosper who entrust their affairs to a woman – cited when Benazir was running for office, Mernissi notes how this was suddenly remembered after Ayesha's failed coup against Ali in 656. The fact that a woman had led what was regarded as the first *fitna* (civil war) gave men an excuse to speculate that female leadership results in chaos. *Hadith* were often invented to add authority to men's opinions. Mernissi suggests that this is exactly what Abu Bakra, the narrator, did (Mernissi 1991, pp. 50–1; 1998, p. 116). Ayesha was pardoned, remaining an honored mother of the believers. Women, though, were discouraged from taking part in public life, secluded, and reserved for domestic, child-rearing duties. Mernissi argues that this departed from earlier tradition when Muhammad consulted women and preached gender equality. His wives' advice was often the deciding factor in "thorny negotiations" (1991, p. 104). It was after his death that misogyny "very quickly reasserted itself" (1991, p. 75; 1998, p. 125). She writes of Muhammad's time as one in which women "had their place as unquestioned partners in a revolution that made the mosque an open place and the household a temple of debate" (1991, p. 10). No few *hadith* express Muhammad's fondness for women, such as "paradise lies at the feet of a mother."

In *The Forgotten Queens of Islam* (1993), Mernissi set out to show that Muslim women had in fact occupied positions of power before Benazir. The stories of these women go unsung, rubbed out "of official history" (p. 2). They are nonetheless available in "yellowed" tomes. She recounts the stories of women who at times in Muslim history exercised power, often against the odds, sometimes through intrigue. As well as regents ruling for infant sons, there were women who ruled in their own right. The problem for men in contemporary times is that women's entry into the public domain breaks convention, shattering the veil designed to separate them. Among the stories Mernissi tells are those of Sultana Radiyya, who "took power in Delhi in the year ... 1236" and Shajarat al-Durr of Cairo, "who gained power in ... 1250." The traveler and jurist, Ibn Battuta, describes her rule with no hint of censure. Al-Durr defeated the French king, Louis IX. Mernissi omits to mention the Begums of Bhopal, a succession of four female rulers of the princely state during the British Raj from 1819 until 1926.

Supplementing Mernissi's work on *hadith*, Wadud offers a detailed analysis of such Qur'anic verses as 2:223 and 4:34–5 that can be interpreted to prohibit women's leadership, asserting male superiority over women. This, she says, depends on how the verses are interpreted. At 2:223 the word *"darajah"* (rank, raised in rank) is used. This is the same word that Muslims to the right of Mawdudi use to justify rule by an elite, such as a royal family or *ulama*, scholars whose knowledge of Islam raises them a degree above others (see such verses as 6:165, 12:76, 43:32, 58:11). Other verses are cited to question the principle of majority rule, such as 5:100, 6:116, 12:21, 12:103. Wadud argues that *darajah* here does not support the universal subjugation of women to men, nor does "prefer" (*faddalah*) at 4:34–5. Rather, within the partnership of marriage, men and women are *co-equal trustees* of life. Yet men cannot bear children, so when wives give birth, they perform a biological task that men cannot. To compensate, men use physical strength and earnings to protect and provide for their wives. They do so as co-equal partners, when the other partner is vulnerable and dependent (1999, pp. 73–4; 1998, p. 135). In describing the Queen of Sheba, the Qur'an expresses no negativity *because she was a woman ruler*, which, says Wadud, supports her interpretation that the Qur'an does not elevate men over women. Men and women are co-equal caliphs (2:30), having accepted the "trust" (*amanah*) of stewarding creation, which the heavens, earth and mountains refused (33:72) (1998, p. 138). There is no reason why Muslim women should not choose to support themselves if they wish; they are not *obliged* to depend on men (1999, pp. 66–7).

Verses 34–5 also appear to permit wife beating. Some Muslim men argue that they do indeed have the right to beat their wives. Others cite various traditions that limit this to a type of playful gesture using a rolled-up handkerchief or a toothbrush (Saeed, p. 131). Wadud and others find it preposterous that Muhammad, who respected women and loved his wives, condoned wife beating of any description. No *hadith* has him hitting a wife. Wadud argues that the word that men render "beat" can also be translated as "to separate" or as "striking out in a new direction" (1999, pp. 73–4). The same word is used in the Qur'an to describe a partition between heaven and hell (57:13). It does not necessarily denote violence. In fact, Islam prohibits wife beating. Referring to the reference in 4:3 to "those whom your right hand possesses," which men inevitably translate as "concubines" so that some Muslim societies have allowed limitless concubinage, she says that this word can also refer to existing wives. Instead of reading "two, three, or four wives and those concubines whom your right hand possesses" it could read "two, three, or four or be content with your current wives." Men, not women, translate and interpret Qur'anic verses to perpetuate women's subordination to men. Turning to the controversial verses on seclusion (33:53) and veiling (33:59), Ahmed argues that the context refers exclusively to Muhammad's wives. In early Islam, only they wore the veil (pp. 53–4). An eminent conservative scholar, Al-Ghazzali (1917–96) supports this, arguing that compelling women to veil is prohibited. Women are not required to veil when praying or during the *hajj*, nor should Muslim women attempt to imitate the "mothers of the believers" (Muhammad's wives) (Afkhami, p. 71). According to this position, there is no reason why Islamic practice and international human rights should not harmonize. The Qu'ran requires modest dress for men and women (7:26).

Some male scholars support "position two." Muhammad Iqbal (1877–1938) argued that what is eternal and immutable is the spirit, intent or principles (*usul*) of the Qur'an, not specific applications or penalties. Iqbal argued that every generation of Muslims, "guided but unhampered by the work of its predecessors should be permitted to solve its own problems" (1930, p. 160). False reverence for the past, what salafists call *taqlid* (imitation), "and its artificial resurrection" is "no remedy for a people's decay" (p. 151). Salafists such as the Wahhabis and the Taliban claim to be *resurrecting original Islam*. The Salafah were the earliest generations of Muslims, close to Muhammad. Their Islam is *essentially ahistorical*. The ideal lies in a perfect, *utopian past*. Iqbal saw Islam as progressive and dynamic, reflecting the nature of God and the Qur'an (Iqbal 1998, p. 263). We can move "upward to receive ever-fresh illuminations from an Infinite reality" which "every moment appears in a new glory'" (p. 123). Men and women, as God's *khilafat*, might one day become God's partners, so God can rest from God's work, even if briefly. Life is in process, evolving toward realizing its potential. Until humanity progresses, God's potential remains dormant within God's being, waiting for us to become co-workers (p. 13).

Although famous for his poetry, Iqbal criticized Sufis for wanting *baqa* (union) with God, neglecting responsibilities to steward the earth and to act justly, rejecting the circumference (this world) for the radius, the spiritual route or path to God. The Sufi "spirit of total other-worldliness … obscured man's vision of a very important aspect of Islam as a social system" (1998, p. 257). Like Ṭāhā, Iqbal speaks of the "evolution" of Islamic law (1998, p. 262). He celebrates *firaq* (separation) of the human from the divine so that cooperation and partnership can develop. He openly acknowledges such influences as Whitehead, Nietzsche and Bergson. As we shall see in Chapter 2, Iqbal admired Turkey's new "republican spirit," saying that she alone of Muslim states had "shaken off its dogmatic slumber" (1998, p. 262). He supported the ideals of democracy, although for him Islamic law, reinterpreted for new circumstances, would be at the center of a Muslim state. He did not share Muhammad Jinnah's or Atatürk's secular vision.

On gender, Iqbal repeated some of the justifications for the differential in inheritance, since "the responsibility for maintaining" a woman is placed on men (1998, p. 265). He also called for a new look at the law in the light of "modern economic life," suggesting "we are likely to discover, in the foundational principles, hitherto unrevealed aspects which we can work out with renewed faith." The "superiority of males over females" was, he said, "contrary to the spirit of Islam" (p. 265). Such men as the Sudanese reformer, M. M. Ṭāhā, executed in 1985, and his protégé, An-Na'im, advocate a view of Islam that prioritizes the ethical spirit or intent, represented by the Meccan verses, over the particular applications found in the Medina passages. They view the former as Islam's real, permanent, universal message of truth (*haqiqa*), the latter as temporary concessions. These were allowed due to human weakness, men's inability to accept what God intended. Ṭāhā and An-Na'im refer to this as "'*aqida*" (dogma). Ṭāhā says that neither the veil, nor polygamy, nor slavery, nor the sword were "original precepts in Islam" (1987, pp. 137–43; 1998, pp. 276–7). Discriminatory verses such as the right of men to marry up to four women, the right of men to marry a Jewish or Christian wife while women can only marry Muslims, men's right to unilateral divorce while women must petition a court, the requirement that women marry another man before remarrying a divorced husband while men can remarry at will, difference in inheritance and testimony rules, must be repealed. They should be replaced with laws that reflect the ethical principles of the earlier, Meccan passages *and meet international human-rights standards* (An-Na'im, p. 233).

Qasim Amin (1863–1908), whose *tahrir-al-ma'ra* (liberation of women) was published in 1899, saw unveiling as the key to the social transformation of women (Ahmed 1992, p. 145; see Amin 2002). Fellow Egyptian Muhammad Abduh (1849–1905), the leading reformer, championed women's education. Egypt's colonial ruler, Lord Cromer (1841–1917) supported unveiling and desegregation yet opposed Abduh's plans for female education, raising school fees that made it more difficult for boys as well as girls to attend school. At home, he chaired the Men's League for Opposing Women's Suffrage (Ahmed 1992, p. 153) but he regarded what he saw as women's ill treatment as a "canker" eating into "the whole system of Islam" (Ahmed 1992, p. 153). This view, so ubiquitous among nineteenth-century writers about Islam, remains popular. Yet earlier European notions of Muslim women were different. Kahf (1999) shows that "the explicit association of Islam with the oppression of women does not reach full fruition until the eighteenth and nineteenth centuries" (p. 8). Earlier, Muslim women were depicted as bold and powerful, and as those who "could enter Europe as an equal" with men, "and even more than equal" (p. 5). In this period, women's representation was not "linked to the veil" (p. 6). The veil and the harem simply "do not exist in medieval representations of the Muslim woman and are barely present in the Renaissance" (p. 8). Later, forfeiting this power and equality, the Muslim woman was confined to the harem, where "her figure shrinks in subjectivity and exuberance." It became "the quintessential victim of absolute despotism, debased to a dumb, animal existence" (p. 8). Kahf links this change to the development of European colonialism and the creation of a type of self-serving "negative female ideal" in the Muslim space, which gave "disparate social groups within changing European societies ... a single social image they could agree to disparage" even as they struggled with new concepts of gender. This, in turn, helped shape a fiction of a "Western, not-Oriental, identity" (p. 7).

William Muir may have had this "not-Oriental identity" in mind when he looked at Muslims in India and complained that they neglected women's education at a time when "the long struggle for women's education was barely begun" in Britain (Daniel 1966, p. 279). Like Cromer (who cites him), Muir thought Islam incapable of reform, thus other nations might progress but Muslim societies could not adapt "to varying time and place" or "keep pace with the march of humanity, direct and purify the social life and elevate mankind" (1915, pp. 599–60).

Farid Esack, whose work as a gender commissioner in South Africa helped that country's rise up the scale of gender empowerment, argues that the Qur'an is about liberation. Uplifting the oppressed and marginalized is the main Muslim task. Realization that the anti-apartheid struggle was about justice and freedom *for all people*, not only for Muslims, encouraged him to look for keys to read the Qur'an "in such as way as to advance the liberation of all people" (1997, p. 78). He calls for a "gender jihad." Reading the Qur'an as pro-liberation, for Muslims who struggled against apartheid and injustice to "succumb to interpretations of the Qur'an that perpetuated the subjugation of women was tantamount to legitimizing the illegitimate" (1997, p. 242). Gender-equal-unfriendly interpretations need to yield to those that establish gender equality, he says. Before his Birmingham doctorate, he trained at conservative Pakistani *madrassas*.

In their writings, Fatima Mernissi and Leila Ahmed speak of women's Islam. This Islam allows individual thought, imagination, freedom to explore meaning and purpose. Ahmed is adamant that restrictive Islam, limiting or controlling access to the Qur'an and people's thought, is not *women's Islam*:

> The women ... had their own understanding of Islam ... different from men's Islam, 'official' Islam ... Islam, as I got it from them, was gentle, generous, pacifist, inclusive, somehow mystical ... of inner things ... So there are two quite different Islams, an Islam that is in some sense a women's Islam and an official, textual Islam, a 'men's Islam'.
>
> ...
>
> [Women did] not have a man trained in the orthodox (male) literary heritage of Islam telling them week by week and month by month what it meant to be a Muslim, what the correct interpretation ... is ... Rather, they figured things out for themselves ... nor did they believe that the sheikhs had an understanding of Islam superior to theirs. (1999, pp. 121–3; 124)

As Islamic history progressed, political authorities wanted to control Islam, demanding obedience, says Mernissi. Rulers saw independent thought as a threat. Such thought, represented by various schools of rational philosophy and by Sufis, more or less went underground or was hounded out of existence. As dissent and individual thought became *fitna*, violent rebellion became the sole method to express dissent or challenge misrule: "fanatical revolt was the only form of challenge which survived within a truncated Islam" (p. 37). "Individuals' use of reason," says Mernissi, "means weakening Islam and serving the enemy' (1992, p. 39). Islam became the *Islam of the palace*: enforced, unitary, male dominated. Nafisi, in *Reading Lolita in Teheran* (2008), remarks that democracy is stifled in Iran because "the freedom to imagine and the right to use imaginative works without restriction" is lacking, suggesting that the "right to free access to imagination" should be added to the Bill of Rights (pp. 338–9). Mernissi also calls for freedom to imagine, likening the "Imam" to a "cosmic watcher" whose job it is to ensure that "the vessel of Islam continues to sail on a hostile planet" with any "outpourings of the imagination" condemned "as a deadly attack." Perhaps, she says, it will be a Salman Rushdie rather than a scientist who "creates" his fiction "from imagination, the most indomitable refuge of individuality" (p. 90) whose work will "be the arena of future sedition" (p. 134).

Position Three: The Call to Abandon Islam

Mernissi, who self-identifies as a Muslim, represents "the aspirations of women who, while remaining Muslim, wish to live in modernity" (Sow, p. 33). Afshari (2003) thinks her efforts to "explain away" such highly restrictive verses" as 33:53 are no more convincing than traditional, misogynistic interpretations. He accuses Ahmed and Mernissi of trying to place ninth-century jurists and modern feminists "on the same epistemological footing." Rereading into Islam's origins modern feminist and postmodern notions and assumptions, they run "the risk of anachronism by contributing contemporary political meaning to antecedents far removed in time." Terms such as gender equality, egalitarianism or freedom of the individual are all derived from modern secular ideology and cannot be *discovered* in Islam's past. For Afshari, Islamic feminism is an oxymoron. Bangladeshi novelist and former practicing physician, Taslima Nasrin, who fled the country following a *fatwa* (opinion) that she should be killed in 1994, also targets Ahmed and Mernissi. She disagrees that the Qur'an can be interpreted *positively for women*: "How can one interpret the Qur'an positively on the question of women – when it says that men are superior?" (2000, p. 72). What is needed is a uniform civil code applicable to women and men, "religion and human rights, religion and women's rights, religion and freedom cannot coexist" (p. 72). All religion should be replaced with universal human values.

Moghissi (1999), in a prize-winning book, found it difficult to concede the *viability of an Islamic feminism*. She argues that the subjugation of Muslim women by men, which she takes as the actual reality within Muslim society, gets excused as *culturally appropriate* under the postmodern rubric that we "should be more accepting" of practices which are unacceptable *here* "but admissible *there*" (p. 5). Charmed by difference, she says, Muslim women are encouraged to "cling to an Islamic path" that has no chance of success (p. 121). Gains made in Iran under the Shah were lost, with more women in work but *in low-paid jobs* or in the "coercive apparatus designed to control and police other women" (p. 114). Women being whipped and imprisoned for failing to veil "find the dress code anything but empowering" (p. 5). This is a response to the claim that wearing *hijab* liberates and empowers women, freeing them from slavery to fashion, the need to dress to sexually attract men. Nafisi points out that when the choice to wear the veil was made freely, it was a "testament to faith," a "voluntary act." Once demanded by law, the act of wearing the scarf lost meaning. Now, everyone is *forced* to wear it (p. 13).

Conclusion: In Defense of Position Two

Are progressive, gender-equality-friendly interpretations of the Qur'an implausible? Must we regard male-centered interpretations of the Qur'an as correct? Must we accept the authenticity of *hadith* against which Mernissi musters convincing evidence? Mernissi argues that *hadith* should be examined carefully to "disinter our true tradition from the centuries of oblivion that have managed to obscure it" (1991, p. 64). Indeed, says Mernissi, due to the acknowledged existence of fabricated *hadith*, Muslims are encouraged to "question everything and everybody" (p. 76), although the elite try to supervise this (p. 10). Her work followed traditional critical methods, examining the *isnad* but also paying attention to *matn* (content), asking whether Muhammad would have said what the *hadith* says he did. Given his love of women, would he condone, as several *hadith* do, wife beating (see Bukhari, Book 72, *hadith*, 43, MM, Vol. 1, p. 693)? Must *daraba* be translated "beat" when a reading that does not condone wife beating is available? Does *Ma malakat aymanuku* at 4:3, which for some justifies unlimited concubinage, really do this? Or does this refer to existing wives who must be cared for equally? Mernisssi's rejection of the "conversation stopping" *hadith* was validated when a petition to remove Benazir from office before the Pakistani Supreme *Shari'ah* Court failed. The tradition was deemed "weak." A vote of four to two "with one abstention" ruled that "Bhutto could continue as Prime Minister" (Krook, p. 70). Krook comments that Shi'a "took a different view" from those who opposed Benazir, "arguing that Islam did not prohibit women from ruling" probably because Shi'a Imams trace their lineage to Muhammad through his daughter (Krook, p. 70).

The fact that five Muslim women achieved high office through constitutional methods suggests that "position one" voices did not control the political processes of the four Muslim-majority states. I find arguments in favor of gender-equal, human-rights-harmonizing interpretations of Islam convincing. It seems to me that some men find it convenient to read Islam differently. Yet it is not so long ago that women in the Christian world "belonged" to their husbands, or that similar notions about women's roles predominated. It was not until the mid-nineteenth century that married women in the US were allowed to own property. Quite recently, writing about barriers to women entering politics in the US, Morin observed that some men think women do not "have the ability to be political" or that their "place is in the home" (pp. 8–9). Once elected, women were less likely than men to gain prestigious committee chairs (p. 8). The same attitude opposed women's suffrage, which it took campaigning, acts of civil disobedience and time in prison by leading suffragettes to achieve. Queen Victoria, who might have supported the female franchise, opposed it. She sounds like Mawdudi, "Let woman be what God intended; a helpmate for a man – but with totally different duties and vocations" (Helsinger *et al.*, p. 60). If, with Soroush, we are able to recognize human-rights ideals as a cross-religious standard, despite their Western pedigree and reservations about their complete universality, why should Islam not be in harmony with them? *Islah* (reform) has a long history in Islam, despite Cromer's famous dictum that "Islam reformed is Islam no longer" but "something else." Cromer then cited Muir; Christian nations might advance but Muslims would remain stationary (1916, p. 229; see Muir 1915, p. 603). Why should Cromer and Muir define Islam? Reform refers to our understanding of Islam. As revealed truth, Islam remains immutable.

Choosing, unlike Nasrin, to respect religious beliefs, I am of the view that an available and plausible pro-equality, pro-peace interpretation is preferable to equality-denying, conflict-prone options. The view that the Qur'an contains eternal principles, that its *real message* should not be confused with *circumstantial, time-limited, particular applications*, makes sense. A book that speaks both to the seventh century and to the twenty-first century should be scrutinized carefully, to interpret the *same content* for a *different context*. Far from "subverting its universality," this locates universality in "the willingness of the faithful to hear the Qur'an speaking to them in terms of their deepest and most painful reality at all times" (Esack 1997, p. 255). When we ask the Qur'an for guidance in the particularity of our circumstances, we find that there is "no end" to "god's promise to disclose" (p. 111). It does not have to be a closed text, controlled by others for *their interests*. It can become *our text* for *our context*. Esack is all too familiar with how some co-religionists, such as the Taliban, see the text but he fails to see what they see. They call themselves "seekers" yet supply violence and subjugation of women to the text. Esack says that while the Qur'an answers the questions posed of it, the weight of verses supports a "profound commitment to life," "the creation of a peaceful society based on justice and compassion" (2005, p. 192). Certain that this is the picture found there, he hesitates to claim *absolute certainty*, lest he commit the same error as the Taliban, who approach the text confident that they *already possess the answers*. Certainty, he says, belongs only to God. We need to approach the text with a profound sense of God-consciousness (*taqwa*), to which I add "and with a deep commitment to the *humanum*, to the cause of human solidarity." Where Muslim states have taken action toward gender equality, there is little reason to see Islam as hindering or discouraging this, depending on interpretation. At worst, Islam might be neutral.

Legal reforms, such as those in Morocco and Bangladesh (see Chapter 5) adopted by Muslim legislatures and rulers, are clearly informed by "position two." Can we be so confident that non-Western cultures and Islam represent major obstacles to women's empowerment, while Western culture supposedly represents a less formidable barrier? Does this fit facts? Does the "not-Occident" picture of Islam color the way many, including liberals, see the Muslim world? Polarizing Islam and global human-rights standards favors the "clash of civilizations" thesis, which some people prefer. Representations that see Muslim women's achievements as counter-cultural aberrations, explained by "special circumstances" and "dynastic ties," leave "our superiority" and "their inferiority" assumptions unchallenged. People allow that Barack Obama's election signifies race-equality progress in the US but disallow Benazir Bhutto's career any relevancy for gender equality in the Muslim world.

The next chapter turns to Benazir, to her country, Pakistan, and to related issues of culture, gender and Islam. Her career is set in the context of Pakistan's struggle for national identity, against military rule, and to establish a stable democracy. Pakistan's tendency toward internal instability and regional separatist aspirations introduces the loss of East Pakistan, which became Bangladesh, where our second Muslim woman leader was elected. Benazir's view was that, "it is not Islam that is adverse to woman rulers" but "men" (1998, p. 111).

Chapter 2

Benazir Bhutto and Pakistan

Setting Parameters

Image 1: Benazir in Washington, DC, 1989.
Source: public domain.

In this chapter, after a summary of the literature used to research it I go on to sketch the political context in which Benazir's career took place. This traces the origin of the idea of Pakistan, through to the state's creation by partitioning India in 1947, through subsequent debates about identity, the role of Islam and the nature of the state. Benazir's career is set within the struggle for democracy, as well as against some of the issues with which she had to deal. A table lists alternating periods of civilian and military rule, locating Benazir's narrative within this wider story. Her career is subsequently outlined, with reference to arguments for and against her role as a woman head of government. Her self-description as "daughter of destiny," and her commitment to continue her father's work, were major factors coloring her politics and achievements. At least two others, Hasina and Megawati, have shared this sense of destiny and commitment to restoring their fathers' tarnished images. Finally, questions listed in the Introduction are explored.

Benazir has her critics. However, she emerges as a courageous woman whose career led the way for others to follow. Of the five women discussed, she was the first to serve as head of government in a modern Muslim state. She was also the world's youngest leader at the time.

Pakistan sees itself as a leader within the Muslim World, as an "ideological miracle" not "a geographical landmark." Its political interests embrace "the entire Muslim world" (Cohen, p. 172). Muslims in Asia and Africa would emulate Pakistan's achievements, and look to it for inspiration. The idea of creating an "Islamic army" was part of the country's self-understanding. Benazir once said that what she most wanted to be remembered for, in addition to toppling a military dictator and "heralding a world of democracy in Pakistan," was what she "did for women," which takes us to the heart of this book's concern (Horton and Simons, p. 189).

Surveying the Literature

For the "idea of Pakistan" and issues surrounding the birth and development of the new state, I consulted a range of sources. I found Cohen (2004) informative, readable and comprehensive with a very useful focus on Islam's role. Other texts consulted for political and historical background include Ahmed (1997) on Jinnah's vision for Pakistan, Gandhi (1986) on some of Pakistan's ideological forefathers, Jones (2002) for more recent events, and such texts as Johari (1993) and Jaffrelot (2004). Chapters in Mitra *et al.* (2004) on the Muslim League (ML) and Pakistan People's Party (PPP) proved very valuable. For biographical information on Benazir, I consulted the *Encyclopæda Brittanica Online*, her 1989 autobiography *Daughter of Destiny*, and material in Horton and Simons (2007). For her personal take on Islam, I used her posthumously published 2008 book and her earlier "Politics and the Muslim Woman" (1985), reproduced in Kurzman (1998). Benazir's ideas are easier to access than those of the other four women. Thompson's work was also consulted. On gender issues in Pakistan, I turned to Krook (2009) and Rai (2009), cited in my previous chapter. Other sources are referenced as appropriate. Cohen's book is an academic text written from a foreign policy perspective. He visited Pakistan many times during the "forty-four" years between starting and finishing his research. Especially interested in proliferation, security and arms control issues and in the militaries of India and Pakistan, Cohen has testified before the US Senate Foreign Relations Committee. Jones writes as a journalist who spent 1998 to 2001 in Pakistan working for the BBC. Ahmed, as in all his work, draws on anthropological training. The specific text referenced here was part of a wider project involving a film, a documentary and two books. His research included conversations with many involved in India's partition. Bettencourt (2000) on violence against women in Pakistan contains useful statistical data. She summarizes all relevant legislation up until 2000, focusing on the retrogressive phase under Zia. She compares this with obligations and commitments under international law.

Sadly, Benazir is no longer alive, tragically assassinated in December 2007. She was poised to win the subsequent election, the third restoration of democracy in Pakistan's history. Instead, her widower emerged as president, with their son as leader-in-waiting. Regardless of criticisms of her administrations and charges of corruption, she showed courage and determination. Her editor, who calls her the "bravest person" he knew, points to the value she attached to finishing her 2008 book, in which she penned her ideas on Islam, "her cherished religion," and on the urgent need to win the battle between "democracy and dictatorship, extremism and moderation" (pp. vii–viii).

Political Background: The Idea of Pakistan

Alternating Civilian and Military Rule

First Civilian Period
Liaqat Ali Khan (first prime minister), 1947–51; Khawaja Nazimuddin, 1951–3; Muhammad Al Bogra, 1953–5; Chaudhry Muhammad Ali, 1955–6; Huseyn Shaheed Suhrawardy, 1956–7 Governor-General, Jinnah, 1947–8; Khawaja Nazimuddin, 1948–51; Ghulam Mohamad, 1951–5; Iskander Mirza, 1955–6, became first president (1956–8)

First Military Period (began under Mirza)
Ayub Khan, 1958–60 (second president); Yayha Khan, 1969–71
(third president)

Second Civilian Period (first democratic restoration)
Zulfikar Ali Bhutto, 1971–7 (Benazir's father) (fourth president,
1971–3, ninth prime minister 1973–7)

Second Military Period
Zia al-Haq, 1977–88 (sixth president)

Third Civilian Period (second democratic restoration)
Benazir, 1988–90 (11th prime minister), 1993–6 (13th prime
minister, excluding caretakers)
Nawaj Sharif, 1990–3 (12th prime minister, excluding caretakers);
1997–9 (14th prime minister)

Third Military Period
Pervez Musharaf, 1999–2008 (10th president)

Fourth Civilian Period (third democratic restoration)
Benazir assassinated, December 27, 2008, during the election
campaign
From 2008: Asif Ali Zardari (Benazir's widow) (11th president);
Yousaf Raza Gillani (19th prime minister, excluding caretakers)

Source: Adapted from Jones, p. 226.

Benazir's two terms in office took place during the *third civilian period*, which lasted from 1988–99, when a military coup took place. Her father dominated the *second civilian period*, 1971–7, which also ended with a military coup. He began as president, becoming prime minister after reinstating that system of government. Both Bangladesh and Pakistan have oscillated between prime ministerial and presidential systems. Hasina's father sandwiched the presidency with being prime minister. Their careers, of course, overlapped. Benazir and her father each helped to restore democracy, which, as the self-styled daughter of destiny, Benazir saw as continuing her father's legacy.

Why has Pakistan experienced military rule interspersed with civilian-led democratic restorations? To answer this question, we need to trace the origin of the "idea of Pakistan" that led to the state's creation. Islam was a crucial component in this story. Debate about Islam's role, combined with competing ideas about the nature of the state, delayed the writing of a constitution, resulting in alternating prime-ministerial and presidential systems, military and civilian rule. How, too, did the army assume such a central and powerful role? What aspects are particularly relevant to Benazir's life? What issues did she have to deal with? What factors especially impacted her political career?

Antecedents to the Idea of Pakistan

The seeds of Pakistan's partition from India as a Muslim homeland were sown over a long period of time. Some claim "Pakistan was born the day that Muslims first set foot in India" (Cohen, p. 25). However, since Muslims came as rulers in the eleventh century and by 1290 dominated "nearly all of India" (Cohen 2004) there was no need then to partition off distinct Muslim territory. It was loss of power under the British that really led to Pakistan. The reality of British power resulted in different responses among India's Muslims; some chose cooperation, some conflict, others seclusion. I explored these responses in my 2005 book (pp. 180–4). In reverse, the Deobandi movement opted for isolation, having as little to do with the British as possible. The famous *madrassa* was founded in 1866. Those who chose conflict, influenced by Wahhabism, blamed the corrupt, Hinduized, syncretistic Islam of India as they saw it for their political decline, declaring a *jihad*. India was now *dar-al-harb* (house of war). Proponents of conflict trekked to the nearest Muslim land, Afghanistan, under Sayyid Ahmad Saheed Barelvi (1776–1831) and declared jihad. The cooperative response is closely associated with Sir Sayyid Ahmed Khan (1817–98), to whom what can be called a "systematic ... argument for what eventually became Pakistan" is traceable (Cohen, p. 25).

It was largely a consequence of events that took place in India during Sir Sayyid's life, to which he responded, that produced Pakistan. However, the British were primarily responsible for the actual event of partition. The catalyst was the war or revolt of 1857, which contributed to Khan's ideas but which also resulted in the British applying their divide-and-rule policy to how they dealt with Hindus and Muslims; that is, as two distinct communities.

No one argues that Hindu–Muslim relations were always positive before 1857. However, writers point out that harmony did exist, especially under Akbar (1542–60). Gandhi (1986), a grandson of the Mahatma, surveys this story. Hindu and Muslim teachers attracted disciples of all faiths, so that "if Islam rode across India with the sword and spoke from the throne, it also walked with the Sufis and spoke in gentler tones from the hut" (p. 12). What became Bangladesh, in the east, was majority Muslim long before any invaders arrived. Sufi missionaries won converts by peaceful preaching, tailoring their message to the religious environment around them. The north-west of India, what became Pakistan, was conquered early, lying on the corridor into India. Some regions "experienced the militant, exclusivist side of Islam, with the destruction of Hindu temples." Elsewhere, Islam was "relatively benign and inclusivist" (Cohen, pp. 15–16). The north-west would later regard its Islam as purer, less contaminated than Bangladesh's. Gandhi suggests that the problem for Hindus was that *Muslims loved India* but *did not worship her*, which hampered Muslims from fully sharing Hindu sentiment and loyalty (p. 14).

Under the Moghuls (1526–1858), Muslim political power in India reached its zenith. Map 2 indicates the largest extent of the empire under Aurangzeb (1618–1707), a very zealous Muslim ruler.

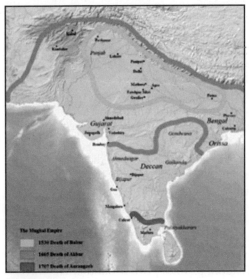

Map 2: The Mughal Empire

Then, starting not long after his death, the British began to displace the Moghuls as India's rulers. What became Pakistan, West and East, were formerly Moghul territories, united in a single Muslim state. They continued to be part of the same state under the British Raj. The difference was that they were no longer Muslim ruled.

The British expanded their territory in India, often siding with one Indian ruler against rivals. They extended their influence, acquiring additional territory or securing protectorates, which *de facto* incorporated territory into the Raj. Their Indian empire began when the British East India Company became agents for the Moghul emperor in Bengal, which they effectively ruled from 1757. By the mid-nineteenth century, they more or less took over wherever they wanted to, using a ruler's alleged incompetence, or lack of an heir whom they recognized, to annex territory. This increasingly alarmed Indians. Rumors about plans to flood India with Christian missionaries, to pollute Hindu and Muslim soldiers by giving them beef and pork fat to oil their rifles, fueled the 1857 revolt. The Moghul emperor, now a puppet of the British, supported the insurgents, many of whom were Muslim. For some, this was a *jihad* to restore Muslim power. *Fatwas* (opinions) were issued proclaiming this. The revolt was squashed, the last Moghul emperor, Bahadur Shah II, exiled, the East India Company wound up and India placed under direct British rule. From 1877, Queen Victoria adopted the title "empress of India." Sir William Muir chose the Hindi version, *Kaiser-I-Hind*. Despite his hatred for Islam, he was a personal friend of Sir Sayyid, who remained loyal to the British. Regarding Indians as *not yet ready* for self-government, wards needing a guardian, the "moral" justification for colonialism became popular. This owed much to Indian-born British poet and novelist, Rudyard Kipling's notion of the "white man's burden." Evils in Hindu and Muslim society had to be abolished. Reports on India's "Moral and Material Progress" were submitted annually to parliament, as if colonialism was really motivated by something other than profit! The claim that without their peacekeeping presence in India, Muslims, Hindus, Sikhs and so forth would slit each other's throats was invariably raised against demands to grant India independence. There would be a bloodbath. Gandhi, in frustration, once thumped the table, telling Lord Wavell, viceroy from 1943–7, that "if India wants her bloodbath she will have it," meaning that Indians had the right to order their own affairs. A bloodbath would be *their problem* to prevent or deal with (Brendon, p. 409). Lord Mountbatten, Wavell's successor, was tasked to quit India as soon as possible, regardless of any "bloodbath" that might follow.

British Anti-Muslims

Blaming Muslims more than Hindus for the revolt, British attitudes toward the former hardened. Muslims, wrote Sir William W. Hunter in his 1871 report, could not be trusted because they had a religious duty to rebel against infidel rulers. Khan disagreed. Responding to Hunter, he said that since Muslims were free to practice their *din* (religion) in India it was incorrect to say that India was no longer part of *dar-al-islam* (Muslim; lit. House of Islam). Muslims were honorbound to protect and preserve the "security" they enjoyed under British rule: "as long as Musulmans can preach the unity of God in perfect peace, no Musulman can, according to his religion, wage war against the rulers of his country" (1871, p. 81). Khan tended to stress the religious aspects of Islam, regarding the alliance of the religious and the political as *linked with circumstances*, not *automatically applicable*. Muslims would benefit most from collaboration with the British, from studying Western science and learning. To facilitate this, he established what became Aligargh University.

Often described as a secularist, Khan's use of this term in the context of Muslim thought requires clarification. Khan saw Islam as the "perfect religion" (2002, p. 302). He believed Muslims had a destiny to fulfill and wanted to secure a glorious future for them. Muslims needed to distinguish "pure Islam" from "later doctrinal elaboration" (2002, p. 299). His ideas embraced the entire Muslim world, not only the *quam* of India (the Muslim community). In speaking about the *quam*, he identified Muslims as a distinct community, whose interests differed from Hindus'. The Revolt impacted Hindus and Muslims differently. Hindus came out "unscathed" but "to the Muslims it was a total disaster" (Dar, p. 81). Khan fell short of advocating a partitioned-off state but set the stage for a "separate status" (Cohen, p. 25). He predicted Hindus and Muslims would fail to cooperate, becoming increasingly hostile, "I am convinced that both communities will not join wholeheartedly in anything … hostility between the two communities will increase immensely in the future" (cited by Gandhi, p. 27). This may have become a self-fulfilling prophecy.

The Two-nation Thesis

The British began to deal with Hindus and Muslims separately. In 1909, when they established a limited system of representation to provincial legislatures, separate electorates were established. This fed rivalry, driving a deeper wedge between communities. In 1905, when

the British decided to partition Bengal into East and West, the Muslim
League was founded in Dhaka, the new capital of East Bengal, where
the Muslim majority would form a government, to represent their
interests. Hindus agitated against partition, which effectively gave birth
to the *swadesh* (self-rule) movement. Bengal was reunified in 1911.
Meanwhile, Muslims had experienced power and liked it. Although
many distinguished Muslims remained within the Indian National
Congress (founded 1895), the larger independence movement, others
identified Congress as Hindu. The League would represent Muslims.
Political parties now looked to the interests of their own particular
community rather than to that of the country as a whole. When Bengal
was reunited, Muslims had 117 seats of the 250 in the Assembly.
(Chapter 3 provides a more detailed discussion of the League's role in
Bengal.) As the two communities drifted apart, securing privileges – such
as reserved posts and job quotas for their members – violence on the
streets increased. This hindered efforts by Muslims such as Muhammad
Jinnah – before he committed himself to "the idea of Pakistan" – to
work toward a single, independent state. Jinnah's early political career
was as a champion of Muslim–Hindu unity.

Pakistan Named

Muhammad Iqbal, the poet-philosopher-politician, formally proposed a
separate Muslim homeland in India's north-west at the 1930 ML congress
in Lahore. Iqbal's Islam was progressive but reinterpreted *Shari'ah* was
central to his concept of "spiritual democracy" (Iqbal 1998, p. 269).
Inspired by the achievements of Turkey, the new republic would be a
model for the whole Muslim world. Each Muslim state would first reform
itself, then form a League of Nations (p. 261).

Europeans nationalism failed because it was racist. Iqbal allowed those
who know the tradition some role in "helping and guiding free discussion
on questions relating to law," following the model of the 1906 Iranian
constitution, which set up a "separate ecclesiastical committee ... to
supervise the activity ... of parliament" (pp. 266–7). However, authority
vested in a single person was alien to Islam (2002, p. 312). The state's ethos
would be distinctly Islamic. Unlike Khan, Iqbal saw religion and politics
as inextricably related, not "two sides of the same coin" but "a single, un-
analyzable reality" (1998, p. 258). "All is holy ground," he said, citing the
hadith, "the whole earth is a mosque" (p. 258).

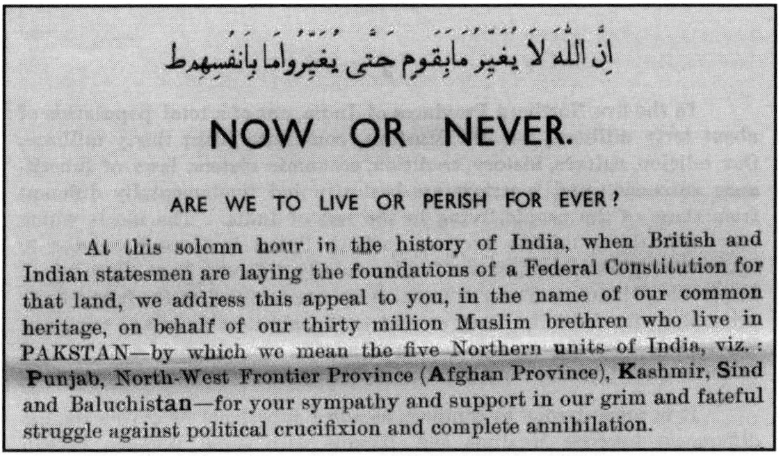

إِنَّ اللَّهَ لَا يُغَيِّرُ مَا بِقَوْمٍ حَتَّى يُغَيِّرُوا مَا بِأَنْفُسِهِمْ ط

NOW OR NEVER.

ARE WE TO LIVE OR PERISH FOR EVER?

At this solemn hour in the history of India, when British and Indian statesmen are laying the foundations of a Federal Constitution for that land, we address this appeal to you, in the name of our common heritage, on behalf of our thirty million Muslim brethren who live in PAKSTAN—by which we mean the five Northern units of India, viz. : Punjab, North-West Frontier Province (Afghan Province), Kashmir, Sind and Baluchistan—for your sympathy and support in our grim and fateful struggle against political crucifixion and complete annihilation.

Image 2: Rahmat Ali's *Now or Never* (1933), written as a student at Cambridge. Source: public domain.

Iqbal recruited Mawdudi to the "two nation" campaign. He moved to be geographically closer to Iqbal, although their ideas about Islamic governance diverged (Adams, p. 106). Yet there are similarities. Mawdudi's ideas are described below. Others also took up the separate homeland idea. In 1933, three Cambridge students put details to the geographical contours of what they named Pakistan – from Punjab, North West Frontier Province, Afghan Province, Kashmir, Sindh and Baluchistan – which Rahmat Ali described in *Now or Never*. The very large Muslim population of Bengal and substantial communities elsewhere were left out. Only the North West was included. Ali later explained that Muslim Bengalis, who, despite increased tension with Hindus, still enjoyed close cultural ties with them, might want to form their own Bangistan.

Ali then proposed a federation of states, called the country or commonwealth of Dinia, a series of geographically dispersed states spread across India. It does not take too much reflection to see that this radical proposition had minimal chance of success. At least one of the proposed states, Osmanistan – centered on Hyderabad, where the Nizam ruled a mainly Hindu state – would try to join Pakistan. On the other hand, while Kashmir, ruled by a Hindu prince, was from the start targeted as Pakistani, the prince opted for India, appealing to Nehru for help when Muslim irregulars crossed the border. Nehru agreed to send troops provided Kashmir joined India. It became a source of major conflict between Pakistan and India. In 1940, after Jinnah' attempt to

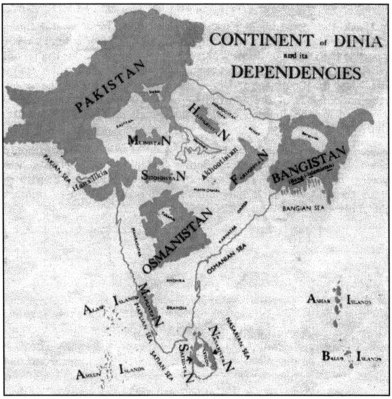

Map 3: Choudhary Rahmat Ali's map of "Dinia".
Source: From *India: The Continent of DINIA or the Country of Doom* (1946),
at http://www.shelleys.demon. co.uk/dinia.htm; public domain; reproduced
with the permission of Tom Shelley.

reach a deal with Congress failed (1938), he declared for Pakistan, his
stance becoming official League policy. The failed deal would have
given Muslims separate seats and recognized the League as the *sole
representative* of Muslim concerns. The 1935 Government of India
Act had already made several concessions to Jinnah, hoping to appease
him. Creating a Central Assembly where Muslims had a third of the
seats, it delegated more authority to the provinces. This was informed
by the paternalistic idea of a gradual transition from colonial to self-rule
(as a client state). In the 1937 elections, though, the League did not
perform well. Other Muslim parties, independents and factions split the
Muslim vote. Many Muslims remained loyal to Congress.

By 1946, the situation had changed. The campaign for Pakistan, based on the claim that Hindus would persecute Muslims in an undivided India, grew in popularity. The League won 75 percent of the Muslim vote in what they saw as a plebiscite in favor of Pakistan, gaining 460 out of the 533 Muslim seats in the central and provincial elections (Ahmed 1997, p. 112). In the Assembly, the League gained 30 seats, Congress 57, with "Sikhs and independents " making up the rest (Ahmed 1997, p. 113).

Partition

The postwar Labour government in Britain decided that Britain had no choice but to "quit India," which Indians had demanded for half a century. Lord Mountbatten was instructed to oversee Britain's departure. Agreeing to partition became expedient. Millions crossed the Indian–Pakistani borders, Hindus and Sikhs into India, Muslims into Pakistan, thousands under compulsion. Tens of thousands died as violence erupted. In the end, Muslim-majority East Bengal *did become* part of the partition plan. The complex story of exactly how that happened is explored in my next chapter. There was, however, significantly less movement and loss of life in the East, where substantial minorities remained on both sides of what was now *twice-divided* Bengal. On May 14, 1947 Pakistan became a reality, with two provinces, West and East, divided by India, which almost completely surrounded East Pakistan. There were always questions about the wisdom of this geographical arrangement, an issue that will surface later in this book.

Pakistan: A Muslim State?

With one foot in the military and cultural achievement of past Muslim empires, Pakistan was nonetheless faced with the daunting task of creating a unified state from disparate elements. Under the British, Pakistan's various regions had belonged to different administrative units. Pakistan has no single language, or ethnicity. There were Punjabis, Baluch, Sindhi, Pashtun and Bengalis. Migrants, known as Mohajirs, needed to be assimilated. Cohen describes Punjabis and Bengalis as the largest linguistic-ethnic groups. Baluchistan was the biggest region. "Ethnic and linguistic groups, identified by cultural markers, often claim they are a people or a nation" and "seek independence … greater autonomy" and may "move back and forth between these goals" (p. 201). This happened in Pakistan, where separatist movements emerged in Baluchistan, the Swat Valley and elsewhere, even among the Mohajirs. In addition, there were (and continue to be) Sunni–Shi'a tensions (see Jones on sectarian deaths, p. 24). In the east, a call for greater autonomy ended when Bangladesh was born. In turn, this encouraged insurgency in Baluchistan. Swat, bordering Afghanistan, had historically enjoyed quasi-independence under local Khans and, to this day, has not really reconciled itself to Pakistani rule. Pakistan's vision was to be a unified state, where Islam would glue different peoples together. Yet discussing Islam's role in terms of governance and law was initially avoided. Jinnah's vision was always liberal. He admired Atatürk, describing his death as a "great blow to the Muslim world" (Johari, p. 164). His Pakistan, though, would not be quite a Turkey-style secular state, since Islamic values were central to his vision. Today, the vision of Islam-oriented parties in Turkey may be close to what Jinnah had in mind. However, when asked whether he would implement *Shari'ah* law, he hesitated. Whose version should he choose (Jones, p. 12)? Democracy and religious freedom, too, would be cherished. "Islam," he said, "believes in democracy" although this would be established on the basis of "Islamic ideals and principles" (Ahmed 1997, p. 197). Again, the question emerged: whose interpretation? Ahmed dismisses accusations that Jinnah could not even pray properly (p. 195). Some criticize him for drinking alcohol and eating pork. Ahmed says that this was and remains commonplace among the "liberal" class of which he was a member (p. 200).

The problem of deciding what role Islam would play made it difficult for Pakistan to write and ratify a constitution. Meanwhile, Pakistan continued to be governed by laws from the Raj. Finally, a constitution was approved in 1956, although it would soon be suspended by the first military regime. Declaring Pakistan an "Islamic Republic," the 1956 constitution replaced the Governor-General with a president. Uncertainly about the constitution helped push Pakistan in an "authoritarian direction" (Cohen, p. 57). So did external conflict with India and internal instability, as diverse communities pulled in different directions. A quick shift to a more federal system might have avoided some of these problems. However, Pakistan's leaders, civilian and military, consistently insisted that Pakistan was "one, united Pakistan." Asked "about the possibility of introducing a multinational Pakistan" in which the different regions would be "entitled to local self rule," Zia said: "We want to build a strong country, a unified country" (Cohen, p. 205). The idea of Pakistan as a revival of ancient empires, an example for other Muslim states, was constantly in play. Military coups were justified in the name of preserving national unity.

Claims that Pakistan was not yet ready for democracy, that Pakistan needed to be "tutored" as an "extension of the Raj," also made constitutional decision making difficult (Cohen, p. 60). Should power be vested in a single man, or shared with others in a cabinet? Successive constitutions referred to *Islamic ideals and principles* but regimes hesitated to introduce these. They could not agree on "which Islam would be widely acceptable" (Cohen, p. 66). Constitutions followed in 1962 and 1973. Zia introduced major amendments in 1985. "Islamic" was dropped from the 1962 version, then reinserted. Benazir's father drafted the 1973 constitution. That of 1962 strengthened the presidency, while that of 1973 vested more authority in the prime minister (Cohen, p. 58).

Pakistan's Islamic identity was also integral to the Objectives Resolution, passed in 1949, which became the preamble of future constitutions. This states that while sovereignty is God's, he has delegated authority to the people of Pakistan within limits prescribed by Him (Cohen, p. 168). The Objectives also stated that steps would be taken to enable the people, individually and collectively, to order their lives in accordance with the principles of Islam found in the Qur'an and *Shari'ah*. The Resolution clearly declared Pakistan's Islamic identity but fell short of saying that *Shari'ah* would *be the law*. The 1973 constitution defined Muslims as believers in the finality of God's prophet, denouncing Mirza Ghulam Ahmad, founder of the Ahmadiyyah, as a fraud. Mawdudi incited anti-Ahmadiyyah protests in Lahore in the 1950s, receiving a death sentence for this, later commuted to life imprisonment. He was subsequently released.

Some objected that Western-style democracy was unsuitable. A constant theme, especially from successive military rulers, was that Pakistan was either not yet ready for democracy or did not want it. "Basic democracy" at local level might be allowed. Perhaps transitional steps could be taken, or Musharaf's "guided democracy" adopted, similar to Sukarno's in Indonesia. (Parallels in Bangladesh will be discussed in a later chapter.) The military emerged, from the beginning, as a strong player, built up to prosecute conflict, primarily over Kashmir, with India. When the Maharajah chose to join India, war began, followed by a UN-moderated settlement. Pakistan-occupied territory became "Free Kashmir" (Azad Kashmir). Huge early investment in the military, says Benazir, saw "approximately 70 percent of the Pakistani budget spent on defense" (2008, p. 167).

As a result of this investment in the military, civil society did not receive the encouragement or funds needed to develop a firm foundation. Benazir comments, "there can be no democracy without a civil society, and no civil society without the rule of law" (2008, p. 292). Democracies, too, "do not spring up fully developed overnight" (p. 88). Seeing itself as guardian of the nation's security, internal and external, and increasingly self-defining as an Islamic institution, the army has played a major role in politics, taking power on three occasions. Cohen describes the process by which an originally secular army became "Islamic," both in terms of the dress, piety and practices of soldiers and with respect to their worldview. The military approaches strategic issues from an Islamic perspective, making alliances within this context, and tends to see the non-Muslim world as anti-Muslim (p. 117).

Pakistani military and civilian regimes have recruited Islam for their own purposes, starting with Ayub Khan, though he dropped "Islamic" from the country's name. He turned to reformist Islam, promulgating the Family Law Ordinance of 1961. This liberalized marriage and divorce proceedings. It does not go as far as reforms suggested by "position two" but it does go some way in that direction.

Zulfikar Ali Bhutto

Bhutto "seized on the idea of an Islamic Pakistan" (Cohen, p. 169). The 1973 constitution strengthened Islam's position. His Pakistan People's Party (PPP), formed in 1967 as an alternative to the League, adopted as its motto "Islam is our faith, democracy our polity, socialism our power. All power to the people" (Shah, p. 159). Bhutto split with Ayub when expected social reforms and democratic restoration did not happen. The Objectives Resolution established "Islamic social justice" as a goal; Bhutto began by talking about Islamic socialism. Later, he changed "Islamic socialism" to "equality as preached by Muhammad" when challenged that he was preaching anti-Islamic ideas (p. 161). During his campaign, the slogan was "bread, clothes, housing" (Shah, p. 161).

Ayub handed over to Yahya Khan on March 25, 1968. Responding to demands to end military rule, Khan promised elections. Regarded as Pakistan's *first free and fair elections*, these took place on December 10, 1970. The PPP won 88 seats. Sheikh Mujib's East Bengali Awami League, with 136 out of 313 seats, won more seats than any other party but not an absolute majority (Molla, p. 232). No government emerged. Bhutto and Yahya feared that Mujib would impose a constitution on the country that would end national unity, while claiming to devolve power. On March 25, 1971 Mujib was imprisoned and the war for Bangladeshi independence began. This story is taken up in Chapter 3. After the war,

Yahya Khan resigned and Bhutto became president. Defeat tarnished the military's image as protectors of national unity. It was finally time for civilian rule, although Bhutto was chief martial law administrator until April 21, when he lifted martial law. He replaced senior generals and began to prepare a new, democratic constitution, convening the assembly on April 14. His legitimacy as leader was, however, derived from the 1970 election.

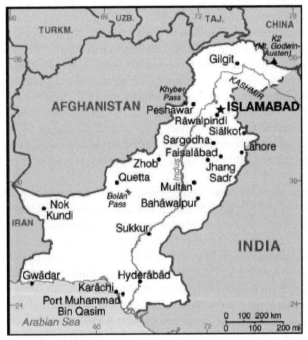

Map 4: Pakistan after Bangladesh seceded following Bhutto's becoming president. Karachi Benazir's birthplace is on the coast to the south; she was assassinated in Rawalpindi (north). Notice the border with China.
Source: public domain.

Jones caricatures Bhutto's political use of Islam as insincere, saying he fooled no one (p. 16). Ahmed (1977), compares Jinnah's eating and drinking habits with Bhutto's, commenting that the latter once admitted that he "drank," though he did not "drink the blood of the poor" (p. 199). Benazir is much more positive, describing the 1973 constitution as the "most Islamic." Her father, she points out, established the Ministry of

Religious Affairs, printed the first "error-free" Holy Qur'an in Pakistan, lifted restrictions on pilgrims traveling to Mecca, introduced Arabic language programs on television, and made Islamic studies compulsory in school. He oversaw the name change of the Red Cross to Red Crescent in Pakistan (1989, pp. 90–91). The 1973 constitution criminalized drinking, gambling and charging interest. Some see these as mere cosmetic concessions to Islam.

Throughout her career and writing, Benazir represented her father as democracy's champion. "My father," she wrote, "was the first to bring democracy" to Pakistan (1989, p. 16). The 1973 constitution was a "model democratic framework" (2008, p. 186), reducing the president's role to that of an "honorific head of state" similar to that of the "British monarchs." The central assembly and provincial legislatures form a College to elect the president. Critics accuse Bhutto of authoritarianism, crushing dissent, appointing sycophants to office, then rigging the 1977 election even though he was the favorite to win (Jones, pp. 227–9). Despite his appeal and intellect, he managed to "generate mass opposition" (Cohen, p. 145). Jones says that he wanted to rule for life (p. 229). His use of liberal Islam to support his socialist agenda mirrored Ayub's earlier recruitment of reformist Islam.

Bhutto had risen to prominence under Ayub, representing Pakistan at the United Nations in 1957. From 1958 until 1962 he was energy minister. At the UN and in this post, he was the youngest ever appointee. From 1962–6 he was foreign minister, and from 1964–6 he was also ML Secretary-General. Under reformist-oriented leaders, Pakistan adopted a pro-Western stance, reacting against India's close relationship with the Soviets. During these periods, such "moderate Islamic states" as Turkey and Iran under the Shah were her natural "allies and role models" (Cohen, p. 71). Bhutto was quickly faced with a separatist war in Baluchistan, sending the army to crush this. On the one hand, he wanted to "whittle away" the army's "claim to be the sole defender of Pakistan" (Cohen, pp. 140, 145), which did not win him any friends among the military. On the other hand, he used the army to "assert his authority in the provinces" (Jones, p. 228). Partly, he was responsible for fomenting troubles in Baluchistan by dismissing in 1973 the provincial government there, "in which the PPP had no representation," appointing a PPP ministry instead (Jones, p. 133). A civil war had waged there from 1962–8. The new war lasted until 1975. Earlier, insurrections took place in 1948 and 1958, each lasting a few months (Cohen, p. 220).

Bhutto's domestic policies attempted to weaken feudalism, extend land ownership, nationalize industry and improve civil service efficiency. Cohen says that he "damaged the economy" (p. 145). His foreign policy was to seek a new relationship with China, with which Pakistan shares a border, distancing Pakistan from the US. His rhetoric was populist and "anti-American" (Shah, p. 157). To strengthen Pakistan's status, he launched the "Islamic bomb" project that led to Pakistan matching India's capability. Pakistan thus became the first and so far only Islamic nuclear power.

Bhutto saw himself as the People's servant, despite his aristocratic background. The army, however, was growing more and more uneasy, unused to civilian control. As he asserted authority, the army feared it would be permanently marginalized. In the dubious 1977 election, Bhutto won 115 out of 200 general seats, 58.1 percent of all votes. Nineteen seats were uncontested because the opposition boycotted the election in Baluchistan, due to the war. Mawdudi's JI won nine seats within the National Alliance (which won a total of 36; 31.9 percent of votes) but had expected more based on "its apparent popularity" at the time. Mawdudi called for fresh elections. Bhutto met with him, hoping to defuse the situation, promising Islamic measures; "activities proscribed by Islam would be against the law" (Nasr, p. 99). He asked Saudi Arabia to act as referee. After a month, Bhutto was "amenable to new elections" but his army chief of staff advised caution. The army would not accept some opposition demands, such as releasing prisoners who had fought against them (Nasr, p. 100). Bhutto had promoted General Zia on October 11, 1976 as army chief *above several senior officers*, so presumed Zia's loyalty. Zia had his own plans. On July 5, 1977 Zia arrested Bhutto, charged with corruption and conspiracy to commit murder. Put on trial, Bhutto was found guilty and executed on April 4, 1979. Here, Benazir's story begins, her father having asked her to speak at various rallies in his place, then to continue his mission (Thompson 2004, p. 42).

Benazir: Restoring Father's Legacy

Benazir describes how her father instructed her during jail visits. "I want you to go the frontier," he said. She was to take his Mao cap with her (a gift from the Chairman himself), wear it while speaking, then place it "on the ground," saying, "My father said his cap should always be placed before the feet of the people" (Bhutto 1989, p. 153). A Day of Democracy was called to protest his arrest, before Benazir and her mother were also detained. On December 10, 1977 the Supreme Court ruled Zia's presidency legal, due to the unstable, volatile political context. This was similar to a decision legalizing Ayub's rule in 1958.

Ayub also won a referendum on his presidency, receiving 80 percent on February 17, 1960 on a yes-or-no vote (Cohen, p. 7). Cohen says that the judiciary has compromised its credibility by repeatedly validating dictatorial rule, which also made it easier for "civilian governments to break the law" (p. 58). One explanation may be that judges were often Mohajirs, who had a strong "ideological commitment" to Pakistan. On December 1, 1984 Zia held a mock referendum on his presidency, claiming a 95 percent yes vote.

Benazir was born in Karachi on June 21, 1953. Her mother, Begum Nusrat, is an Iranian Shi'a, her father was a Sindhi Sunni. Her grandfather, Sir Shah Nawaj, chief minister of a princely state, tried to take his state into Pakistan but was prevented by Indian intervention. Benazir attended a Catholic convent school in Karachi, then university at Harvard (1969–73) and Oxford (1973–7). She graduated with degrees in Comparative Government and in PPE (Philosophy, Political Science and Economics). She would later receive several honorary doctorates and awards for her advocacy of human rights and democracy. This pattern was similar to her father's, who graduated from Berkeley (Politics), then from Oxford (Law). He also passed the bar examination at Lincoln's Inn, London. At Oxford, Benazir was elected President of the Union Society (1976), a platform that has launched the careers of many British politicians ranging from H. H. Asquith to W. E. Gladstone to Edward Heath, all prime ministers. She had intended to enter the Foreign Service but her father's execution propelled her into politics. She became PPP chair in 1983. Her mother, who chaired the party from 1979–83, was later a cabinet minister and deputy prime minister in Benazir's government. Benazir married Asif Ai Zardari – at the time, a businessman – on December 18, 1986. They had two daughters and a son. Benazir made it clear to Asif's stepmother before they married that as a politician her life would not revolve around him, to which she replied "Asif has his own work" (Bhutto 1989, p. 356).

Between 1979 and 1984, Benazir was frequently under house arrest. From 1984–6, she lived overseas, still opposing Zia. An unelected dictator was ruling Pakistan, with democracy again suspended. Mass human-rights abuses were taking place, inspired by a version of Islam that repulsed her. Mainly conducting her campaign against Zia outside Pakistan, she "cultivated civil society all over the world" (2008, p. 191). Ironically, while Benazir petitioned US senators and human-rights activists for support, the US was sending Zia billions of dollars in aid to fund support for Afghan insurgency against Soviet occupation, Pakistan becoming the third largest recipient of US aid, after Israel and Egypt (Bhutto 1989, p. 121). This led to an increase in the size, power and influence of the ISI (the intelligence service), as well as in the illegal arms trade and the growth of radical groups using violence to achieve Islamist goals (2008, p. 193). Pakistan and the world became less safe. Zia consolidated his power, Benazir says, with US money (2008, p. 193).

Zia made the idea of an Islamic Pakistan, his *Nizam-i-Islam* (Islamic order) his goal, claiming a universal validity for his system (Riaz, p. 138) He did not like democracy so had no interest in restoring civilian rule. There is little doubt that even after holding non-party elections and promising to allow party elections in time, he intended to "hang on to power" for the rest of his life (Jones, p. 273). He may have seen himself as a caliph, to whom loyalty is owed once appointed. Or, he may have taken the view that by enforcing *Shari'ah*, the state automatically became genuinely Islamic. Sayyid Qutb, the influential Muslim Brotherhood thinker, appears to have assumed that legitimate Islamic order automatically follows implementation of *Shari'ah* (Bennett 2005, p. 40). Unlike Mawdudi, Qutb saw democracy as *totally alien* to Islam.

In the non-party elections of 1985, Zia appointed a compliant civilian prime minister, Mohammed Khan Junejo. At the same time, he inserted a clause in the constitution permitting presidents to dismiss governments and dissolve parliament (Amendment 8). Zia used Islam to justify his rule. In 1980, with parliament suspended, he set up an appointed consultative assembly of 284 members, establishing a *Shari'ah* Supreme Court Council to determine whether laws were acceptable or repugnant to Islam, while the Islamic Ideology Council advised on balancing Islam and modern life.

After years in the political wilderness and several jail sentences, Mawdudi became popular. Benazir calls him Zia's "spiritual father' (2008, p. 68). Members of his party accepted significant posts, as did compliant ML members. Mawdudi, who never accepted the legitimacy of military rule, qualified his support. In his view, members of the *Shura*, together with the amir (leader), should be elected, not appointed. His party joined "the Movement for the Restoration of Democracy" (Cohen, p. 178). Zia claimed one-man rule was appropriate for Muslims, who had one God, one Prophet and one Book (Turner, p. 144) Mawdudi, however, consistently supported parliamentary governance and party political elections. He and others criticized Zia for placing himself above the law, even above the *Shari'ah*, which he interpreted himself, rather than allowing those versed in the law to do so or after wide consultation. Zia did not think

Shura binding. Mawdudi was emphatic that Islam does not vest authority in a single individual (1999, p. 170).

Mawdudi started campaigning for his version of an Islamic state about six months after Pakistan's birth. His writing sets out detailed ideas about "theo-democracy" (1999, p. 160), much of which Zia adopted. We find these ideas in his 1955 book and the 1999 chapter. He agrees with Iqbal that the caliphate can be vested in an elected body, always emphasizing that the task is not *law making* but interpreting and *applying God's law*. Western democracy vests sovereignty in the people, he said, Islam only recognizes God's sovereignty. He was happy to see this recognized by the 1956 constitution (Adams, p. 110). He repeatedly asserts that *people* means "the whole community" (1999, p. 168) not the "dictatorship of any person or group" (1999, p. 170). His more conservative understanding of *Shari'ah* differs from Iqbal's progressive view. Candidates for election should not self-nominate. A neutral institution would select them from a pool of pious candidates. Although he opposed self-appointed authorities, there is a question here about who would decide concerning those who qualify as pious and those who do not.

Mawdudi called Bhutto an infidel, as his heirs did Benazir (Bhutto 2008, p. 69). He disallowed, then allowed, non-Muslim representation, since the constitution would preclude any laws repugnant to Islam (1999, p. 167). Mawdudi wanted revolution but believed this should be societal, from the *bottom up*. He did not incite armed revolt, or indiscriminate violence against non-Muslims, nor did he endorse autocracy. He encouraged anti-Ahmadiyyah protest but did not demand the death of its members. Benazir and others cite him incorrectly on "jihad of the sword"; he did not justify *unprovoked aggression* (Mawdudi 1996, p. 3; Bhutto 2008, p. 246). I do not place Mawdudi on the far right although he was far to Benazir's right. I define "left" as those who support democracy, harmonizing Islam and global human-rights standards. Bhutto spoke of a "left–right" divide, "reactionary Islam and progressive Islam" (1998, p. 107).

All agree that Zia clothed himself in Islamic dress to legitimize martial rule. Zia's program was consistent with his goals, so it was difficult for Mawdudi to refuse any cooperation. Zia's strategy of creating a "Statist Islam" aimed to produce and control a discourse to marginalize all others, "including that of democracy" (Riaz, p. 139). His Hudood and Zina Ordinances introduced amputation for theft and stoning for adultery, required four male witnesses for adultery and rape (*Zina*), and made flogging a common punishment. His Law of

Evidence (1984) required two female witnesses in any legal case involving oral testimony, when one man's suffices. Benazir describes these measures and their impact on women in some depth (1989, pp. 314–15). Many men went free since rape is rarely "conducted in public" so, without a confession or four eyewitnesses, victims cannot prove their case. Benazir refers to a blind girl who, unable to summon witnesses to her rape, was found guilty of adultery, publicly lashed and sentenced to three years in prison (p. 316). Yet there are *hadith* recording Muhammad accepting one eyewitness for rape (Hashmi, p. 51). Hashmi refers to a tradition that Ali would have been prepared to try Uthman's killers based on one woman's evidence but "on grounds of political expediency (to avoid a civil war) … refrained from trying the murderers." Ayesha's rebellion followed, because Ali failed to bring Uthman's assassins to justice.

Zia set steps in motion to make veiling and seclusion compulsory. The 1961 Family Law was rejected as Western inspired (Esposito and Voll 1996, p. 113). Amputation was actually never carried out because doctors refused to supervise (p. 111). In 1985, Zia's civilian prime minister tabled a *Shari'ah* Bill intended to give legislative legitimacy to the Hudood Ordinance. Before this was passed, Zia died in a plane crash (August 17, 1987).

Party political elections had already been scheduled and Benazir was back in Pakistan (April 10, 1986). She led her party to victory in the November 1988 election, defeating the faction of the ML led by Nawaj Sharif, a bitter foe. Benazir's father had nationalized the Sharif family's factory. The League suffered from association with military rulers, who appointed members to posts even when party politics was suspended. It was traditionally a party *for Muslims*, not an Islamist party, but Sharif's faction moved toward Islamism. Benazir describes this faction as pro-Zia (1989, p. 390). She won 92 seats, a plurality. The Islamic Democratic Alliance, dominated by Sharif's League and organized, according to her, by the ISI, won 55, the next largest bloc. Sharif, a protégé of General Zia, served as Chief Minister of the Punjab during 1885–8 (Cheema, p. 145). There were 20 reserved seats for women in that parliament out of 237 seats in all (10 were reserved for non-Muslims). Benazir and her mother won open seats. As discussed in Chapter 1, some opponents, not least of Mawdudi's party, said that a woman leader was contrary to Islam. The president did not immediately ask Benazir to form a government but "called different leaders" to try to "cobble together a coalition" (2008, p. 197). "Despite all the odds," she says, she was "finally sworn in."

Benazir points out that Mawdudi had supported Fatimah Jinnah in 1965, so his heirs stood on thin ground opposing her (2008, p. 70), given that Islamists had not objected to the constitution's guarantee of gender equality (1989, p. 392; Articles 25 and 27). She repeatedly stated that Islam is not opposed to women leaders; men, not Islam, object. Nothing in Islam, she said, citing the Qur'an's positive reference to the Queen of Sheba (27: 23) and the *hadith* "paradise lies at the feet of the mother" (1989, pp. 42–3), discouraged her from pursuing her political career. Anticipating Mernissi's detailed work on women leaders, she wrote, "Muslim history was full of women who had taken a public role and performed every bit as successfully as men" (1989, p. 44). Islamist objection to her serving as prime minister, she says, was political, not theological (2008, p. 70).

After her election, the *Shari'ah* Supreme Court ruled she could remain in office. In her campaign, she vowed to secure peoples' rights, freedom and democracy (1989, p. 329). Claiming to be both leader of the PPP and "a symbol of democracy" (2008, p. 191), she did not hesitate to depict herself as a strong Muslim woman, standing on her predecessors' shoulders. "People think I am weak because I am a woman," she said. "Do they know that I am a Muslim woman?" "Muslim women have a heritage to be proud of," she continued. She had the patience of Bibi Khadijah, Muhammad's wife, the perseverance of Bibi Zeinab, the sister of Imam Hussein, and the courage of Bibi Aisha, who "rode her camel into battle at the head of the Muslims." The daughter of martyr Zulfikar Ali Bhutto, and sister of Shah Nawaz Khan Bhutto – who, named for their grandfather, had died in France in mysterious circumstances (1985) (pp. 332–3) – Benazir blamed Zia for her brother's death (2008, p. 191).

Zia used her unmarried status against her, placing her "under surveillance" to try to catch her in a compromising situation with a man (Thompson 2004, p. 44). She responded by agreeing to an arranged marriage (1987). When she became pregnant, Zia tried to find out the child's due date, calling local elections for that day, which he thought would handicap her campaign. Actually, she had "lied about the due date," resulting in one reporter commenting that this was "the first election to be timed for gynecological consideration" (Thompson 2004, p. 44). Bhutto's version is slightly different, suggesting that Zia's agents miscalculated the date, so her unborn son's political prescience foiled him (1989, p. 386).

Benazir's first administration lasted until August 6, 1990, when the president intervened, using Amendment 8. Although only ratified by the 1985 non-party political parliament, the amendment was used three times until 1997, when the thirteenth amendment annulled it. In 2003, the seventeenth amendment partly restored this power; it now requires Supreme

Court approval. Sharif won the next election, with 137 seats to the PPP's "absurdly low" 44. Benazir attributes the election result to intelligence service rigging (2008, p. 203). She became leader of the opposition (also an elected post).

During 1991, Sharif passed a modified version of the *Shari'ah* Act, removing "any protections previously granted to women" (Krook, p. 71). However he found himself locked in a power struggle with the president, who dismissed him on April 18, 1993, alleging corruption. Sharif refused to go. The Supreme Court overruled the president. Sharif was reinstated on May 26 (Cheema, p. 146). A standoff ensued, which ended on July 18 when, following an army-brokered deal, both resigned (Cheema, p. 147). In the October 24 election, the PPP won 86 seats, Sharif's faction 73. With the support of independents and smaller parties, Benazir defeated Sharif in the vote for the office of prime minister, 121 to 72. Her second term began. In November 1996, accused of corruption and mismanagement of the economy, her ministry was again dismissed. Once again, Sharif succeeded her, also battling corruption charges. In this election, he soundly defeated the PPP, winning 135 seats to its 19.

During her administrations, Benazir released political prisoners and lifted restrictions on trade unions, the media and students associations. Reversing her father's policy of nationalization, she privatized publicly owned utilities (2008, p. 1999). She promoted micro-credit programs, placed women's rights and minorities' rights at the top of her agenda, and reached out to India over a nuclear treaty, attracting the charge of being an "Indian agent" from the *Jamaat* and the League. Even friends abroad were "vilified in the Urdu press as 'Hindu-Zionist' conspirators" (2008, p. 201). Benazir claims also to have stimulated the economy, making Pakistan one of the ten top "emerging markets of the world" (p. 206). Jones, however, says otherwise, commenting that her and Sharif's only fiscal success was "running up huge levels of foreign debt" (p. 231).

Benazir worked during her time in office to renew the Pakistan–US relationship, which had weakened following the Soviet withdrawal from Afghanistan. She negotiated a concord with the US on "no-export-of-nuclear-technology" (Bhutto 2008, p. 200), despite criticism from the army, which believed she shared too much sensitive information in doing so (Cohen, p. 146). She tried hard to avoid clashing with the military – Cohen, indeed, accuses her of failing to curb the ever-increasing "power and influence of the ... much expanded intelligence services" (p. 147) – but she faced a powerful foe (2008, pp. 200–1). There were al-Qaeda-linked plots on her life (p. 205) and an al-Qaeda-funded attempt to vote her government out of office. PPP members were offered million-dollar bribes. On September

20, 1996 her brother, Murtaza was "gunned down in a police shootout" in front of her house (p. 209).

On the positive side, Benazir committed herself to empowering women, opened women's police stations, extended educational opportunities, and "made dramatic reforms in women's rights." She appointed several women to her cabinet, created a Women's Development Ministry, a Women's Development Bank and university women's studies programs (2008, p. 2000). She allowed women to compete in international sports, which Zia had banned. New schools were built and women trained to teach family planning and health (p. 206). Again, she saw her gender policy as perpetuating her father's legacy. He opened the Foreign Service, police and civil service to women, named a woman as governor of Sindh and as deputy speaker of parliament, and encouraged his wife to "take a more active role." She went to the 1975 UN conference on women in Mexico, where she was elected vice-president. Bhutto appointed the first woman head of a university and allowed women to read the news on television (1989, p. 91). The 1973 constitution also reserved one female seat on the Islamic Ideology Council (Krook, p. 63).

Yet Benazir surprised some, who saw her as a Westernized liberal through and through, when she spoke against abortion at the Cairo population conference, excusing "abortion only in the rarest of circumstances." "Regrettably," she said, "the conference's document contains serious flaws in striking at the heart of a great many cultural values, in the North and in the South." Western cultural and religious hegemony was trying to impose adultery, abortion, sex education and other such matters on individuals, societies and religions which have their own social ethos" (Moghissi 2005, pp. 228–9).

Benazir is widely criticized for failing to tackle corruption. She always dismissed charges of corruption against her and her husband as politically motivated. According to Jones (pp. 232–4), both Bhuttho and Sharif became very wealthy during their terms, and it is not clear exactly how they did so. Benazir is also said to have spent too much time trying to restore her father's image, appearing unwilling "to forgive and forget her father's death" (p. 147). Cheema says she was "obsessed with avenging her father's death" (pp. 165–6). She writes of how it was his imprint on her that kept her going: "Endurance. Honor. Principle" (1989, p. 123). Sharif diverted funds back to the military away from "the social sector," reversed many of her reforms, restricted unions, reimposed press censorship, reduced the educational budget and closed down the women's population control centers she had established (2008, p. 203). However, as opposition leader, Benazir successfully blocked a harsher version of the *Shari'ah* Act (p. 204).

On October 12, 1999 Musharaf became military ruler, dismissing Sharif who had appointed Musharaf army chief in October 1998. Subsequently, Sharif tried to remove Musharaf after military disaster in Kashmir (the Kargil conflict of May 1999), for which each blamed the other. The sequence of events sounds familiar. Musharaf was disinterested in democracy, except in its "guided" guise, in *Shari'ah* or in Islamist ideas. He decreed that Benazir and Sharif could not seek third terms. Corruption charges against Benazir and her husband led to conviction in 1999, overturned in 2001 by the Supreme Court, citing political motivation (Jones, p. 235).

Exile followed, technically voluntary, although Benazir did not feel safe in Pakistan. She was willing to negotiate some type of power-sharing deal with Musharaf, although details remain vague. Musharaf also clashed with the judges by requiring an oath of loyalty, as had previous military rulers. He dismissed the chief justice for corruption, causing controversy about judicial independence, guaranteed by the Objectives Resolution. The Supreme *Shari'ah* Court ruled in 1999 that he could be president provided he stood down as army chief and called elections within three years (Kukreja, p. 280). On April 30, 2002 he staged a "mock referendum," declaring "himself President for five years" (Bhutto 2008, p. 213). He claimed 98 percent of the votes, again following a familiar pattern (Cohen, p. 154). Elections followed (October 2002), won by a loyal faction of the League (118 seats to the PPP's 80). The government conveniently passed a law allowing him to keep both jobs. He intended to introduce legislation to give the military a constitutional role as "guarantor of a quasi-democratic system." Musharaf called this "guided democracy," described by others as "army-backed quasi democracy." He planned to establish a military-dominated National Security Council as the sole authority on matters of security and defense (Kukreja, p. 281). Similarity between this, the military's constitutional role in Turkey and in Bangladesh are discussed in later chapters. Independently wealthy through business and commerce, the army has had little experience of subordination to civilian authority.

Musharaf did, however, repeal many anti-women laws through the Protection of Women Act, 2006. Recognizing the heinous nature of Zia's *Zina* Ordinance, the Act stated: "The Zina Ordinance has been abused to persecute women, to settle vendettas and to deny basic human rights and fundamental freedoms" (http://www.pakistani.org/pakistan/legislation/2006/wpb.html). However, internal and external pressure on Musharaf to step aside in favor of genuine civilian government made his position untenable. On October 2, 2007 he resigned as army chief. A few days later, October 6, he stood in a presidential election, winning by a large margin. He now promised free and fair elections.

In October 2007, Benazir returned to Pakistan to contest the forthcoming election, which she was widely expected to win. Musharaf had granted a general amnesty to politicians and officials in office between 1996 and 1999, so Benazir and Sharif could both contest seats. While campaigning, however, she was assassinated in Rawalpindi on December 27, 2007, following an earlier attempt when 179 people had died (2008, p. vii). In the election (February 18, 2008), the PPP won 97 seats, rival factions of the ML 71 and 42. Musharaf stepped aside (August 18, 2008). Her husband, included in the amnesty, was elected president (September 9). Their son, Bilawal Bhutto Zardari, whose political debut predated his birth, currently attending Oxford, became PPP co-chair.

Some characterized Zardari as the "real prime minister" during Benazir's ministry (Thompson 2004, p. 49). Zardari had progressed from being called "Mr Five Percent" to "Mr Ten Percent" for the "commission he reportedly asked for in return for approval of industrial projects" (Cohen, p. 252). Benazir called this a smear tactic, doubting it "would have been used against a male prime minister" (2008, p. 201). The Supreme Court annulled the amnesty on December 2009, raising questions about Zardari's political future.

If dynasty explains Benazir's career, it is even more difficult to imagine that Zardari would have become president except as Benazir's widower. Despite "having his own work," he capitalized on his marriage to win Assembly seats in 1990 and 1993. During Benazir's second term, he held overlapping portfolios. Some say he faked his degree (candidates must be graduates). He won both the 1993 election and a Senate seat (held 1997 until the 1999 coup) from his prison cell. In 1993, he took his minister's oath the day he left jail. He spent 1990–3 and 1996–2004 in prison on a range of charges including blackmail and murder, so although he held office during these years he did not actually occupy his seat. None of the cases resulted in conviction despite almost 11 years behind bars.

The Issues

What role did Islam play?

Some Pakistanis chose to play the "Muslim women cannot lead a state" card. When women's election to parliament was first discussed, a few wanted to establish a separate women's assembly with power to deal only with women's and general welfare issues. This did not happen

(Krook, p. 61). Indeed, "position one" voices may have received publicity disproportionate to their influence. Benazir says that the Saudis used to buy thousands of Mawdudi's publications to "dump them into the sea because too few people wanted to read them," at least before Zia's coup. After that, his popularity increased (2008, p. 52). In 1983, a commission reported to Zia that the position of head of state in an Islamic country should be restricted to men. Women standing for reserved seats should be over 50 and have their *husbands' permission*. Zia did not act on this recommendation, which was almost certainly "directed at Benazir Bhutto," then *single and under 50*. He banned all current party leaders from standing in 1985 but also doubled the number of reserved seats (Krook, pp. 67–8).

Javed Iqbal, former Supreme Court Justice, the poet-philosopher's son, says that the "preponderant majority of Pakistani Muslims are moderate ... and believe in cultural pluralism" (Cohen, p. 86). Cohen adds, "the dominant Islam practiced in Pakistan is strongly influenced by Sufism" and there is little sign that radicalism is attracting much support (p. 196). In contrast, Wahhabi Islam in Saudi Arabia and elsewhere disapproves of Sufism and dislikes pluralism within and outside Islam. In support of her own ideas on gender and democracy, Benazir cites the Qur'an on *Shura* (consultation) (3:159; 42:38); the principle of *ijma* (consensus) (2008, p. 71); and Muslim scholars such as Soroush (p. 65), Asghar Ali Engineer (p. 47) who leads the progressive branch of the Ismaili Bohras (Sh'ia), and the former Indonesian president, Wahid (pp. 292–3). Categorical in her belief that "Islam and democracy are compatible" (2008, p. 68), she eloquently argues in favor of "position two." Furthermore, she claims, Islam requires that government be *benevolent* (p. 73).

Benazir was knowledgeable and passionate about her faith, about "true Islam in contrast to the perversion ... espoused by extremists and militants and the caricature that is too often accepted in the West" (2008, p. 20). She rejected this from "the core of her being as a Muslim" (p. 16). Men and women, she said, are equal in Islam. Jones is wrong to claim that Benazir kept her "modernist outlook" a "secret" (p. 18). Men's interpretation, she said, perverts Islam. Describing her *umrah* (voluntary *hajj*) in Mecca, she speaks movingly about how she felt burdens lifted as she prayed for her father, brother and supporters still in prison (1989, p. 322). She was raised to "read the Qur'an in Arabic" (1989, p. 45). Islam did not prevent her from leading her nation. Twice, enough people, not an absolute majority but sufficient for her to gain office in a parliamentary system, voted for her, rejecting "position one" thinking. The *Shari'ah* Supreme Court also upheld her right to lead. In comparison, patriarchy is more embedded in the Arab world, where pro-gender equality factors found in Asia are less evident. However, given certain conditions, if Islam trumps culture, which many Muslims claim, Arab Muslims can also move in the right direction. Where civil society and democracy are healthier, where regimes are committed to gender equality, where "position two" has found a welcome, progress occurs.

What role did culture play?

In her own upbringing, albeit in a Westernized domestic context, nothing in Benazir's cultural background discouraged her from pursuing her chosen career. She points to the extraordinary record of South Asian women leaders who preceded her (1989, p. 125). The Indian National Congress had chosen women presidents as early as 1917 (Annie Besant) and 1925 (Sarojini Naudi, succeeding Mahatma Gandhi, later first female governor of an Indian state). Boys were not favored over girls in Benazir's family (1989, p. 42). She was taught that she *could do and be whatever she wanted.* She points to "Mughal women" as "strong personalities who had a say in government through their husbands and fathers" (2008, p. 160).

It is easy to identify cultural and religious factors in the subcontinent that negatively impact women, from the ancient *Laws of Manu* to the assumptions and practices that Bettencourt describes. On the other hand, women in places like the Swat valley are very powerful in the domestic, if not public sphere, evidenced by anthropological research. When men bully them they refuse to cook. Men often sulk off to their clubhouse, so much so that *supposedly all powerful men* "are surrounded by animosity in their" own homes (Lindholm and Lindholm, p. 234). Even conservative Muslims interpret the Qur'an's alleged permitting of "wife beating" at 4:34 as a playful slap, not as justifying anything more violent. Aspects of Indic culture emphasize the female divine, the wife as the "strength" (*sakti*) of the male deity. It is not so long ago that women in the West were told to stay home but *did not.* Women in Pakistan know they have a right to enter the public square, and *do so.*

There is still much to achieve but successive regimes, military and civilian, have pursued the reserved seat measure to strengthen female representation in parliament. Zia increased reserved seats from 10 to 20 in 1984; Musharaf tripled them in 2002. There are currently 60 reserved seats; 16 women occupy open seats. There are 17 out of 100 reserved seats in the Senate and about 20 percent in provincial assemblies. Musharaf abolished separate elections for minorities, a move welcomed by minority leaders who felt that such elections placed them outside the political mainstream (Krook, p. 75). They retain 10 reserved seats; 17 Senate seats are reserved for technocrats and *ulama*. Civilian regimes failed to renew the reserved provision; when Benazir won her 1993 election, she was one of just four women. Another was her mother. The percentage of women in parliament dropped from 10 percent to less than 1 percent (Krook, p. 74). In 1997, five women won seats. When 60 seats were reserved in 2002, 13 women won open seats (Krook, p. 76).

Benazir argues that many anti-women practices are cultural or tribal, not Islamic (2008, p. 48). The same can be argued in relation to seclusion and veiling, both of which might derive from Sassanian tradition (Ahmed 1992, pp. 14–15; Hashmi, p. 41). Both practices were subsequently hung onto Qur'anic verses that were intended to relate exclusively to Muhammad's wives. Certainly, neither women as men's "property" nor honor killings have Islamic warrant. Islam does not permit people taking the law into their own hands, although some do. The notion of *izzat* (honor) is cultural. Dealing with alleged breaches – always committed by women, never men – by killing transgressors contravenes Islam's stress on mercy. Available data records female fatalities of close to 1,000 per annum, many murdered by their own relatives for alleged "reasons of honor." "Male dominance," says Bettencourt, "and commodification subjects women to violence on a daily basis in Pakistan" (p. 4). As appalling as these statistics are, they do not actually support the idea that Pakistani culture per se oppresses women or prevents full gender equality. Subconscious racism and assumptions of inalienable difference between "us" and "them" informs some views on other cultures as obstacles to gender equality, while "our" culture is less problematic. This posits that Pakistani culture *must be a hindrance because it is non-Western and inferior*.

On the positive side, two women have served as High Court judges, Majida Rizvi (later chair, National Commission for the Status of Women) and Khalida Rashid Khan (now an international criminal tribunal judge). On March 19, 2008 the first woman Speaker was elected, namely Fahmida Mirza, a physician, whose striking resemblance to Benazir immediately caught media attention. None of this could have occured if culture was an absolute obstacle. Could it be that seeds within culture and Islam, properly nurtured, allow gender equality?

What role did a dynastic tie play?

Thompson argues that dynastic ties *secured* Benazir party's leadership due to the *then absence* of a male heir. Later, when Murtaza returned from exile, November 1993, even her habitually supportive mother thought he should replace her (Thompson 2004, p. 48). Benazir felt let down but did her mother change her stance because she thought a male leader was more appropriate or because she feared that Benazir's life was threatened? After Murtaza's murder, his wife "took over his faction of the PPP," standing "for parliament against Benazir." Thus another woman became a leader (p. 48).

I do not think that dynasty alone explains Benazir's career. She not only had a vocation to enter politics, but also had talent, acumen and skill. Her education was highly relevant. Nor do I think that George W. Bush's career can be explained solely with reference to his father's, although that played a critical part. It was not unusual for a Pakistani woman to enter politics through a family tie. Krook writes, "those women who did obtain office typically served as surrogates for their fathers, husbands or sons, whose illness, death, exile or imprisonment prevented them from continuing their own political careers" (p. 77). Succeeding a dead male relative has been common in the US, so this cannot be put forward as somehow peculiar to Pakistani culture, as if this is radically different. Disqualified by the 1970 Ordinance (which required a university degree to stand for parliament), some men nominated "female relatives who were better educated or who did not have criminal records" (p. 83). Benazir's career may be less unique than those who would explain it solely in terms of *extraordinary circumstance* suggest. How else, they say, could a Pakistani Muslim woman become head of government, which culture and religion oppose? It must be an aberration!

Did gender play a significant role in Benazir's rise to power?

Thompson suggests that after the martyrdom of Bhutto, regarded by party loyalists as a pro-democracy hero, the choice of a woman to challenge Zia, a military dictator, was a good tactical move. Leading non-violent protest, Benazir symbolized the personal cost of commitment to justice. Meanwhile, Murtaza led violent resistance, dividing gender roles. She may have seemed less threatening to rivals within the PPP, who were able to rally around her more easily than had she been male. Thompson, though, points to a tendency to turn from a quest *for justice* towards one for *revenge*, which can poison the political climate.

Did gender play any role in Benazir's exercise of power?

Benazir's commitment to women's empowerment and human rights could be characterized as gender inspired, although men can share these commitments. In dealing with the military, her gender was almost certainly *perceived as a weakness*. The military had overthrown and killed her father. Her account of how she tried to neutralize the ISI is complicated. Somehow, the general she wanted to dismiss had his duties transferred to Military Intelligence, via the president and army chief (2008, p. 202). Anyone, male or female, would naturally feel vulnerable in such circumstances. Being the daughter of the slain leader, however, added to her high social status, and "made it more tolerable to break with traditional female roles" (p. 43). Here, the combination of dynastic tie and gender helped her political career. Drawing on her own unsullied past when she entered the arena, she "promised to cleanse the soiled public realm with private, familial virtue" (p. 36). On the other hand, while on the campaign trail her "suffering" and that of her family enabled her to rise "above the barrier of gender" (1989, pp. 154–5). Perhaps all who represent men and women need to develop some degree of transgendered consciousness.

Is there any particular relationship between Benazir's gender and her strengthening of democracy in Pakistan?

Men in Pakistan have tended toward autocratic power, sidelining democracy, suspending civil liberties and jailing dissenters. The argument that *women are more democracy prone than men* is debatable but the reality is that *women have led democratic reforms across Asia*. Benazir's record is ambivalent but the problems have nothing to do with authoritarianism. For Zia, she could *not have seemed as threatening as a man*. Through her, too, her father's dubious democratic record was recycled, enabling his legacy to rise above an "ambivalent past." Benazir portrayed herself as a "caring sister" of the poor (p. 43). Femininity, somehow, stressed the "moral character of the struggle against dictatorship" (p. 36).

Does the post-colonial context have any bearing on Benazir's career?

Benazir was confronted by challenges such as those posed by Pakistan's nature as a fractured, even failing state, separatist movements, and the military's strength due to conflict with India. All flow from the colonial legacy. She feared the "Balkanization" of Pakistan (2008, p. 211). Cohen thinks that Pakistan could become a rogue state, where arms are sold, borders unpatrolled, schools and healthcare unfunded, and taxes uncollected. Possible "futures" for Pakistan are discussed in Chapter 5, when we encounter similar issues in Bangladesh.

Did Benazir promote women's issues and rights?
Yes, her record speaks for itself. With 22.5 percent of parliament being women, much has been achieved. Benazir praised and promoted the role of women's organizations, not only in Pakistan but also globally, as vital for past and future progress (2008, pp. 293–4).

Conclusion

Benazir's election, the appointment of senior women judges, and the accomplishments of other Pakistani women, do not exhaust what needs to be done for gender equality in Pakistan. However, they represent important milestones. Even if neither culture nor Islam were a positive help, the argument that they presented *insurmountable obstacles* to women's representation cannot be sustained. Benazir ought to be remembered *exactly as she wanted to be*, "for what she did for women," especially for Muslims. Some *are* oppressed. Oppression, though, is not the *whole story*. Those who insist otherwise do so for their own purposes.

Chapter 3

Khaleda Zia and Bangladesh

Image 3: Begum Khaleda Zia.
Source: public domain.

Setting Parameters

In 2005, *Forbes Magazine* ranked Khaleda Zia the 29th most powerful woman in the world. She is associated with restoring democracy after Bangladesh's *second military phase*, alongside her political opponent, Sheikh Hasina, with whom she was then collaborating. Since 1991, they have alternated in power, a unique political story. With three female-led administrations completing full terms in succession, Bangladesh passes one test of democratic legitimacy, despite other shortcomings. In comparison, no Pakistani administration has yet completed a full term before a military or presidential intervention.

Pakistan and Bangladesh enjoy different status in economics, military strength and strategic significance. Pakistan, located where the Middle East meets Asia, borders China and has a long conflict with India. Like India, it has nuclear capability. War in Afghanistan – aimed at ousting, first, the Soviets, then the Taliban – has resulted in Pakistan attracting a great deal of media attention. People want to know who Pakistan's leader is, whose finger might push the button. They are less curious about who leads Bangladesh. Threatened by climate change and renowned for floods, Bangladesh is unthreatening and strategically unimportant. Several analysts argue that it could become a threat if militant Islamist groups gain strength there, turning the state into a terrorist refuge and arms depot. Yet Bangladesh deserves more media exposure for what it has achieved. It has enjoyed a steady, if slow, annual growth in GDP (roughly 4 percent per annum, reaching 5.7 in 1998), similar to the US's during Reagan's administration. Despite challenges of poverty, development and ecological dangers, Bangladesh is also a major contributor to UN peacekeeping missions. A Bangladeshi, Muhammad Younus, originated micro-credit, co-winning the Nobel Peace Prize in 2006 with the organization he founded, Grameen Bank.

As the second Muslim woman to lead a government in the modern world, Khaleda stands in Benazir's shadow. To some degree, this is true of all four women who came after Benazir. There are interesting differences as well as similarities between Khaleda and Benazir's careers. Although the PPP has an Islamic hue, it is less "Islamic," more secular, than its main rival, the Muslim League. The League was not originally an Islamic party but shifted toward Islamism under Sharif. In Bangladesh, of the two main parties, Khaleda's BNP is distinctly more Islamic. Of the three parties – the PPP, BNP and AL – the AL is the most explicitly aligned with pluralism and secular values, with the PPP in the middle. It is less surprising that the PPP or AL chose a woman leader, given their leftist ideological leanings. The PPP and AL have identified themselves with socialist ideas. Although the BNP is center right, currently little actually separates it from the AL on fiscal policy. However, when Bangladeshis elected Khaleda, they were also voting for a party allied with Islamist Islam. They chose *that party* and its *woman leader* over the more secular party, also led by a woman. This reinforces the contention that Islam per se is not a barrier to women's participation in politics. On the ground in Bangladesh, voices echo my "position one."

Members of the Bangladesh branch of Mawdudi's party expressed opposition to women leaders. Yet that party has cooperated with both women, gaining seats in Khaleda's cabinet. Working with her, accepting her authority and the *legitimacy of her leadership*, it cannot unambiguously oppose her. Khaleda's success on two occasions shows that many Muslim people do not perceive there to be faith-related obstacles to supporting a woman leader.

Like Pakistan, Bangladesh has alternated between civilian and military rule. Khaleda's husband, Zia, was its first military ruler. Benazir's father had not assumed power through a coup, but questions about his authoritarian style compromise his democratic legacy. Zia did not stage the coup that brought him to power but stepped in to restore order. Initially disinterested in restoring civilian rule, he copied the methods used by Pakistan's military leaders to legitimize his rule. Later, founding his own party, he launched what many regard as a genuine shift toward democracy, despite allegations of election rigging. Following his assassination, his civilian vice-president won a fair election, only to be ousted by Ershad, the second military ruler.

Khaleda entered the political arena in opposition to Ershad, whom she blamed for her husband's death. Hasina has a grudge against Khaleda's husband for complicity in her father's death – a rift that poisons their relationship. Did Zia's ambiguous democratic record impact her career? Alongside Hasina's and other parties, including *Jamaat* (JI), Khaleda campaigned to end military rule and restore democracy. Aspects of her legacy – and she is an active politician – raise questions about her leadership style, whether she has compromised democracy or not. We should not assume that women are automatically democracy's gift.

Feuding between Khaleda and Zia, parliamentary boycotts when in opposition, and failure to play the role of "loyal opposition," are all dubious elements in both their legacies. On the positive side, they developed a two-party system that promises greater political stability. Like Pakistan, Bangladesh has had to deal with Islam's role and with that of the military. So far, no regime has shifted as close to an Islamist form of Islam as Pakistan has. Legal accommodations to Islam have been relatively cosmetic. The Constitution is less Islamic, with no reference to *Shari'ah*. Under Mujib, Bangladesh was secular. Zia and Ershad pursued Islamization policies. Yet Ayub's 1961 Family Law Ordinance is still in force in Bangladesh, unchallenged by any Bangladeshi regime, although there have been new laws concerning women. Most laws date back to the Raj. The 1860 Indian Penal Code and the 1898 Code of Criminal Procedure cover many areas. With modification, these remain Indian law as well. Bangladesh's law of evidence is the 1872 Act. The country has not experienced the same level of demand as Pakistan to Islamize its legal system. The British legacy rather than culture or religion must be blamed for most legal obstacles to gender equality.

Analysts argue that Islam has become part of the political landscape in all four states. This raises issues about how women handle their Muslim identity, how they dress and promote their image, and how they use Islamic language and symbols? Perhaps not surprisingly, Khaleda has a reputation for being the more pious of the two. Hasina, though, has also contributed to the accommodation of Islamic language and symbols in the public square. Islamist parties have mushroomed. Some have radical agendas. Some engage in or incite violence, often against minorities. All this undermines the heritage of pluralism and coexistence, and makes Bangladesh less stable and safe. Numerically, these parties are small, winning few votes.

JI is the only Islamist party that has enjoyed electoral success. Despite accusations to the contrary, it stands for constitutional politics. Some members are active in promoting interreligious harmony. Party literature affirms that a *Jamaat* government would work for the emancipation of all people, "regardless of caste, creed and colour," from poverty and exploitation. The party would collaborate with all "democracy-loving" people (Party Manifesto 2001).

However, is Bangladesh today less viable a state due to Khaleda's alliance with Islamists? Nightmare scenarios suggest the possibility of Islamists seizing power through "systematic ... murder, intimidation and the assassination of key political and social leaders and personalities in the field of culture who stand for modernity, moderation and secularism." Such parties stand no chance of "capturing power ... through election" but Karlekar fears that Khaleda's BNP government created a climate favoring their growth (p. 278).

This chapter begins with a brief literary review. It then discusses political background. Khaleda's career follows. Finally, it turns to issues listed in the Introduction. Obviously, political background is relevant for both Khaleda and Hasina, so Chapters 3 and 5 overlap. To avoid unnecessary repetition, this chapter focuses on Zia–Khaleda aspects, Chapter 5 on Mujib–Hasina aspects. Overlap also occurs because the women are rivals. Since Zia began Bangladesh's Islamization process and his widow leads a party with distinct Islamic identity, this chapter prioritizes issues surrounding Islam and gender. Chapter 5 prioritizes cultural considerations that may shed light on why Bangladesh, supposedly patriarchal, has chosen women leaders and made considerable strides on gender issues. Of course, religion and culture overlap. Indeed, they are part of the same matrix.

Are there lessons from the religion–culture matrix in Bangladesh to transfer into Arab space? As in Pakistan, there is still much to be done. Yet legislation has addressed some important gender-related areas. Both women would score highly on any gender empowerment measure. Some claim that their elite status and "special circumstances" as surrogates for dead male predecessors separate them from non-elite women, whose lives have not improved very much. Chowdhury (1994) thinks that Khaleda and Hasina's careers are "best explained by their kinship links," describing Bangladesh as a "patriarchy" (p. 94). Yet there is evidence of more ordinary women, with no dynastic ties, entering politics too and having led successful political careers. What follows challenges any attempt to minimize the significance and impact of Khaleda's career.

Literature Survey

For details of Khaleda's life, I consulted the *Encyclopædia Brittanica Online* and biographical entries on the Council of Women World Leaders and Bangladesh Nationalist Party websites. The chapter on the BNP in Mitra *et al.* was very useful, both for references to Khaleda and for the broader political and historical background. On politics in Bangladesh and the role of Islam, I am especially indebted to Baxter (1998), Chowdhury (2003), Riaz (2004) and Karlekar (2005). Benazir's 2008 book also contains relevant information, although I use this more for Chapter 5.

Chowdhury applies lessons on democracy from the US to South Asia, analyzing Pakistan, Bangladesh and India. He argues that the development of a two-party system in Bangladesh was positive. However, a way needs to be found to normalize how the opposition functions, to encourage leaders to be better democrats. Their feuding, he says, lets down the Bangladeshi people, who show their preference for democracy by voting in large numbers whenever given the chance. Chowdhury sees parallels in how military rulers in Pakistan and Bangladesh accuse civilian politicians of corruption and how they use Islam to legitimize their regimes.

Riaz and Karlekar fear for the Talibanization of Bangladesh. Riaz usefully compares the increasing influence of Islamism in Bangladesh with the situation in Pakistan and Indonesia. I do not myself, however, see Islamists gaining a high level of popular support in any of these states.

For gender in Bangladesh, two books that use fieldwork cover the material extremely thoroughly, Hashmi (2000) and Shehabuddin (2008). Shehabuddin focuses on rural women, suggesting that rather than being pulled in different directions by secular-oriented agencies and Islamist parties vying for their votes or sympathies, they skillfully manipulate a middle path. Interviewing women affiliated to *Jamaat-e-Islami* (JI), she discovered that they too do not necessarily subscribe fully to all *Jamaat* ideas. Nor when pious Muslim women vote for a non-Islamist party do they think that they are also voting *against Islam*, despite what propaganda tells them. Many are shaping an Islam to meet their own needs.

Much literature identifies animosity between NGOs and their efforts to empower women and Islamists. Several books explore the issue of violence to women and the role of village courts, or *salish*, which apply Hudood laws, use the two-for-one testimony rule and require four witnesses for rape and adultery, although they have no legal authority to act in these matters. Hashmi says that "hardly anything Islamic about the judgements can be found" (p. 131) and that the courts enable certain local elites to exert power over subordinates. Village elders run these courts, gaining financially from the verdicts they pronounce (p. 137). Their misogyny is "not necessarily synonymous with peasant culture" but stems from a "little tradition" of rural power politics outside the "mainstream" (pp. 93–4). Women "in general despise them" (p. 94). He argues that better-educated *ulama* and others do not share their views, although some "who, aware of the *mullas*' incomplete knowledge of Islamic texts and history, condone their activities" because these "safeguard their vested interests" (p. 91). Riaz says these courts have "no legal status" (p. 76). Hashmi refers to various ordinances recognizing the traditional village system of arbitration courts but says their "jurisdiction is strictly limited to minor civil and petty criminal offences" (p. 103). Use of *fatwas* against NGOs, writers accused of "blasphemy against Islam" and women who take part in NGO activities or work for their programs is widespread. Those who deal with NGOs are condemned as infidels. Some *fatwas* denounce women for voting. NGOs are "wrecking Islamic cultural values," in conspiracy with Christians and Jews (Riaz, p. 123). The number of *fatwas* issued led to some *ulama* being dubbed "*fatwa* mad" or *fatwabaz*. The High Court (2001) ruled that only state-appointed judges can issue *fatwas*, since they are legal opinions and "the legal system of Bangladesh empowers only the courts to decide all questions related to legal opinion on the Muslim and other laws in force" (Riaz, p. 86). This has not stopped *fatwas*. Riaz says that the combined objections to this ruling of the rural mullah and Islamists suggest that the latter do have ties with the former, while some have argued against any direct relationship (p. 9).

On legal aspects, Hossain (2003) – with the 1961 Family Law Ordinance and the 1939 Dissolution of Muslim Marriage Act as an appendix – is detailed and informative. Hossain and others support a Unified Family Law for all Bangladeshis. I return to the 1961 Ordinance in Chapter 5.

A search on the internet found sites and texts containing many laws relevant to gender, including Sections 175–6 of the 1860 India Penal Code on rape, and relevant clauses of the Evidence Act (1872). Much internet material can be found, also covered by Hashmi and Shehabuddin, on violence toward women in Bangladesh. One source here is a report on women and violence in Bangladesh, Pakistan, Egypt and the Sudan, useful for comparison across these Muslim spaces although somewhat dated (Marcus 1993). Marcus observes that, at the time of writing, "few studies on the scale and nature of violence against women in Bangladesh" had been carried out (p. 3). However, he notes, "the battering of women within the household appears to be widespread throughout Bangladesh" (p. 5). Violence against women occurs. It must be recognized, not denied or minimized as somehow culturally acceptable. However, millions of women are also *not being brutalized* every day, millions of Bangladeshi men *do not hit women*, and millions of Bangladeshis reject and *condemn violence toward women*. Figures cited include approximately 500 reported rapes per annum, about the same number of abductions, and about 30 cases of acid attacks. Marcus does not specify statistics for wife beating but another source cites approximately 3,000–4,000 per annum (ADB Country Briefing Paper, Bangladesh, 2000).

As horrific as such statistics are, they do not represent every household in a country of some 150 million. We need to be cautious before making misogyny and violence toward women a national characteristic, as if these are widely condoned. Action has been taken, including new legislation, such as the Woman and Children Repression (Special Provisions) Act (1995), replaced by the Repression of Cruelty to Women and Children Act (2000) and the Violence against Women and Children Act (1998). In 1996, the Permanent Law Commission was mandated "To recommend, after examination, necessary reforms of the existing laws and enactment of new laws in appropriate cases, in order to safeguard the rights of women and children and prevent repression of women."

I also used Thompson (2004) on female leaders and democratic restorations in Asia; Rai (2009) for reserved seats in Bangladesh; case studies in Commonwealth Secretariat (1999); and Nelson and Chowdhury (1994). *Women in Politics: Voices from the Commonwealth*, a report by the Gender

Affairs Department of the Commonwealth Secretariat, explores the contributions of three Bangladeshi women politicians who have no dynastic ties. Finally, Begum's 2006 *Asian Profile* article is an excellent analysis of image- and party-ethos issues with respect to both Bangladeshi female leaders.

Alternating Civilian and Military Rule

First Democratic Period
First president, Sheikh Mujib-ur-Rahman, 1971–2; prime minister, 1972–5; third president, January to August 1975
Second president, Abu Sayeed Choudhury, 1972–3
Fourth president, Mohammad Ullah, 1973–5

First Military Period
Fifth president, Khondaker Mostaq Ahmad, August–November 1975 (self-proclaimed)
Sixth president and chief martial law administrator (former chief justice), Sadat Mohammad Sayem, November 1975–April 1977
Seventh president, Ziaur Rahman, 1977–81

Second Civilian Period (first democratic restoration)
Eighth president, Abdus Sattar, 1981–2; former vice-president

Second Military Period
President Hussain Muhammad Ershad (1981–90) (technically ninth president March 24–7, 1982, then chief martial law administrator until December 1983); eleventh president 1983–90
Tenth president, F. M. Ahsanuddin Chowdhury, March 1982–December 11, 1983

Third Civilian Period (second democratic restoration)
Twelfth president, Chief Justice Shahabuddin Ahmed, 1990–1

After return to prime ministerial system, subsequent presidents are ceremonial elect by parliament.

Prime Minister Khaleda Zia, 1991–6 – two elections 1996: February 1, boycotted by opposition; June 2 (some count her as having served three terms)
Prime Minister Sheikh Hasina, 1996–2001

Prime Minister Khaleda Zia, 2001–6
Interim (military supported) chief advisor, Fakruddin Ahmed,
2007–January 2009
Prime Minister Sheikh Hasina, from 2009

The Political Background: Origins of the "Idea of Bangladesh"

Tracing the origins of Pakistan to the development of an idea is common, but this is less so with Bangladesh. Shared history in pre-partition India – the "two-nation" theory and the act of partition itself – represents overlap between their stories. Yet Bangladesh did not secede only because, as East Pakistan, it was ill treated by West Pakistan or because Islam did not unify Pakistan's diverse peoples. Those would be negative reasons for founding a separate country. Before Pakistan's creation, issues of culture in relation to religion in Bengal and whether East Bengal would want to join Muslims in the North West of India given their cultural differences, were already alive. Bangladesh may not fit the "imagined community" model quite as neatly as Pakistan but ideas about statehood predate its birth. Pakistan turned out to be more or less what people wanted. However, when people dreamed of an independent, sovereign state in the geo-political space where Bangladesh is now situated, they had a larger entity in mind, one that included the whole of historic Bengal.

The idea that became Bangladesh is traceable to the pre-partition period, when the possibility of a united Bengali nation, east and west, was seriously proposed. Rahmat Ali named this Bangistan. That state would have had a Muslim majority but a large Hindu minority bound by a common language and culture. It would have valued cross-religious ties and Islam would not have been sidelined. It would have been close to Jinnah's vision, whose Pakistan would officially recognize Islamic values but would not be an Islamic state per se.

The idea of Bangladesh as a unified state – what is now West Bengal and Bangladesh – is rooted in the failed partition of 1905. Conventional wisdom has it that Bangladesh's secession from Pakistan saw culture trump religion. I myself subscribed to this, writing that Bangladesh separated "almost entirely to assert cultural independence" (2005, p. 251). I now think otherwise. Islam remained a vital component of life for the majority of Bangladeshis. Respect for Islam did not diminish.

What people reacted against was an Islam that failed to treat them justly, equitably; that dishonored their cultural identity. Injustice, exploitation and political disempowerment, not disillusionment with Islam, drove secession.

The real aim of the 1905 partition was to isolate Hindus in the east, where many well-educated pro-independence agitators lived, from their colleagues in the west. Adding additional territory to the west and taking some away, the British reduced the overall proportion of Hindus, making them a minority on both sides of the new border (Hardy, p. 149). The east also gained territory. This was classic divide and rule, neutralizing Hindu leadership of the self-rule movement and winning the Raj Muslim support (Baxter, p. 39). Muslims liked the arrangement; they would form an administration within the limited scope of powers then delegated to provincial assemblies. The stated reason was that Bengal was too large to govern as a single unit, although the British had done so since 1757. It was, they said, the size of France with a population as big as France and Britain's combined (Hardy, p. 148).

Hindus throughout India reacted negatively; partition was arbitrary, dividing an ancient, culturally homogenous province. If the British could divide Bengal, no region was safe. Secret terrorist organizations began to operate. Bengal as "motherland" was epitomized by the goddess Kali, the "goddess of power and destruction, to whom they dedicated their weapons" (Metcalf and Metcalf, p. 155). Partition was revoked in 1911. Additional territories were subtracted. Delhi became the capital of India instead of Calcutta. Dhaka reverted to municipal status. It got a university in compensation. While few Muslims campaigned against partition, some remained proud of their wider culture. In that culture, Hindus, Muslims and others lived for the most part in harmony, singing the same songs, reading the same poetry, honoring each other's saints, artists and writers.

This harmony dates from when Islam first reached Bengal. We see this in the Sufi flavor of Bengali Islam. I elaborate on this stream or current of coexistence, tolerance and openness in later chapters. The creation of the Muslim League, separate electorates, the Government Act of 1935 and the movement for Pakistan ran against this current. On the other hand, while communitarian violence did happen, due to the traditional harmony between communities this was less common in Bengal (Karlekar, p. 38). Muslims, however, continued to pursue their separate political interests. After the 1937 election, they were able to form a government. Although the Muslim League did badly (39 seats), Fazlul Haq (1873–1962) – whose Krishak Shamrik Party won 36 seats –

entered a coalition with them, conceding two cabinet posts. Independent Muslims won 45, a smaller Muslim party 5, with Hindus and others making up the rest of the 248 seats (Jalal, p. 27).

As the idea of Pakistan gained impetus, Bengali Muslims enjoyed running Bengal. In 1946, in the election-plebiscite on Pakistan, the Muslim League won 114 against Congress' 86 seats. There were 2 independent Muslims. Now, the League formed its own ministry, under Huseyn Shaheed Suhrawardy (1892–1962), later Prime Minister of Pakistan. Cultural unity was badly damaged. Yet, as Indian independence dawned, many Bengalis still preferred a sovereign, unified Bengali state over dividing Hindu- from Muslim-majority areas. This was what Rahmat Ali had expected. Despite growing tensions between Hindus and Muslims, people throughout India suspected Bengalis

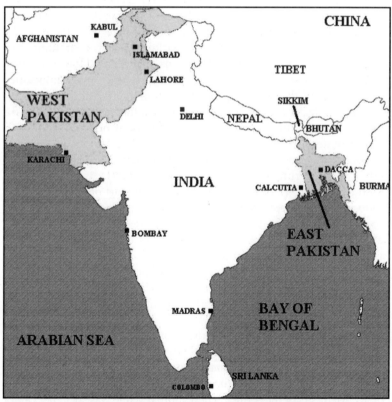

Map 5: West and East Pakistan, 1947–71, separated by India.

would choose ethno-linguistic-cultural unity. I would add "religious" – coexistence and Bengali spiritual tradition are inseparable. Mountbatten ruled this out, disallowing the option on the basis that other provinces would want independence too (Hasan, p. 311). Ali's Dinia would be a nightmare scenario. For the partition vote, the legislature divided into separate Hindu and Muslim chambers. If one chamber voted for partition, that result carried, regardless of how the other voted. When the Hindus voted, fear of becoming a minority in Pakistan produced a 58 to 21 vote *for partition*. The Muslims refused to vote to partition Bengal. Instead, they voted on whether the *whole of Bengal* should join Pakistan or *remain in India*. They voted 166 to 35 in favor of the former. The Muslims of Bengal indeed preferred ethno-cultural unity. Denied the option of independent statehood, they tried to take their whole province – the size of France – into Pakistan.

The Hindu vote vetoed the Muslim's preferred choice and Bengal was repartitioned. West Bengal joined India; East Bengal, Pakistan. Sizeable minorities remained on both sides – about 20 percent in the east, 25 percent in the west. During the population transfer, communitarian violence resulted in hundreds of thousands of fatalities. However, fewer fatalities occurred in the east than elsewhere, since more minorities stayed home. In the north-west about 7 million crossed the border in both directions, a movement of 14 million. In the east, as few as a million crossed, although another four followed between 1947 and 1964 (Chatterji, p. 105). Later, an incident when Hindus in Kashmir were accused of stealing a relic from a mosque fomented communitarian animosity, triggering more migration (Novak, p. 91).

On May 14, 1947 Bengalis found themselves part of Pakistan. Some 1,000 miles separated them from the larger province, although more people lived in the east. More GDP was generated there – from the now-defunct jute industry. Islam was meant to glue Pakistan's people together. Instead, constitutional uncertainty, debate on Islam's role and questions on how the state should be governed drove people apart. Islam hardly had a chance to do its job. East Pakistan was linguistically and culturally homogenous. Multi-ethnic West Pakistan, though, soon faced separatist insurgency.

Conflict with India pushed Pakistan in certain directions, including drifting toward authoritarianism and heavy military expenditure. Islam, seeing all Muslims as equal, demands social justice, which the Objectives Resolution recognized. Unfortunately, West Pakistan treated East like a colony. Members of the former, where more revenue was spent per capita than in East Pakistan, dominated the army, civil service and party political leadership. A proposal to make Urdu the single national language in September 1950 further aggravated tension between the two. Ahmed (1997) says that West Pakistanis treated Bengalis as racially inferior. Karlekar refers to West Pakistan's "feudal arrogance," to the "vested interests of ... business men and industrialists" that exploited the East (p. 41). Soon after partition, famine struck East Pakistan. Due to inadequate response, it continued until 1951. Fazlul Haq, who left the League in 1941, complained about authoritarian leadership (p. 41).

Bengali separatism started on February 21, 1952, when soldiers killed four students during a pro-Bengali language demonstration. The newly formed Awami League under Mujib and Haq's leadership united against the Muslim League, winning the 1954 election, 228 seats to 10. (The Awami League's emergence and details of its agenda are taken up in Chapter 5.) At this stage, greater autonomy was the goal, or an equitable distribution of resources and power. An independent state was not the issue. Sadly, instead of working out a form of federalism to satisfy not only East Pakistan but other ethno-national groups too, West Pakistan responded with increased repression. Public meetings and demonstration were prohibited, press freedom restricted, and imports of books and films from West Bengal – even the broadcasting of Tagore's songs – banned.

The songs and poems of Rabindranath Tagore (1861–1941), the Hindu reformer and Nobel Literature laureate, are universally loved by Bengalis across religions. My sister-in-law is a nationally renowned Tagore artist who has performed on state television.

Mujib's six-point program, launched in 1966, would have given East Pakistan control of West and left only defense and foreign affairs in the hands of the center. The states, with "their own currencies," would have dealt with all other areas, including taxation (Bhutto 2008, pp. 177–8). Benazir says this would have "constitutionally dismantled the state" (p. 178).

When the first free and fair election took place in Pakistan on December 7, 1970, Mujib won 160 seats to the PPP's 81 and should have formed a government. Yahya Khan and Bhutto, however, prevaricated. Bhutto argued that East Pakistan could not impose a constitution on the whole country but needed the consent of all "federating units" (2008, p. 177). He was not prepared to lead the opposition, either, with Mujib in power. A crackdown on East Pakistan followed. On March 25, 1971, soldiers fired on and killed 300 students, Mujib was imprisoned and Zia, then an army major, declared Bangladesh's independence following a telegram from Mujib (p. 122).

Map 6: Bangladesh today.

A bloody war followed. Bengali freedom fighters battled Pakistan's better trained, better equipped army. Atrocities, rapes – perhaps as many as 425,000 (Karlekar, p. 47) – murders of civilians and minorities took place on a massive scale. India's intervention finally ended the war. A new nation was born on Victory Day (*Bijoy Dibosh*) December 16, 1971, with Mujib as president. When a prime ministerial system was subsequently instituted, with a ceremonial presidency, he became PM. (Details of Mujib's regime are taken up in Chapter 5.)

When Bangladesh adopted a constitution (November 4, 1972), it proclaimed that the state was "secular" and "socialist." Riaz says that a "ban was imposed on the use of religion in politics" (p. 5). I return to what Mujib meant by "secular" in Chapter 5. However, Mujib had a wartorn and soon flood-devastated country to govern. Refugees were returning from India. Factions were pulling in different directions. The *Jamaat*, supporting Pakistan, had run the Islamabad-imposed emergency government "as provincial ministers in charge of revenue, education, commerce and industry, and local government" (Shehabuddin, p. 66).

Committed to "unity of the state," JI was unsympathetic toward "ethnic and linguistic sentiment" (p. 61). It alleged a communist plot to dismember Pakistan. This "continues to have repercussions for" *Jamaat's* "participation in the political arena" (p. 67). Its leader raised large sums of money to fund the war. Some collaborators were suspected or accused of "rape, murder and torture" (Karlekar, p. 49). JI started a campaign to reunite with Pakistan.

In the first parliamentary election, March 1973, the Awami League won almost all seats, 293 out of 300 (there were 15 reserved seats for women). This may have been rigged or it may have reflected the enormous popularity Mujib still enjoyed. Effectively there was no opposition (p. 12). Mujib announced the formation of a party of national unity, the Bangladesh Peasants, Workers and Peoples League (BAKSAL). On January 25, 1975 parliament approved an amendment to the constitution introducing an executive presidency, which Mujib assumed (Molla, p. 225). The severe flood in 1974 resulted in a state of emergency (December 28); Mujib became president on January 25, 1975. For some, this compromised Mujib's democratic credentials. Chowdhury regrets that Mujib did not emulate George Washington, and "show a strong commitment to consti-tutional government" (2003, p. 30). On August 15, 1975 some army officers assassinated him and his family. Hasina and one sister were overseas, so survived. Others assassinations followed on November 3 when "the entire top leadership of the Awami League" was wiped out (Karlekar, p. 50). This sets the scene for Hasina's assumption of the party's leadership; the story of which is continued in Chapter 5. As we shall see, she sees events differently, defending her father's legacy. It also sets the scene for Zia's rise to power.

Zia's Regime

The volatile situation that followed saw a series of "coups, counter coups, killings and counter killings, chaos and confusion" and two short presi-dencies, all over an 84-day period. Khondaker Mostaq Ahmad appointed Zia, now a war hero, army chief after the first coup. After the next coup, he was imprisoned from November 1 to 7. Released, he stepped in to restore order (Riaz, p. 20). A familiar process of legitimization followed, with Zia winning a referendum by 76.63 percent, which Chowdury calls "farcical" (p. 36). In June 1978 he stood against a contender, General M. A. G. Osmani, and claimed a 76 percent to 21 percent victory (three other candi-dates had a 3 percent share).

Zia may or may not have had long-term plans for restoring democracy at this stage. With strikes and demonstrations to deal with, he "told the nation" that "he was a soldier, not a politician" and that his government was "interim" (Hossain 2004, p. 198). Changes to the constitution followed. Beginning what analysts call an Islamization process, Zia replaced "secular" with "faith in Almighty Allah" and "socialism" with "economic and social justice," the latter change responding to World Bank requirements for "economic liberalization" (Shehabuddin, pp. 71–2)

The *bismillah* (in the Name of God) was added above the preamble and the official nationality changed from "Bengali" to "Bangladeshi," stressing *difference* not *sameness* with Hindu-majority West Bengal, whose people are also Bengalis. Zia's changes "linked the identity of the nation" with its "territorial limits" (Riaz, p. 35). (The difference between Bengali and Bangladeshi will be discussed further in Chapter 5.) Two considerations impacted Zia's changes. First, Bangladesh had neither the "ideological base" for secularism nor the "economic resources to carry out a socialist economic policy" (Chowdhury 2003, p. 26). Second, there was some pressure from the Arab world for Bangladesh to declare Islamic identity. Zia attempted a balancing act, appeasing oil-rich Arab states to attract aid while trying not to alienate Western donors. Riaz suggests that this shift also sought to legitimize the coup against Mujib by establishing it as an expression of Bangladeshi nationalism, not Mujib-style Bengali nationalism (p. 34). By establishing 1975 as the real birth of the nation, he "minimized" the role civilians had played in "achieving ... independence," maximizing the military's role (Riaz, p. 35). A constitutional amendment legalized all ordinances passed during martial law (Riaz, p. 37). The country remained and remains the People's Republic (not Islamic).

Zia's economic policies were free market, in line with World Bank and IMF policies, in contrast to Mujib's centrally controlled system. He ended press censorship and allowed political parties to function, founding his own – the Bangladesh National Party – on September 1, 1978, deputizing vice-president Abdus Sattar as the main organizer. Zia tried to improve law and order, while his 19-point program aimed to stimulate the economy. He stood for election on June 3, 1978 against an Awami League opponent, winning 76 percent of the vote. Chowdhury says that both Zia and the second military ruler, Ershad – the latter more so – took vote rigging to new levels (Chowdhury 2003, p. 37). Yet Zia was a charismatic leader and genuinely popular, for which I can attest (I was working in Bangladesh during his presidency). He worked hard to combat poverty, leaving Khaleda a positive legacy from which she benefited: "Zia's efforts are remembered by many rural poor to this day and have played an important role in maintaining

electoral support for his party, even helping to bring his widow to power."
He "drew praise for his efforts to further the cause of women"
(Shehabuddin, p. 73). On other hand, military rule "allowed women and
men little opportunity to exercise democratic rights" (Shehabuddin, p.
157). However, his rule coincided with the UN Decade for Women and his
second five-year plan (1980–5) gave special attention to women in development strategy. He set up the Ministry for Women's Affairs and increased
the number of reserved seats to 30. He appointed women police, who wore
"shirts and trousers like" their male colleagues (Shehabuddin, p. 72). When
the Saudis objected that women should not be visible to the public, he
reassigned them to "duty inside checkpoints or traffic booths" (p. 73). The
Saudis recognized Bangladesh after Zia removed "secular" from the constitution (p. 69). He introduced other Islamic measures, such as compulsory
Islamic studies at primary and secondary levels, regulations to standardize
madrassa curricular, and broadcasting the call to prayer on state media five
times a day. His cabinet included collaborators and "people with close ties
to religious organizations" (Riaz, p. 36). He established the Ministry of
Religious Affairs and in 1979 lifted the ban on religious parties. His BNP
won the 1979 election, 270 seats out of 300.

Zia survived various plots and assassination attempts until May 30,
1981, when I remember the shock of hearing the news on my radio that he
had been killed in a failed coup attempt. I was expecting a guest that day
from Chittagong, where the murder took place. I liked Zia. I thought he
was sincere about transitioning to democracy.

Sattar became acting president. Under the constitution, he was required
to hold elections within 180 days. The BNP considered whom to nominate.
Sattar was respected but old. Various party members, including the former
prime minister, Shah Azizur Rahman, and the General Secretary – a close
friend of Zia's – Badruduzza Chowdhury, were eligible but could not agree
between them. Sattar emerged as a compromise candidate, winning the
subsequent election, held on November 15, 1981, against an Awami Party
contender (65.2 percent) (Chowdhury 2003, p. 120). This may be a unique
instance of an originally military regime transforming itself into a democratic
civilian one (Hossain 2004, p. 202). Sattar resisted pressure from the army
chief, Ershad, to give the army a "constitutional role in governance"
(Chowdhury 2003, p. 38). Claiming that the government was incompetent
and corrupt, Ershad seized power on March 24, 1982. I was present in
Bangladesh during these events. After a very brief democratic interlude,
Bangladesh entered its second military phase. Where Sattar failed, due to
no fault of his own, was in lacking charisma.

Khaleda: Championing Democracy against Military Rule

Sattar appointed Khaleda vice-chair in March 1983. Born in 1945, she attended high school in Dinajpur, then Surendranath College. She married Zia in 1960. From then until becoming party leader, she was a homemaker and First Lady with no active political role, though she may have expressed her views in private. Sattar retired as BNP leader in February 1984. Again, the same men vied for the job. Some who might have contested were now aligned with Ershad, so were out of the running. Khaleda, already vice-chair, was nominated by Jahan Ara Begum, Vice-President of the Executive Committee, who emphasized that while she "would be entering politics on the basis of kinship, she would have to pass the test of competent political leadership" (Commonwealth Secretariat, p. 34). Subsequently, Jahan, who mentored Khaleda politically, served in her government. This suggests that Khaleda was consciously chosen as a unifier whose leadership would attract support, if for no other reason than the expected sympathy votes she would gain. Alternatively, the party might have planned to control her. Khaleda, however, proved to be a strong and popular politician, a crowd puller. Her public appearances drew people "like a magnet," something that other BNP leaders "cannot do" (Begum, p. 274).

Khaleda successfully built on her husband's popularity to identify herself with the "people," making it clear that she represented "them first." Her style, whether in office and opposition, continues to perpetuate her self-image as the "people's mouthpiece," just as she was during the days of the "democratization movement" (p. 275). Her clothes, however – expensive silk saris – denote nobility, royalty; thus she moves among the people as a "Queen coming down to the level of the populace" (p. 277). The use of Begum before rather than after her name indicates that she "belongs to an aristocratic family on her husband's side." Non-elite Bangladeshi women place Begum after their names, and wear cotton saris (Begum, p. 277). During the 2004 flood, she "was daily seen going to ... affected areas ... distributing relief, speaking to the people" (Begum, p. 275).

The Ershad Years

Ershad prioritized Islamization, promising to make "Bangladesh an Islamic country" (Riaz, p. 37). Similar sentiment emerged after Mujib's death, when Major Dalim declared, "Sheikh Mujib has been killed. Praise God. Bangladesh is now an Islamic Republic" (Shehabuddin, p. 69). Ershad spoke about introducing *Shari'ah* law. Chowdhury tends to see Zia and

Ershad's pro-Islam policies as mere expediency, to legitimate their rule through state control of discourse, trumping other understandings of Islam or democratic ideals of governance (p. 139).

Like Pakistani dictators, Ershad did not think democracy a suitable system of government. However, following Zia's example, he formed his own party, which attracted some members of the BNP's leadership. In March 1985 he held a referendum on his presidency, claiming a yes vote of 94.15 percent. That month, both Khaleda and Hasina were arrested (Khaleda was to be detained seven times in all under Ershad). In largely uncontested local elections, his party swept into power. In 1986, he allowed party elections for parliament, his party winning 153 seats to Hasina's 73. This was the first election when women won general seats. The BNP boycotted. Smaller parties won 39, independents 32. With 10, JI was the third largest. The communists won 5 seats. Hasina became leader of the opposition, but rarely attended parliament.

In August 1986 Ershad, still army chief, resigned that post to contest a presidential election in October, which both the BNP and AL boycotted. Not surprisingly, Ershad won. Parliament validated his victory and approved Amendment 8, which established Islam as the state religion. Shehabuddin says that, fearing repercussions for women and minorities, secularists and women's groups were the "first to protest" (p. 73). Islamists also objected, condemning the amendment as "hypocritical." They wanted an Islamic state, not a "declaration of Islam as a state religion" (Riaz, p. 38). Opposition parties led strikes in protest, to which Ershad responded that they were striking "against Allah, his prophet, and religion" (p. 39). In July 1987 he gave the military representation on local councils, moving on his contention that the army should have a constitutional role in governance. Similar to arrangements under Sukarno's "guided democracy," this also resonates with Musharaf's ideas in Pakistan. Musharaf and Ershad both complained about the incompetence and corruption of civilian rulers. Chowdhury remarks that it is difficult to prove such allegations when made by a military ruler, though what we do know is that Ershad himself was corrupt (Chowdhury 2003, p. 3). Ershad in fact made allies with the very politicians he accused of corruption (p. 380). Such allegations represent an "old trick" used by the military when seizing power.

The Democracy Restoration Movement

Opposition to Ershad picked up speed. Strikes followed. Hasina resigned from parliament in March 1987, entering an uneasy pro-democracy alliance with Khaleda and JI. When Ershad held elections in March 1998, with all main opposition parties boycotting, his Jatiya Party won 252 seats (out of 300). However, as dissatisfaction with his blatantly illegal regime increased, resignation was really his only option (December 6, 1990). He was immediately arrested for corruption. Found guilty, he went to jail, from where he still won seats in parliament.

Ershad made few if any policy changes from Zia's 19-point program, so did not seize power for ideological reasons. Continuing economic decentralization, he encouraged private investment and attracted foreign capital and aid (Chowdhury 2003, p. 39). Chowhdury says that Zia and Ershad established "military-bureaucratic" regimes in "the old Pakistani tradition" because they thought that the military could rule better than civilians (p. 36). Bangladesh inherited a "politicized military" from Pakistan (Chowdhury 2003, p. 127). Ershad's regime experienced so many strikes and disruptions, however, that Bangladesh's development was retarded. A new beginning was required.

On the Campaign Trail

The BNP–AL alliance ended when Ershad, whom Khaleda blamed for her husband's death, resigned. The two women leaders were opponents in the 1991 election. The alliance between Khaleda and JI, though, continued through the election. What role did Islam play? Khaleda's party has a distinctive Islamic hue, while Hasina's BNP is more secular and left of center, though no longer really socialist. The two parties now differ little on economic policy but adopt opposing policies on several key issues. The AL wants to improve relations with India, stresses Bengali nationalism and draws more on cultural symbols. Emphasizing Bangladeshi nationalism, the BNP draws mainly on Islamic symbols. Some implications of these differences are explored in Chapter 5.

Hasina and Khaleda dress differently. Khaleda wears a separate chiffon *duppatta* (scarf) on her head, which some see as "very Pakistani." She also wears chador "to cover the upper part of her body" (Begum, p. 277). Hasina is perceived to have covered up" only after performing the *hajj*, which critics say she did to prove her piety (Shehabuddin, p. 171). Both use Islamic language on the campaign trail, hence Shehabuddin writes about "God on the Campaign Trail." The BNP incorporates the *Kalimah* "there is no God but God" in its slogan, before "vote for the sheaf of rice in the name of God." The sheaf is the party symbol. AL copied the *Kalimah*, adding "but you are the master of the boat," that is, of its symbol.

JI says that a vote for it is a vote for Islam. JI member, Delwar Hossain Saidi, said that not voting was wrong but that Muslims must cast their ballot for a party planning to "establish Islam" (cited in Shehabuddin, p. 173). Saidi encourages women to vote but also preaches a "position one" view of gender, denouncing women's liberation as the "harbinger of doomsday." Opponents of polygyny are agents of the West; Saidi "is opposed to female leadership in any sphere of life" (Hashmi, pp. 88–9).

While Khaleda and JI were collaborating, the JI Press published a book in which M. Ruhul Amin declared that God created man to protect woman. "Women were not intended to be responsible for millions of households," he wrote, "by taking charge of an entire state" (Shehabuddin, pp. 167–8; citing Amin, p. 2). Mawdudi's followers may forget that he once supported a woman politician.

Several female JI activists told Shehabuddin that they could not under-stand how any self-respecting woman would "ever want to run for public office" or why they should do so when "there are men who can run" (p. 218). There should be no question, they said, of a female prime minister when men were available to do the job. Others, though, were unhappy with being told to vote for men. JI has not yet nominated a woman for election to an open seat, although it supports women voting and accepted two reserved seats in 1991. Women, as they voice their needs, compel the party to change some "rhetoric and strategies" (p. 220). The effort to win women's votes has led the party to consider "non religious, worldly policy areas" because this is what women want (p. 220). Both secular-oriented organizations and Islamists target women, who, skeptical that either can deliver their promises, skillfully negotiate between the two options.

Many women approve of NGOs programs because they give them "confidence and financial benefit" and access to learning. Critics say NGOs damage Islamic values, encouraging women to work alongside men. Since micro-credit programs usually involve women working at home, some Islamists approve of them (p. 135). Others argue that micro-credit is not really empowering; women end up working in "low-paid enterprises such as making handicrafts or raising poultry" (p. 141). *Fatwas* denounce NGOs, including Grameen Bank, claiming that Mohammed Younis has betrayed the country to foreigners. NGOs, like the East India Company, entered under false colors, intending to take over the country. The company came to trade but stayed to rule. NGOs target "mothers and sisters," aiming to "ruin them socially," "enticing them out of their homes," "inciting them against their husbands" by undermining their authority (p. 123). One paper published a cartoon in which a wife sets off outside, instructing her harassed-looking husband, "sweep the house, heat the food, wash my sari and petticoat and dry them in the sun, and don't 'get out of line' or I'll tell the NGO" (p. 123).

Khaleda's First Term

Khaleda won the 1991 election, governing until 1996 (BNP 140 seats, AL 88, Jatiya 35, JI 18, others 19 including 5 communist). She is said to have preferred the presidential system but agreed to amend the constitution to re-establish prime ministerial government, with a ceremonial president. Her critics call her authoritarian. One minister, for example, was dismissed for showing too much initiative (Chowdhury 2003, p. 111). The president was forced to resign on June 21, 2002 for failing to honor Zia's tomb on his death-date anniversary. He had also refused to ratify her nominee to an important post (Karlekar, p. 223). Khaleda rarely attended parliament, often announcing policy at meetings without having consulted anybody (Chowdhury 2003, p. 82). She monopolized state radio and television. The AW tended to boycott parliament. Organizing strikes, they alleged that the election had been rigged and constantly called for Khaleda's resignation. Bills were passed "without the participation of the opposition" and de facto a one-party system emerged (p. 82). Even budget sessions went unattended. This behavior compromises a parliamentary system's effectiveness, where the opposition is meant to challenge and scrutinize legislation.

A less adversarial, more conciliatory approach is needed. Bangladesh would benefit from leaders learning to negotiate, bargain and resolve difference peacefully without calling a strike, hartal. The opposition should be listened to and included in the legislative process. "The challenge to democratization in Bangladesh comes from the political sector," says Chowdhury, (2003, p. 100). Leaders let down the people, who consistently choose democracy when given the chance. Some research suggests that Bangladeshis like charismatic leaders, who command their loyalty and who they look up to as "superior." This may be why voters prefer elites to non-elite. The concept of a "loyal opposition" is problematic if allegiance is given to a single leader. Bangladeshi leaders "place themselves on an unequal position of hierarchy and fail to discuss nationally important issues as equals not as rivals" (Hussain and Khan 2000). Power is idealized as "arising from human consent freely given" and authority as "stemming from unquestioning recognition that some other person is superior ... and worthy of respect" (p. 208). Chowdhury fears that both leaders' conduct invites military intervention. Having tasted power, the military likes it. They now wait for any excuse to re-enter the arena (p. 127).

The 1996 Elections

Khaleda called a sudden election on February 15, 1996, without consulting the opposition. The AL boycotted the election, which Khaleda won (278 seats out of 300), commencing a second term. Counted as the sixth parliament, it lasted only 12 days. Some see this as another sign of indifference toward democracy. Leaders in Pakistan and Bangladesh assume that once they win an election they have the right to rule forever (Chowdhury 2003, p. 99). Between the two elections, Hasina made common cause with JI, whose alliance with Khaleda floundered after the 1991 election, when they did not get cabinet posts. A military coup was foiled in April. The demand was for a constitutional amendment establishing a neutral caretaker government between parliaments to supervise the next election. This amendment, the thirteenth, was passed on March 26. A caretaker government under a retired chief justice had supervised the 1991 election, but with no constitutional mandate. In the second 1996 election, on June 12, Hasina won with 146 seats to the BNP's 116. Ershad's Jatiya kept 32 out of 35. Its manifesto promised *Shari'ah* law and punishment of those who denigrate Islam or the prophet (Riaz, p. 44). The more radical Islami Okiya Jote, which allegedly has terrorist links, contested 59 seats, winning 1. JI lost 15.

The 2001 and 2008 Elections

After Hasina's first term, 1996–2001, Khaleda won by 193 to 62 seats. JI, again allied with the BNP, gained two posts in the cabinet having again won 18 seats, matching its 1991 result. Six women won open seats. Khaleda' alliance included the IOJ and Ershad's Jatiya. When Khaleda's second term ended in 2007, both women faced corruption charges and were banned (later rescinded) from standing for re-election. Both spent times under arrest and in voluntary exile but charges were dropped, dismissed or ruled as inadmissible. Both Khaleda's sons, Tarek Zia and Arafat Rahman Koko, said to be multi-millionaires, were also arrested on money laundering and other charges. Finally, after two years of caretaker government supported by the military and a massive effort at voter registration, elections took place. Photo-ID-cards had been issued to all eligible voters. Perhaps the Bangladesh military sees its role as similar to that of the Turkish military, which is tasked with defending the constitution. Hasina won her second term. Khaleda, re-elected BNP chair, became leader of the opposition.

Fears expressed by some that Islamism is gaining ground appear unfounded. Despite many more Islamist parties post-democratization, some calling for a South Asian caliphate, some linked with terrorist organizations, not even JI did well, retaining only two seats. Again, the BNP was part of an Islamic Alliance. The AL won 230 seats, the largest post-1991 majority. Jatiya (including Ershad) retained 27, this time allied with Hasina, who awarded the party a ministry. The BNP won 30. Karlekar say that JI is becoming "kingmaker," wielding influence when the BNP is in power. Without gaining additional seats of its own, it can pressurize the BNP to introduce desired measures. With two seats and the AL back in power, this seems unlikely. Despite conciliatory gestures from Hasina, who offered to share power if the BNP cooperated with her government, the BNP has boycotted parliament since the election, claiming it was rigged. However, after Hasina's husband died on May 10, 2009, Khaleda visited her home, personally expressing condolences. Reports say that the two women rarely meet.

Khaleda's Administrations

Khaleda continued decentralized polices, and encouraged foreign investment and industries such as garment manufacturing, where 80 percent of workers are women. She adopted IMF recommendations, lowered inflation (less than 4 percent), increased tax revenue, "shrunk the current account deficit of GDP to 3%" from 7 percent "two years ago," promoted private enterprise and the market economy, and reduced state intervention (Chowdhury 2003, p. 40). Labor conditions and wages were improved. She introduced free, compulsory primary education and no fees up to grade ten for girls, established girl's scholarships, and set up a "food for education" program. She promoted micro-credit for village women. In early 1991, she responded competently when a cyclone hit Bangladesh and later during floods (Chowhdury 2003, p. 40).

Khaleda increased reserved seats to 45 in 2004, although critics say she had promised more (64) and that this was an arbitrary number. The reserved seat provision lapsed between 1987 and 1990, after which 30 were restored. In the interim, representation dropped to less than 1 percent. In 1991, 36 women stood for open seats and 8 were successful. When Khaleda started her second term, the percentage of women in parliament was about 13 percent, the same as in the USA, where there are no special measures but many other healthy pro-gender factors (Commonwealth Secretariat, p. 28). Incidentally, candidates in Bangladesh can stand for multiple seats. Khaleda has contested and won five three times, a record for any MP. Ershad won five seats from his jail cell. Despite guilty verdicts, he remains a significant political player. He has apologized for his wrongdoing and begged forgiveness. His continued success might indicate public cynicism about corruption in a climate where everyone accuses everyone else.

The Issues

What role did Islam play?

Despite protest from supporters of "position one" and objections by women supporters of *Jamaat*, women leaders keep winning elections. Khaleda's party has a distinctive Islamic ethos. She herself has a personal reputation for piety. Shehabuddin found that many women "counter the objections of Islamist groups" on dress saying that they "observe *purdah* in their own way," or that it is a "state of mind," refusing to be intimidated (p. 156). Some use earnings to "buy *burkas* or adopt other forms of Purdah." The polarization between Islam and modernity is false, since there is no "single, unchanging Islam." Many rural women fuse these two, bringing about "further democratization of social, economic and cultural power" (Shehabuddin, p. 30). They are not passive objects of secular-modernist or Islamist subjects but make their own choices. The state's "ineffectiveness compels them to fend for themselves," to choose "what best serves their interest" (pp. 13–14). The majority question exclusion from the public square, precisely because *there are women prime ministers* and a growing number *of NGO-supported women in local elected office* (p. 218). Some NGOs are run or staffed predominantly by women, which shows "village men and women alike what women can accomplish" (p. 145). Khaleda is open about her Muslim identity, and has consistently used Islamic language and symbols. Shehabuddin says that personal piety is increasingly necessary in a candidate, which has been a factor in "elections since the restoration of democracy" (p. 168). This results in intense focus on Khaleda and Hasina's "religiosity," as the main contenders'. "Both, of course, are women. Khaleda has made Islamic symbols and language more acceptable in the political arena. She launched her 2001 campaign at a rally with leaders of the Islamic United Front, allied with the BNP, by saying, "we are united to protect the nation, our hard-earned independence and Islam" (Riaz, p. 17). Although *Jamaat*'s position was ambiguous, some members might have thought "special circumstances" described the post-military-rule context.

What role did culture play?

I argue in Chapter 5 that currents in Bangladeshi culture or in the culture–Islam matrix predispose people toward a tolerant, open, pluralist worldview. By extension, this embraces gender equality and women's empowerment. This sheds light on how Arabs and other Muslims might progress on gender, human rights and democracy. Similar currents exist in Turkey and Indonesia.

What role did a dynastic tie play?

Khaleda's tie with the former ruler was the main reason for her choice as party leader. She was also chosen because a fractured party needed someone who could mend it. As wife of the murdered leader, who remained popular, she was well positioned to unify her party and lead it to electoral victory. Her clean record helped. Zia, with a less tarnished legacy than Ershad's, was represented as having restored order, even as effectively founding the nation before transitioning toward genuine democracy. Many remembered his positive achievements (Thompson 2004, p. 45). In terms of lack of experience, Khaleda's position is comparable to that which was faced by Aquino. When Aquino's homemaker status was ridiculed as inadequate preparation for leadership compared with Mr Marcos, she agreed; "I have no experience," she said, "in cheating, stealing, lying or assassinating political opponents" (Thompson 2004, p. 44).

Khaleda's party did not turn to her automatically as a hereditary successor, first choosing Sattar instead. Both were perhaps less *compromise* than *pragmatic* candidates, chosen to unify the party. On the one hand, Khaleda does not constantly invoke Zia's memory, stressing instead what he achieved and planned (Begum, p. 275). On the other hand, she uses the "mystique" and "tragedy" associated with widowhood effectively, suggesting self-sacrifice for the nation, which draws "men and women to her" (p. 277).

Did gender play a significant role in Khaleda's rise to power?

Khaleda's identity as widow of the slain leader was the main element in her rise to power. On the other hand, she still had to establish competence as a leader. Her physical attractiveness helped her career; "people consider her extremely beautiful" (Begum, p. 276).

Did gender play any role in Khaleda's exercise of power?

Khaleda's focus on gender issues and women's empowerment is gender linked. She passed laws on preventing cruelty to women and children. Several women were ministers of state (not cabinet posts). One, Sarwari Rahman, was Minister for Women's affairs. Khaleda does not draw on mother-, sister- or daughter-of-the-nation images. She *does* project a compassionate, caring image, personally distributing food to flood victims, expressing solidarity with the people while also retaining a certain distance. Her reputation for authoritarian leadership may be less feminine. A blend of "attire, name, and physical movements" projects a queenlike image, which people see as "appropriate" for a leader, the type of person who can be trusted, who possesses the right qualities. This evokes "splendor of royalty in their collective memory," reminiscent of the Bengali Nawabs. Khaleda's fair skin, admired in Bangladesh, hints at nobility or mixed blood, such as Iranian or Arab, implying a Muslim pedigree. "She belongs" yet "does not belong to the land," like Muslim royalty (p. 277).

Is there any particular relationship between Khaleda's gender and her strengthening of democracy in her state?
The BNP's choice of its slain leader's widow played on her gender. Some claim she has weakened democracy, due to the dubious nature of her election victory in 1996 and her conduct in office. Yet more men than women perpetuate adversarial tactics. The system needs reform. Khaleda may be victim of cultural assumptions about power and authority, from which gender alone cannot liberate her. On the other hand, this does challenge the notion that *women are naturally more democracy prone than men*. Reports concerning her time in office refer to nepotism, corruption, even to trying to create a BAKSAL-style one-party state (Chakrabarti), of which Hasina is also accused.

Khaleda's son, Tarek Zia, became BNP General Secretary in early 2002. Dubbed "future leader of the party," he may give dynastic continuity (Hossain 2004, p. 215). The AL refers to him as "Queen Khaleda's crown prince," denouncing Khaleda for "mischievous attempts to establish monarchy," of which Mujib had also been accused (AL *Newsletter*, June 25, 2006, "Revolt Agianst Zia Family").

Does the post-colonial context have any bearing on Khaleda's career?
More homogenous than Pakistan, Bangladesh has not experienced large-scale insurgency, though there has been conflict in the Chittagong Hill Tracts. Tension between Muslims and minorities, sometimes spilling into violence, is another issue, which I discuss in Chapter 5. Islamists encourage discord to create instability, trying to weaken the state so that they can take power. The state's weakness is a colonial legacy. It was *never meant to be a stand-alone state*, but to be part of Pakistan. It wanted to remain unified with West Bengal. Extremist activities are explainable because Bangladesh *is* a weak state, not because of Khaleda's openness toward Islam. Islamists feed off people's insecurity, off Bangladesh's struggles against poverty, suggesting that Islamic solutions can solve all problems while others continue to fail. They make a loud noise but have little real support. Civil society in Bangladesh

needs strengthening, which is why the campaign against the 1988 constitutional amendment failed to build a "common platform" (Riaz, p. 96). Neo-colonialism impacts on the country, too, through pressures from the World Bank and IMF. Pressure from the former led to constitutional change. Colonialism impacts how opposition is expressed outside rather than inside parliament. In the Raj, this was how almost all opposition to British rule took place.

Did Khaleda promote women's issues and rights?

Khaleda is committed to empowering women. She increased the number of reserved seats from 30 to 45. She launched or supported other programs in the fields of education, healthcare and economics. There is, however, a long way to go. For example, women hold only 12 percent of all government jobs, a mere 2 percent of senior posts. More can be recruited.

Conclusion

Twice prime minister, twice leader of the opposition, Khaleda has stood at the forefront of Bangladeshi politics for more than two decades. Cohen, who sees Bangladesh as a model for Pakistan, asks what conditions might "turn Pakistan into West Bangladesh" (p. 282). Pakistan sees Bangladesh as too aid-dependent, too influenced by Hinduism, yet it itself would benefit from a similar "lengthy spell of normal democracy" with a government going full term (p. 283). Khaleda has played an important part in achieving what Cohen describes as "a degree of political stability that has escaped Pakistan," even though "governance" in Bangladesh "leaves much to be desired" (p. 281).

Chapter 4

Tansu Çiller and Turkey

Image 4: Tansu Çiller.
Source: public domain.

In 1993, Tansu Çiller became the third woman prime minister of a Muslim-majority state, remaining in office until 1996. Between 1996 and 1997, she served as deputy prime minister and foreign minister. From 1999 until 2002, she exercised considerable behind-the-scenes influence, backing the coalition government, although not formally a member. In 1999, her party won the smallest number of seats (85), one less than the Motherland Party. All coalition parties lost their seats in 2002, as did Çiller's, resulting in her retirement. When Çiller took up office, Benazir was in her second term, Khaleda her first. Benazir and Çiller visited Bosnia together in February 1994. Their images appear on a Pakistani stamp, commemorating a conference in Pakistan of Muslim women parliamentarians (August 1–3, 1995). Çiller's term ended in March 1996, a few months before Sheikh Hasina started her first. So far, Çiller is the only one of the five women featured in this book to have retired from politics. Benazir, of course, was assassinated while actively campaigning for re-election.

As deputy, Çiller was part of a coalition government between her party and a religious, Islamic party. The military compelled their resignation, due to fears that Turkey's secular identity was under threat. Of the four states this book is concerned with, Turkey is the oldest and the only one with an explicitly secular identity. Bangladesh was constitutionally secular for the brief period 1971–3. Pakistan was founded in 1947 but became the "Islamic republic" in 1956, when it ratified its first constitution. However, the Objectives Resolution of 1949 made its Islamic identity explicit. Today, Islamic parties are very much part of the political scene in Turkey, raising questions about Çiller's relationship with her coalition partner. Of the five women in this study, Çiller is the only one without a dynastic tie. She was, though, a protégé of a seven-term former prime minister. The vacancy arose when he moved up to the presidency. Unlike Benazir and the Bangladeshis, but like Megawati, she was an elected politician before standing for and winning her party's leadership. Only Çiller had already served in government. Benazir and Khaleda became PM upon entering parliament. Çiller's gender was a factor. Her political career – as with that of all five women – began during a democratic restoration, in her case not from its very beginning but in the climate it generated. Her gender and clean image were advantageous, given that many senior male politicians had tarnished reputations. She did not come through unscathed however. For some, her candidacy was emblematic of Turkey's *bone fides* as a modern state, ready to enter the EU. Married, attractive, with a successful career outside politics, she represented "modernity," late twentieth-century woman. An academic economist, appointed the youngest ever full-professor in Turkey's history in 1983, she is the only one of the five women who had a career *before politics*. She has the highest earned degree among the five, a PhD from the University of Connecticut, USA.

Despite being the senior of the four states, Turkey (founded 1923) is still dealing with issues of identity and Islam's role in society. Turkey, as a nation-state, emerged from the defeated Ottoman Empire. Founding father, Mustafa Kemal Atatürk, was largely responsible for the *idea of*

Turkey as a state *distinct from* and *unpunishable for* Ottoman errors. In many respects, Turkey was a *new state*, not a continuation of the earlier entity that overlapped its geographical space. That entity was much larger than modern Turkey. Unlike the other states, Turkey was never colonized. It was, though, shaped by colonial realities. Pre-nation-state Turkey, part and parcel of a great imperial power, reacted against outside colonial pressures that weakened the Ottoman Empire, compromising its sovereignty. It also emulated the same European nations that undermined it, distinguishing itself from the empire they helped destroy. The Ottoman Empire became an *object* of European imperial politics, having earlier played as a *subject* in the same arena. Loss of "Turkey in Europe" ended the Ottoman's role as an equal player. It was Atatürk who decided that Turkey would be secular and European oriented. It was Atatürk also who decided that, in a modern state, Turkish women would be equal with men. Remarkably, Turkish men led the way, granting gender equality. Turkish women, unlike British and American, did not have to campaign for this. Yet Kemalism, the ideology that dominated the country until the Second World War, and Turkey generally are described as "patriarchal." Despite theoretical gender equality, lack of a women's movement and men's privileged position in a political system that thrives on patronage, has not encouraged women's political participation.

Atatürk's regime was authoritarian. Considering Turkey not yet ready for democracy, he pursued a policy of guided, gradual transition. This concept emerges, at times, in all four states. It was only after 1950 that Turkey permitted multi-party politics. Unlike the other three, Turkey, at the bottom of the gender empowerment scale, has not introduced any special measures. Two parties, True Path (10 percent) and Motherland (33 percent) have quotas (the former established under Çiller) but both lost all seats in 2002. Several others – none with seats in parliament – have quotas. Both female literacy and GDP (17th) are high. If prosperity, freedom and access to education alone empowered women, Turkey would be further up the scale. Of the four states, Turkey (Rank 3) performs well on the "freedom scale." Indonesia is classed as free (Rank 2.5), Turkey as "partly free" but above Bangladesh (Rank 4) and Pakistan (Rank 4.5), which, with the highest parliamentary representation of women, is lowest. Most Arab states are "not free," although Bahrain, Jordan, Morocco and Yemen rank below Bangladesh in the "partly free" category (Freedom House). Freedom is considered significant for establishing gender equality. This reinforces the argument that, when some pro-gender factors are strong, absence or weakness of others plus the presence of obstacles hinders progress.

There are parallels with Megawati's alliance with an Islamist vice-president and Khaleda's with *Jamaat*. Not only did Çiller align herself with an Islamic party; she also used religious language in her speeches, referring to "being Muslim," "Turkish" and "secular" as a seamless continuity. Comment has been made on her occasional use of a scarf.

Turkey has had episodes of military intervention (1960, 1971, 1980 and the "postmodern" coup of 1997), so the role of the military is an issue in all four states. Reasons given for military intervention are similar, too. The concept of "guided democracy" encountered in Pakistan and Indonesia, which Zia effectively practiced in Bangladesh, was used in Turkey after the 1971 coup. Turkey's military has a special status in law, tasked with protecting the state and the *state's constitution*. Dealing with the army was a major concern for Bhutto. How did Çiller handle this? The role of the military is very sensitive in Turkey where, as in Pakistan and Indonesia, separatist insurgency threatens national unity. Pakistan's Musharaf may have had the role of Turkey's military in mind when he contemplated a similar status for his own. Certainly, he admired Turkey, as had Pakistan's founding father, Jinnah. There is some possibility that Bangladesh's military covet a comparable status, which Indonesia's military enjoyed before democratic restoration.

Turkey, as does Pakistan, sees itself as a role model for other Muslim states. Does Çiller's career feature in this role-model self-image? Did her career promote gender equality? Did she strengthen or weaken democracy? Criticisms of her leadership style sound very much like those against Khaleda. As with Benazir, accusations of corruption involved her husband.

After reviewing the literature, we will turn to the political background. This begins with a table indicating civilian and military periods. The latter have been brief. However, even after the presidency became more ceremonial, several military presidents kept their eyes on civilian leaders. Next, we will discuss Çiller's career, then explore the questions listed in the Introduction.

Reviewing the Literature

Information on Çiller is mainly from her entry in the *Encyclopædia Britannica* online and Cizre's chapter in Heper and Sayari (2002). This chapter and the volume of which it is part express negativity toward her that might fail a test of academic impartiality, if this is possible. The book examines Turkey's leaders, beginning with Atatürk, ending with Çiller, and asking whether they strengthened or weakened democracy. Sayari points out that all party leaders in Turkey exercise "near absolute control ... over party organizations," distributing "patronage" and "enjoying extensive formal authority" (p. 3). The authors then condemn Çiller for acting just like everyone else. Chapters on Atatürk, Demirel – in whose government Çiller was a minister (1991–3) – and Erbakan – her coalition partner from 1996–7 – are referenced below. Çiller's 1995 *Middle East Quarterly* interview with editor Daniel Pipes was also useful.

For broader political and historical background, I consulted a range of sources, including Fromkin (1989), O'Shea (2006), Lewis (2004) and Bryce (2005). Fromkin covers the period leading up to the collapse of the Ottoman Empire and Turkey's creation. O'Shea casts a wider net, exploring the variegated relations between Ottoman and European space. Lewis looks at efforts by Turkish women writers to counter Occidental images of Ottoman women, challenging stereotypes. At least some elite women were subjects, not mere commodities. These women worked to emancipate their fellow women and to "alter the West's conception of the 'Oriental" woman – the term that they use throughout their writing (p. 1). Lewis describes their writing as a "resistant form of cultural production." They refused to be defined by others yet they also wrote for them, so selected and used certain "Orientalist styles, forms and techniques" to rewrite "Western harem literature" (p. 2). "These Ottoman women ... were active in seeking their own liberation in their own terms" (p. 5).

The Occidental depiction of Oriental women created a self-serving polarity between European women as subjects and Orientals as objects or commodities. As Kahf (1999) argued, Oriental women were doubly unfortunate: first, they lived in a degraded society; second, they were subordinate within that society. Bryce takes us further back, to the ancient Hittites, whose queens exercised considerable authority, relevant because Kemalists equated their stance on gender with Turkey's pre-Islamic heritage. The mother goddess was venerated. After their husband's death, several queens ruled in their own right. Metz's Library of Congress Country Study (1995) was also consulted.

On gender in Turkey, I am especially indebted to Yeşim Arat. Her doctoral work at Princeton, which involved "intensive interviewing" (p. ii), was published in 1989. Arat (2005) contains research conducted under the auspices of the Turkish Economic and Social Sciences Foundation, part of a wider project. Her fieldwork focused on women members of the Refah (Welfare Party), which was allied with Çiller. This is similar in scope to Shehabuddin on women members of *Jamaat* in Bangladesh. Müftüler-Bac's 1999 article summarizes much of the ground covered by Arat, whose work she cites. Both address the paradox or puzzle represented by Turkish women's status. Turkey is "said to be the only modern, democratic Islamic country" yet women's empowerment has a long journey ahead (Müftüler-Bac, p. 303). Arat explains how women's enfranchisement was achieved without a "women's movement pressuring for these rights" (p. ii) because men decided that "women's rights were a dictate of the secular, national and democratic republic" that they intended to establish (p. 33).

Turkey "recognized full rights of citizenship" for women before many European states. In the subsequent one-party system, women were nominated as assembly delegates under the same system of patronage as men. In this period, 3 to 4.5 percent of parliamentarians were women. At the time, this was the second highest in Europe, where only Finland had more women legislators. Finland led Europe with the female franchise (1906). By 1918, when the UK gave women the vote, all Scandinavian countries (including Iceland) except Sweden (1919) had already done so. USA followed in 1920. Turkey (1930) was before Spain (1931), France (1944), Belgium, Italy, Romania, and Yugoslavia (1946), Switzerland (1971) and Liechtenstein (1984).

After the introduction of multi-party, competitive politics, the number of women in parliament fell. When Çiller was elected (1991), it was barely 1 percent. In 1995, it was 1.5 percent (8 out of 450). These authors argue that while Turkey has achieved high standards of women's literacy and female employment in some sectors, politics remained almost exclusively a male domain. Patriarchal attitudes relegated women to predefined roles, "developing a stereotype of the Turkish woman" who was to be "self-sacrificing ... pure, honorable, unreachable" (Müftüler-Bac, p. 307). As nurse, teacher and in other appropriate professional roles, she would not "threaten morality or order." As such, she could enter the public space by concealing her femininity, displaying "modesty in attire and behavior" (p. 307). She becomes asexual, every male colleagues' sister (*baci*) (p. 308). Arat's paradox is that men emancipated women because it suited them ideologically, then did little to encourage their political empowerment. Thus, Turkish society remains patriarchal.

Parallels with the granting of women's rights in Indonesia will be drawn in Chapter 6. There, women's energies were channeled into fulfilling tasks within the "nationalist project" that stressed "obligations" over "rights." Women's "gendered responsibilities" centered on the family but they also had to help defend the nation against "neo-colonial oppressors" (Blackburn, p. 98). Sukarno was dubbed "Great Leader of the Revolutionary Movement of Indonesia" (p. 24). The movement consisted of elite women under government patronage, who subscribed to and practiced "Ibuism" (Ibu = mother), the state's gender ideology (p. 25).

Arat explores how language, authority structure and role stereotypes hinder gender equality, despite the absence of legal barriers. (Arat also wrote the Heper and Sayari chapter on Demirel.)The latest democratic restoration began in 1983. New laws were passed removing remaining legal inequalities, making "Turkey's legislation more favorable to women than ... that of several US states" (Keddie, p. 120). This was the immediate context for Çiller's political debut. Nelson and Chowdhury (1994) have a case study on Turkey. Keddie (2007) also contains a great deal of information. She comments that the recent emergence of women's organizations gives them a voice "that does not depend on the state." While many women oppose the "rising tide of Islamism" others support Islamist parties, finding them "more helpful to them with food, health and social services than were secular parties and government" (p. 120). The Welfare Party's victory in 1995 and of successor parties in subsequent elections was largely due to women's support. Success enjoyed elsewhere by Islamist parties, such as Hizbullah in the Lebanon, and the Muslim Brothers standing as independents in Egypt, where the Brotherhood is banned, is equally attributable to their social service and humanitarian programs. Increased women's involvement in Islamic parties is a significant phenomenon. Due to their opposition to "existing regimes," "failed secular Westernizing rule, unsuccessful communism and imperialism," women, leftists and liberals have "allied with Islamists." Some women "adopt *hijab* as a form of protest" (Keddie, p. 164). Although Atatürk banned veiling in public places, government offices, schools and universities, today about 45 percent of Turkish women veil.

Finally, I consulted Raudvere (2003) on women in contemporary Turkish Sufi Islam. She did extensive fieldwork between 1993 and 1998, overlapping Çiller's career. Again, we see Turkish women as actors, shaping their own lives.

Next, we turn to the political background, identifying issues Çiller had to address. I argue that Turkish culture does have patriarchal aspects but that what most hindered gender equality was Kemalist ideology, the *same ideology* that gave Turkish women rights when *few were actively demanding these*. There was, though, an embryonic women's movement in the late Ottoman period. To avoid confusion, I use English names but Turkish initials for political parties.

The Political Context: The Ottoman Legacy

Alternating Civilian and Military Rule within Turkey

Military-Civilian Regime (presidents in italics)
Founding of Turkey: 1923
One party-system (Republican Peoples Party, CHP) 1923–45 (effective from 1950)
Mustafa Kemal Atatürk, first president 1923–38
Ismet Inönü, second president 1935–50
(PMs not listed: executive authority was vested in the president and Council of Ministers but the former dominated the political system; president elected by the Assembly)
Celâl Bayar, third president 1950–60 (Democratic Party) (1950 first genuinely democratic election; CHP lost: DP 470, CHP 69)
Adnan Menderes, prime minister (DP) 1950–60

First Military Coup, 1960
Cemal Gürsel, fourth president 1960–6 (military) (1961 constitution made presidency ceremonial; Democratic Party suppressed)

First Democratic Restoration, October 15, 1961
Ismet Inönü (CHP), prime minister 1961–5
Süleyman Demirel, prime minister 1965–71 (Justice Party, AP, building on the DP)
Cevdet Sunay, fifth president 1966–73 (military)

2nd Military Coup, 1971
Sunay remained president. Demirel was replaced by Nihat Erim, who acted as a non-party prime minister, March 12, 1971 to the next election, October 14

2nd Democratic Restoration, October 14, 1973
Fahri Korutürk, sixth president 1973–80 (non-party; retired Admiral*)
Bülent Ecevit, prime minister (CHP) January 1974–November 1974 (in coalition with the National Salvation Party, MSP under Necmettin Erbakan, who was deputy prime minister)
Sadi Irmak, prime minister, November 1974–March 1975 (non-party)
Süleyman Demirel, prime minister March 1975–June 1977 (AP)
(Erbakan a deputy – four-party coalition)

Bülent Ecevit, prime minister June–July 1977 (CHP)
Süleyman Demirel, prime minister (AP), July 1977–January 1978
(Erbakan a deputy – three-party coalition).
Bülent Ecevit, prime minister (CHP), January 1978–November 1979
Süleyman Demirel, prime minister (AP), November 1979–September
1980

Third Military Coup, 1980
(1981 constitution strengthened presidential powers and military's
role; existing parties banned; ten-year ban on current politicians)
Kenan Evren, seventh president 1980–9 (military, unelected)

Third Democratic Restoration December 13, 1983
(New parties formed in 1983 are seen as successors to those banned;
CHP was allowed to reform in 1989)
*Turhut Özal, prime minister 1983–9 (Motherland Party, ANAP),
eighth president 1989–91*
Three short Motherland administrations October 1989–November
1991
*Süleyman Demirel, prime minister 1991–3 (True Path Party, successor
to Justice and Democratic parties), ninth president 1993–2000*
Tansu Çiller, prime minister 1993–6 (True Path Party, DYP)
Mesut Yilmaz, prime minister March 6–June 28, 1996
Necmettin Erbakan, prime minister June 28, 1996–June 30, 1997
(Welfare Party, successor to MSP); Çiller – deputy prime minister and
foreign minister

Coup by Military Memorandum, September 1997
(Welfare banned; reformed as Virtue Party)
Mesut Yilmaz, prime minister June 30, 1997–January 11, 1999
(ANAP)
Ahmet Necdet Sezet, president 2000–7 (judiciary)
Bülent Ecevit, prime minister 1999–2001 (Democratic Left)
Abdullah Gül, prime minister 2002–3 (Justice and Development, AKP,
successor to the Virtue Party, banned 2001), *tenth president from 2007
(initially prevented by Constitution Court concerned about his stance
on secularism, then allowed after the 2007 election when AKP won)*
Recep Tayyip Erdoğan, prime minister from 2003 (AKP)
** Korutürk served in the Senate and as a diplomat after retiring from
the Navy. He was not part of the current military establishment
when elected president, and had no party affiliation*

At its zenith, the Ottoman Empire was one of the largest contiguous imperial projects in human history, covering most of the Middle East, except Iran and a few smaller emirates. It stretched west across sub-Saharan Africa, then north into the Greek and Balkan peninsulas. Twice, in 1529 and 1648, the Ottomans besieged Vienna, threatening Europe's cultural heart. Apostolov describes the original Anatolian emirate under Osman I (1281–1326) as a "military frontier state" because its polity was always expansionist (p. 30), driven by the conviction that God wants the whole world to be Islamic, a single order of humanity governed by divine law. There is little doubt that the Ottomans were feared in Europe. European–Ottoman rivalry saw a series of wars between these geo-political spaces. Competing religious truth claims exacerbated territorial rivalry. Ottoman expansion was dramatic.

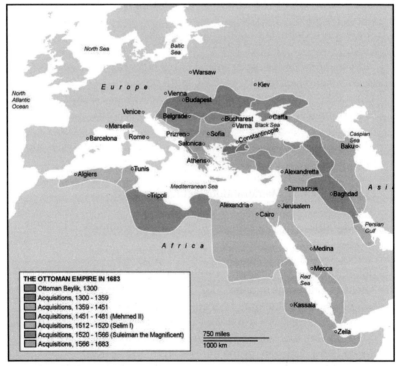

Map 7: The Ottoman Empire. Suleiman's reign was the high point for efficient administration and justice, followed by a decline. Successive sultans ran up debts, neglecting good governance.

The real conflict with Europe dates from the conquest of Constantinople in 1453, ending the Byzantine Empire which, for Europeans, symbolized continuity with the Roman legacy. Despite regarding Orthodox Christians as heretics, the psychological blow was considerable. The presence of what became known as "Turkey in Europe," the Ottoman provinces in Greece, the Balkans and at times Hungary, fueled fear that Europe was under threat. Yet there is another side to the story, explored by O'Shea and others. As well as epochal battles there were "eras of coexistence and commingling," of *convivencia* that set the tune for the *whole period of encounter*, "a continuum of cooperation, audible as a kind of tone upon which the more martial music of narrative history must be played." "Convivencia informed the entire medieval millennium," he says, "even those epochs that opened and closed with battle" (p. 9).

"Selective agenda-driven amnesia" on both sides distorts historical memory. Apostolov discusses how frontier-zones, such as the Balkans, are represented as continually volatile. Yet such zones were "bridges" as well as "buttresses," spaces where "cooperation" occurred (p. 185). Treaties ended many European–Ottoman conflicts. Commerce and trade flourished over centuries, dating from Venetian concessions and colonies carried over from Byzantine times. Later, other European concessions, or capitulations, followed. These included mines, railroads, the postal service, customs and excise, water, power and the ports (Hershlag, p. 49). Even when Venetian–Ottoman wars took place, commerce continued as the Genoese assumed preferred-partner status.

As an empire, the Ottomans differed from most European colonial projects. It was a single geo-political unit. There was, technically, no colony-possessing metropole ruling territories as separate entities, with one system of governance at home and different systems for colonies. As democracy took root in Britain, little or no effort was made to introduce this throughout the empire. That would undermine the colonized status as "objects" rather than "subjects." In contrast, although the experiment did not succeed, when the Ottoman Empire attempted parliamentary government, all male Ottoman citizens, regardless of race or religion, elected the Assembly.

In my view, there is some relationship between how social systems treat minorities and women. Ottoman treatment of minorities was not perfect. However, Jews enjoyed better conditions and greater freedom than they did in Europe. There were fewer if any restrictions on dress or employment (Lewis 1984, pp. 135–6). When Jews were expelled from Spain in 1492, the sultan welcomed them. Many settled in Bosnia, where what has been described as the "*harmonia Abrahamica*" developed, a type of *convivencia* that honored all Abrahamic faiths, refusing to idolize any one tradition as the only true faith (Mahmutćehajić, p. 83). Another writer calls Bosnia "the other Andalusia," where "Islamic humanism" flourished. Muslims promoted "a state for all Bosnians regardless of their religious affiliation" (Duran 1995, p. 31).

One criticism of Ottoman polity was that it dealt with minorities as separate communities (*millet*), so there was little interaction between them. Nonetheless, a consciousness of pan-Ottoman identity evolved. Conversion to Islam was certainly beneficial but non-Muslims did hold high office (Lewis 2004, p. 70). Women's rights, albeit not equal with men's, were protected. Women went or sent representatives to court. "Queen mothers of princes and of sultans were especially powerful" and maintained links with the outside world through servants and their own sons. During crises, it was often women who held the centers of power together (Keddie, p. 54). With "maturity, women as well as men, acquired positions of greater authority," she says. Some women were involved in trade (p. 55).

Recognizing that the administration of the empire needed modernization, a series of reforms began. At its best, the empire was well regulated. This deteriorated as corruption and self-interest pitted local officials against the center, which was often a long way off. Unfortunately, what contributed most to the empire's decline, apart from the cost of expensive wars, were weak sultans whose interest lay in palace intrigue, securing the throne against rivals. At the same time, they wasted money by profligate living. Parts of the empire were neglected. The Tanzimat reforms, from 1836, replaced many laws with the Napoleonic Code, declared all citizens equal, and adopted European commercial and banking practices. From 1876 to 1878, following the 1876 constitution, a multi-national, multi-religious Grand National Assembly met. This was "fairly representative of the religious, ethnic, linguistic and occupational makeup of the empire" (Baaklini *et al.*, p. 13). Nothing comparable existed elsewhere – Indians and Kenyans never sent delegates to the British House of Commons! The Assembly built on an older tradition of informal consultation with subjects, to whose opinions some sultans listened. Laws were always posted, giving governance an element of transparency. Reform, championed by the Young Turks, an alliance of military and intellectual progressives, was set back when Sultan Abdul Hamid II (1876–1909) annulled the constitution. The number of concessions and capitulations had hugely increased to repay heavier debts. Capitulations were quasi-sovereign enclaves. In 1878, at the Congress of Berlin, Cyprus was placed under British administration, Bosnia under the Austrians. A European commission was set up to supervise and control Ottoman finances. In 1882, the British *de facto* seized Egypt, arguing that financial oversight was needed. European-inspired nationalism was now spreading across the empire, causing instability. Ethnic-religious groups demanded independence. The Tanzimat reforms aimed to integrate everyone into the empire: Abd-ul-Hamid's solution was to reassert absolute authority. One by one, beginning with Greece, the Balkan states achieved independence.

During the Crimean War (1853–6), the British supported the Ottomans, becoming protectors as part of their "great game" with Russia. By assisting the Ottomans, they planned to eventually control the empire (Fromkin, p. 27). William Ewart Gladstone revoked this policy. Calling the sultan's regime "a bottomless pit of fraud and falsehood," he withdrew all "protection and influence from Istanbul." The Germans, ambitious to extent their imperial interests, filled the gap (Fromkin, p. 30). In 1908, in an attempt to end territorial loss and European domination, the Young Turks' Committee on Union and Progress staged a revolution. A young captain, Mustafa Kemal, took part. The Grand National Assembly was reconstituted. Adu-ul-Hamid abdicated, succeeded by Mehmed V. The plan was to revive pan-Ottoman loyalty, countering regional nationalisms. Influenced by notions of nationality as mono-cultural, the Young Turks introduced a Turkification process. Instead of winning non-Turks loyalty, which was the Young Turks' aim, this alienated them. In many respects, this went against the ethos that had permeated the empire. The First World War intervened. Germany was initially reluctant to accept an alliance with the Ottomans, who demanded ending all capitulations and a share in the "spoils of victory" (Fromkin, p. 64). However, an alliance began. The Young Turks were more responsible for this than their puppet sultan. They wanted to end European domination but realized that "their domains were in mortal danger" without help (Fromkin, p. 45). British ambitions in the area revived. With France and Russia (later replaced by Italy), they planned which territories they would administer after victory.

Atatürk and the Turkish Republic

Atatürk was one of the few heroes of the war, holding Gallipoli, symbolic as the first Ottoman possession in Europe (since 1253). Both my parents lost an uncle there. A few months before the war ended, Mehmed VI succeeded as sultan. Faced with defeat, he negotiated a treaty with the allies, signed in Sévres, August 10, 1920, reducing his realm to a tiny portion of Anatolia, with territory ceded to Greece, Kurdistan given autonomy, Armenia granted independence and League of Nations mandates imposed for other areas. Europeans would continue to control Turkey's finances. There were other punitive restrictions. Saudi Arabia became independent. The British created Iraq and Jordan. In the face of opposition from the Assembly, Mehmed dissolved it (April 1920). Rejecting the treaty, Atatürk reconvened parliament, denounced the sultan's government, drafted a provisional constitution and set about reclaiming lost territory. Several victories in the war for independence against neighboring Greece and occupying powers resulted in a new treaty, signed July 1923, establishing an independent, sovereign Turkey within Anatolia's historical boundaries. The plans for Kurdistan and Armenia were shelved.

Map 8: Turkey after the Treaty of Lausanne (July 24, 1923). Kurdistan – East of Euphrates.

The sultanate was abolished. Atatürk became president. Officially, the Turkish republic began on October 29, 1923. Initially, Islam was named as the state religion, dropped in 1928. Earlier, the caliphate was abolished (1924). The sultans claimed the caliphate from the Abbasids in 1517, although they did not use the title until later. Mehmed VI's cousin became caliph, only to be sent packing with two thousand British pounds in his pocket. Atatürk did not think Turks should pay for the caliph, given that – at least in theory – he was titular head of the whole Sunni Muslim world, which made no financial contribution.

Adopting secularism as a principle of state, Atatürk set out to transform Turkey into a modern, liberal state, informed by European values. Abolishing all Islamic laws, he adopted the Swiss Legal Code. Turkey is the only

Muslim-majority state where no aspect of *Shari'ah* has legal status. He blamed the sultan for involvement in the First World War, although the Young Turks bore most responsibility. The sins of the Ottomans were *their sins*, not those of the Turkish people. Modernization took many forms. The Western calendar replaced the Islamic. Traditional Turkish dress was discouraged, the Fez outlawed, followed by wearing the veil in public space. The alphabet was changed to Latin. From 1933, any public reading of the Qur'an had to be in Turkish, as did the call to prayer. Religious schools and Sufi lodges were closed. There was a brief attempt to establish a government- or state-formatted Islam when a Faculty of Divinity was opened in Istanbul and Imam-Hatip (Prayer Leader-Preacher) schools started in 1924. These were closed in 1930 and 1933 respectively (see below for subsequent history). Titles of honor were dropped. From 1934, surnames became compulsory. One aspect of modernization was that women and men would be equal. Women were enfranchised in 1934.

Under Atatürk, a one-party system operated, so the CHP apparatus appointed men as well as women. Although a feminist movement had started in the Ottoman period, described by Lewis and others, some Kemalists saw precedents in pre-Islamic Anatolia (Keddie, p. 82; Arat 1989, p. 32). Hittite queens exercised power. In the thirteenth century BCE, Queen Puduhepa of the Hittites co-signed treaties with her husband, King Hattusilis III. She fixed her own seal on some correspondence, indicating that she had "full authority" to make decisions on her husband's behalf (Bryce, p. 287).

Girl's schools began in the late Ottoman period. Halide Edibe (1884–1964), who had links with British suffragettes, started a women's movement (Keddie, p. 81). She fought in the independence war (Lewis 2004, p. 38). As Ruth Barzilai-Lumbroso (2009) observes, drawing on sources used for her UCLA doctoral dissertation: some Ottoman women exercised influence over "the ruling elite" (p. 73). They were "not only passive bystanders" but "powerful and active participants in their own society, different from Western representations" (pp. 76–7). Kemalist historians, mainly male, wanted to contrast modern Turkish women with their Ottoman predecessors, so rewrote history to underscore the freedoms enjoyed by the former, so much so that the "new Kemalist woman" became "the ultimate symbol of Turkey's disassociation from its Ottoman past" (p. 57).

Lewis, Barzilai-Lumbroso and others turn to women's writings to "re-imagine the Turkish woman" in the post-Kemalist context following the 1950 multi-party election (p. 53). However, Atatürk "hastened the process" of female emancipation, taking it further than "existing trends" (Mango, p. 19). Quite simply, "women's rights were a dictate of the secular, national, and democratic republic Mustafa Kemal intended to establish." The question was, would Turkish women now be able to "stride through" the doors of the "private" into the "public domain" (Arat 1989, p. 33)? Arat argues that many patriarchal assumptions remained culturally unchallenged, despite legal equality. In fact, until more recently, some inequalities remained, such as "the husband is formally the representative of the marriage union," "decides the place of residence" and has first claim on custody after divorce (p. 34). Without a strong women's movement to pressure for attitudinal change, ideas about the public domain as men's sphere, the domestic as women's, that "within the family ... the husband is the ultimate authority," remained popular (p. 46). Arat supports this with reference to everyday expressions used in Turkey, similar to "a woman's place is in the home" and other English sayings.

Although the constitution vested sovereignty in the nation, not in a single ruler, Atatürk was authoritarian, often governing through executive orders. He issued many, believing in "immediate change by decree" (Mango, p. 20). He did not think Turkey ready for full-blown democracy, so maintained only its trappings. The one-party Assembly was compliant, consistently re-electing him. Suppressing "all opposition," he had some opponents executed (Mango, p. 12), although for a few months in 1930 (August to November) he allowed the Free Party to operate as a "loyal opposition" (p. 12) His greatest achievement, according to Mango (2002) was that he saw culture and civilization as universal, placing Turkey "on the map as a peaceful member of the world community" (p. 20). He rarely "used the word" democracy, which, says Mango, was actually in retreat at the time in much of Europe (p. 21). Yet he admired France, Britain and the USA, not fascist Spain, Italy or Germany (p. 20). The institutions he established eventually allowed a smooth transition when multi-party politics began (1950), although his own legacy probably arrested democratic development (p. 21).

Atatürk and Gender Reforms

Atatürk saw education as the key to national success, the "engine of progress" (p. 16). He did much to promote this for both sexes. By the 1970s, about 15 percent of medical doctors were women compared with "11.3% for the United States as late as 1978" (Arat 1989, p. 38). A "high percentage of teachers" are women in Turkey, where teaching is "less of a female profession than it is in Western countries" (p. 38). In 1986, 29.4 percent of civil servants were women (Abadan-Unat and Tokgöz, p. 707). Women have occupied senior judicial and diplomatic posts (p. 717). Ultimately, Turks would contribute to "universal civilization" (p. 16). At this point, Turkey was preparing to be a future beacon for the *world*. In contrast, Pakistan's founders saw their new state as a future beacon for *Muslims*.

Arat comments that women who were elected to Turkey's parliament had similar social backgrounds to Turkish men. Some were recruited to "carry on their father's names" (p. 90) which, as noted, occurs elsewhere, including in the US. Most were from families where politics was discussed at home (p. 85), more so than with male politicians. They often came from families where power was shared with men (p. 79). Arat cites Turkish men who wanted to see more women politicians, suggesting that they bring with them compassion and a capacity for bridge-building that can check men's less conciliatory tendencies (pp. 81–2). Her interviews were with male and female politicians. Some men and women differed on what virtues women politicians represent but many agreed that their gender was a "normative justification for more women in parliament" (p. 94). Arat's conclusion was that men *still set the rules* and determine the "parameters within which women exercised political power" (p. 94).

Müftüler-Bac argues that having given women rights, Kemalist ideology failed to fully encourage their political empowerment, because private-public assumptions about gender roles continued. These may have been influenced by "position one" Muslim views, which she summarizes (p. 306). However, she places Turkish patriarchy in a wider Mediterranean context, suggesting that similar gender assumptions dominate elsewhere, "with the possible exception of France and Northern Italy … Mediterranean family structure is based on male superiority and female inferiority" (p. 305). Having taken the protection of veiling from women, Kemalist ideology did *not want* to exclude women from the public sphere but it *did want* to protect them from male sexual objectification. What Kemalists shared with some Muslims was the idea that women in public *threaten social order*, so their visibility should be minimized. Kemalism did this by "developing a stereotype of a Turkish woman: modest in appearance, companion to her male in modernizing the country." Called "sister" by male colleagues, she would be defeminized. This is somewhat different from the idea that women are valued in politics because they take feminine qualities into the arena (Arat 1989, p. 81).

It took over half a century for the percentage of women sent to parliament under the post-1950 multi-party system to rise higher than during the one-party period. The switch to multi-party polities saw another significant change: Islam's return to the public square. Secularism, initially a top-down imposition, was by then generally accepted as non-negotiable. However, people wanted more recognition of Islam in public life. In 1949, the Divinity

Faculty at Istanbul reopened, followed in 1951 by Imam-Hatip schools, whose Islamic curriculum was intended to train prayer leaders and preachers for government employment. In 1959, a Department of Religious Education was set up. By 1962, Istanbul also had a Department of Islamic Studies (Krämer, pp. 60–1).

Multi-party Politics

In 1950, the center-right Democratic Party swept into power, with the now leftist CHP in opposition. In 1961, social unrest, strikes and the threat of civil war provoked the first military coup. There is some evidence that the DP leader, Bayer, encouraged military intervention against the opposition, hoping that the CHP would be shut down (Harris, pp. 50–1). In fact, the DP was suspended, not the CHP, which formed the next government. Several DP politicians were executed. Bayer was given life imprisonment (later pardoned). The new constitution turned the presidency into a more ceremonial role. Within seventeen months, civilian rule was restored.

The 1961 constitution also established the military-dominated National Security Council. The military saw their role as protecting the constitution as well as internal and external security. They did not want to exercise power. They did, however, begin a tradition of installing a military or retired military officer as president, to keep his eye on civilian politicians. After the 1961 coup, the first of two men significant for Çiller's career became prominent. Demirel, her mentor, became prime minister in 1965, heading the Justice Party (AP), which replaced the banned DP, winning 52.9 percent of the votes (Arat 2002, p. 89). This began a long series of periods in and out of power, culminating in his 1991–3 administration in which Çiller was economics minister, followed by his 1993–2000 presidency. Strikes, demonstrations and party rivalry provoked the second military coup of 1971. After democratic restoration, no party could gain a majority, so a series of short-lived coalitions followed.

Islam in the Public Sphere

The second man significant for Çiller's career was Erbakan, founder of the National Order Party (1970). Shut down after the 1971 coup, on the grounds that it challenged Turkey's secular principles, it reformed as the National Salvation Party (MSP). It was in coalition with the CHP government from January 1974–November 1974. Erbakan was deputy prime minister. In a secular country, he had taken his party from nowhere to considerable success. A Sufi, he consulted his sheikh before starting the party, and on other "socioeconomic and political issues" (p. 129). His Naqshbandiyya sheikh inspired interest in "moral development and social justice" (Özdalga, p. 138).

Alliance with the party that had banished Islam to the private domain "was unexpected and controversial." It also showed sensitivity to the "religious propensities of the average Turk" (Tachau, p. 118), respecting the "values" of the electorate. The MSP was not calling for Islamic law but for Islamic values and concepts of social justice to inform politics. Erbakan did talk about reinstating *Shari'ah*, but his ideas here are ambiguous. Özdalga discusses whether he meant the type of negative law imposed by Pakistan's Zia, with *hudud* penalties, or such positive aspects as mercy, justice, reconciliation and benevolence, about which Benazir Bhutto also wrote, citing Soroush (2008, p. 65). Erbakan also spoke a great deal about "helping the poor" (p. 140).

Erbakan opposed Turkey's application to enter the EU, pointing out that Turkey's history was one of "1, 500 years of conflict" with Europe (p. 136). Turkey's natural friends were Muslim countries. In 1995 he was still against joining the EU but supported Çiller's pro-Europe stance during their coalition (p. 136). He wanted to position Turkey as an alternative leader in the Muslim world, although his 1996 trip to Libya "turned into a fiasco" when Gaddafi denounced Turkey's "pro-European orientation" (p. 135). Erbakan spoke of new Muslim alliances to replace NATO and the EU (Turkey had joined NATO in 1952). In the 1970s, his discourse became more radical. He supported the anti-Shah movement in Iran, slogans such as "Khomeini in Iran, Erbakan in Turkey" and "In Turkey the Shariah will Replace Barbarism" appearing on party placards (p. 143). However, his "basic commitment to the democratic process" was "not questioned" (p. 144). He expressed nostalgia for the single caliphate, when Turkey had led the Muslim world (pp. 138–9).

Erbakan also entered coalitions with Demirel, again as a deputy prime minister. Shifts from left to right and back, short coalitions, and strikes and demonstrations provoked the third military coup in 1980. In 1983, democracy was restored under a new constitution. All previous parties were banned. Most politicians were excluded from standing for a ten-year period. The role of the president and of the National Security Council was strengthened. The Council had fewer civilian, more military members. Heper and Güney argue that the military's participation in politics derives from the fact that the Ottoman Empire was a military state. Founders of the republic, too, had military ties. Clearly subordinate to the civilian regime during one-party rule, "it was nevertheless considered the ultimate guarantor of the secular republic" (p. 184). Secular education increased the military's secular orientation, the opposite of the trend in Pakistan. Despite Atatürk's determination to cut Turkey off from Ottoman history, continuity exists. He did not quite start with a *tabula rasa*.

During the 1950s, as Islam resurfaced, the military shared guarding secularism with the CHP. With the proliferation of parties and the CHP's electoral weakness (until 2002), the military became "virtually the sole defenders of the secular-democratic state" (p. 184). The 1961 constitution tasked it with protecting the fatherland and its constitution. The 1983 constitution stated, "the military plays a role in government through the participation of the High Command in [the National Security Council]." Government must "give priority" to NSC recommendations "to maintain the existence and independence of the state" (p. 184). New parties were formed, most of which enjoyed continuity with predecessors. The Justice Party became the True Path Party. The CHP was later allowed to reconstitute itself. Çiller first met Demirel in 1984, introduced to him as "part of the strategy to open up the party to academia" (Cizre, p. 200). The demand was for a new generation of politicians, unsullied by past errors.

Çiller's Political Career

Born in Istanbul on May 24, 1943, Çiller attended the prestigious private American College for Girls (established 1876), where she is said to have hid her family's modest financial status from her friends. Her father, a civil servant, "passed" his "unfulfilled political ambitions" to his daughter (p. 200). Çiller claimed early political interest, wanting to improve the economy. After obtaining an economics degree in Turkey, graduate study followed in the United States. Earning her PhD there, where she also taught, she returned to Turkey. In 1983, she became the youngest full professor, the year of the third coup. Rather snidely, Cizre says that she "gained fame" less through academic achievements than by writing research reports for "influential economic interest groups" (p. 200). This is exactly the type of funded research universities encourage. It led to friendships with politically connected businessmen. Joining DYP, she stood for election in 1991, winning her seat. Demirel, whose ban had expired, formed a center-right coalition. Çiller was economics minister. Demirel also created a Women's Ministry.

In 1993, Demirel decided to run for the presidency, so resigned the party leadership as required by law. His successor would also become PM. Çiller, already party vice-chair, stood against three male candidates and won. She rode a "tide of media support and exposure" (Cizre, p. 201). Many hoped she would attract more liberal voters, so supported "the female option" (p. 201). Cizre suggests that her gender was advantageous, promising a new beginning. As indicated in an earlier chapter, she could distinguish herself from "the partisan, aggressive, self-centered, self-interested, fractious, unscrupulous and constantly wrangling images of male politicians." Instead, she could draw on images of motherhood and sisterhood, of having an "unselfish concern for the nation" (p. 207). This suggests that gender was a dominant factor, perhaps going beyond the defeminized Kemalist stereotype. Remarks cited in Cizre suggest she projected her femininity, not an asexual image. Cultivating the image of mother may have been her way of imitating Demirel, known popularity as "*baba*" (father) (p. 206). Supposedly because he thought her too ambitious, or perhaps, because her performance as economics minister had disappointed him, Demirel did not endorse her candidacy. However, by remaining neutral, he did not actively oppose her either (p. 202).

The issues that faced Çiller's administration were fiscal, membership of the EU and insurgency in the Kurdish region, waged since the late 1970s. Despite her interest in the former, the latter dominated. She wanted to reduce inflation. Privatization of government assets and pro-market polices, though, were accompanied by high interest rates, an overvalued currency and pay increases in the public sector (Cizre, p. 212). The stock market crash of 1994 hindered her efforts. Inflation remained astronomical (150 percent) (Pipes, p. 74). Growth was negative. Her aim was to downsize the state, giving people greater control over their income (p. 211). Social reform would be paid for by tax reform and privatization revenue. On Europe, which Turkey had applied to join in 1987, she ratified the EU–Turkey Customs Union treaty in 1995.

Çiller's biggest challenge was dealing with the military. Demirel, twice removed by the military, played a balancing act, cultivating a relationship with Gürsel, leader of the 1961 coup. He prevented coups in 1962 and 63, then consented to a military successor to the presidency in 1966. This did not prevent his ousting in 1971. After that, he collaborated "not with" but "against the military," ensuring that a civilian, "as opposed to a retired military officer" was elected president, opposing the military's candidate (Arat 2002, p. 95). Korutürk was actually a former admiral. However, retired for 13 years, he was no longer associated with the military command. As president, Demirel "worked hard to keep the military in its barracks" (Heper, p. 224). At issue for Çiller was whether the military was subject to civilian control. Cizre says that she oscillated between anti-militarism, warning the military "that final authority rests with parliament," to praising their role as guardians of the constitution (p. 204). She spent money on modernizing the army and took a hard line on defeating Kurdish insurgency, convincing the US to list the PKK (Kurdistan Workers Party) as a terrorist organization.

Corruption allegations concerned her husband's real-estate business dealings. Tansu had married Özer Uçuran in 1963, when he adopted her surname. The couple, who have two children, became multi-millionaires. There was a pre-1991 scandal involving the collapse of a bank from which they had received substantial loans while her husband was working there. Controversy swirled around an alleged "criminal triangle" linked with the anti-PKK war, involving "politicians, mafia bosses and security forces" (Cizre, p. 205). Guns imported with discretionary funds destined for Kurdish opponents of the PKK, unreported to customs, may have ended up "in the hands of Hizbullah" (p. 205). Çiller allegedly helped herself to funds and benefited financially from privatization deals. Subsequently, charges were dropped or dismissed on technicalities, such as statute of limitations.

February 1994 saw Çiller with Benazir in Bosnia, expressing solidarity with Muslims there, beginning a shift toward an Islam-friendly polity. When the CHP left the coalition in 1995, elections followed on December 24. For the first time ever, the Islamic party, now the Refah (Welfare), won most seats (Cizre, p. 158). True Path came next with 135, only just ahead of ANAP, with 132. The Democratic Left had 79, CHP 49.

Political Opportunism or Skilled Maneuvering?

Although both center right, ANAP and True Path were rivals. Initially, the president was reluctant to invite the Refah to form a government. Meanwhile, Çiller continued until March 1996, when she formed a coalition with ANAP, despite their rivalry. The premiership was to rotate, beginning with Yilmaz. This collapsed in June, due to personal animosity. Being "beautiful," constantly changing her clothes and "posing for cameras," did not qualify her to lead the country, said Yilmaz (Çinar and Özudun, p. 194). Yilmaz and Çiller also faced corruption charges (Heper, p. 235). Çiller then entered a coalition with Refah, in which Erbakan became PM. She continued as a deputy and foreign minister, also the first woman in that post, reaching out to Turkic states in central Asia. Corruption charges would be dropped. Erbakan gained from collaboration with her identifiably secular party. Çiller modified, says Cizre, some Refah ideas. However, the "secular establishment and body politic" disliked her alliance with an Islamic party, launching a campaign against her "wealth, family, character, leadership style" and political dealings (p. 204). Islamist leaders are frequently accused of lacking a genuine commitment to democracy. They use the ballot box, it is claimed, with the aim of changing the system once in power.

Heper and Sayari (2002), considering reasons for earlier alliances, depict Demirel's coalitions with Erbakan as deft political maneuvering, part of his "moderating and conciliatory style" (Arat 2002, p. 96). Çiller's alliance is depicted as expressing "lust for command." The National Security Council demanded action "to contain political Islam" (p. 96). In February 1997, the military issued a memorandum warning the government against compromising secularism, hinting at intervention should it do so. In response, the Erbakan–Çiller coalition resigned. Çiller had some expectation that Demirel might ask her to form a new ministry. Instead, he invited Mesut Yilmaz to do so. Erbakan was banned from politics.

Yilmaz's not especially successful government ended when the 1999 election produced split results. The Democratic Left formed a coalition with the National Movement Party (MPH), the CHP and ANAP, leaving only the successor to the now-banned Refah, the Virtue Party and True Path in opposition. It was Demirel who prevented the government–military clash from escalating (Heper, p. 224). Çiller supported the coalition, emerging as a power-broker within a behind-the-scenes leadership cabal (Kinzer 1999). She was not formally a coalition member.

The next election, 2002, saw all coalition partners lose every seat, as did the DYP. For the first time since its formation, it was outside parliament. So was the CHP. Çiller retired. The Virtue Party was banned as endangering Turkey's secular philosophy. Its successor, the Justice and Development Party (AKP) won a massive, absolute majority (363) in 2002. The CHP, with 178, was the only other party, so it was back in parliament. In 2007, AKP won a second term (341 seats; CHP 112, MHP 71, Independents 26, one a former DYP member).

Under Recep Tayyip Erdoğan, the AKP has pursued pro-Europe moderate policies while committed to Islamic values. Despite military interventions, and banning of parties and politicians, the Turkish people appear to want Islamic ideals influencing society. Imam-Hatip schools, for example, are increasingly popular. There were 45 in 1965. By 1997–8 there were 604, with some female students. Under pressure from the military, as stipulated in the memorandum, Yilmaz abolished the middle-level schools, extending secular education up until "the ninth grade." This was of "paramount importance to the military" (Krämer, p. 62). Çiller opened a record number of Prayer Leader and Preacher Schools "within a span of one and a half years" (Cizre, p. 211). Private religious schools similarly mushroomed in the late 1990s.

The Heper–Sayari volume ascribes Çiller's fall to hunger for power at any cost, resulting in too many compromises, shifting "policies and discourse as the situation warranted" (p. 226). It does not castigate other Turkish politicians for entering coalitions. Hunger for power motivates many people in the political arena, who find ways to remain in office, including unlikely alliances. People may be self-serving, or they may sincerely believe they have a contribution to make. It remains debatable whether Erbakan would have changed the state's secular nature. Heper speculates that perhaps he only wanted to "upgrade religious morality in Turkey" (p. 220). This compares with the BNP's agenda in Bangladesh and with several parties in Indonesia.

Ecevit, who entered a coalition with Erbakan, was convinced that the vast majority of Turks are "adapted to secularism" but remain "bound to" their religion. Their "humanistic outlook" on life emphasizes God's love for all people. His description of this as "Turkish mysticism" reflects Sufi openness, its message of universal love. Ecevit thought religion suffered more than politics when used as a political tool (Tachou, p. 119). Other Turkish politicians have combined personal piety with secularism. Demirel, who belongs to the Disciples of Light movement, prays regularly (Arat 2002, p. 100). Turhut Özal "proclaimed his Muslim identity" publicly "alongside his Western, modern one" (Acar, p. 170). This resembles Benazir, who could not have been more open about her progressive Muslim ideas. Women Refah activists interviewed by Arat spoke of belief in Turkey's secular ethos, which they did not regard as clashing with Islamic values. They "endorsed a unique Islam shaped by the principles and practices of ... secular society." Their "Islam" was not the "threatening Islam that the state attributed to them" (p. 110). They want the state to respect "public expressions of religiosity" (Arat 2005, p. 21) and refused to be "victimized as women," while proudly asserting Muslim identity (p. 23). Some said they would not object if *Shari'ah* were introduced, assuming it would only "hurt wrong-doers." They stressed, though, that what was most important was that "those who come [to power] be democratic" (p. 106).

The Issues

What role did Islam play?
Islam did not hinder Çiller's career, except that her alliance with Refah ended in military intervention. An Islamic-oriented party allied with her, agreed that she would be PM after the next election, so did not object to a woman leader. Currents in Turkish Islam may favor women's empowerment. One Naqshbandiyya branch has a conservative stance on dress, requiring that

women wear complete *chador* when attending *dhikr* ceremonies. Ershad belongs to a similar order in Bangladesh. Other Naqshbandiyya branches have women's circles. There is also a long history of women teachers in Sufi Islam. Most teach women, which is not controversial. Some have taught men. Ibn Arabi (1165–1240) acknowledged two female teachers.

Rabia (717–801) taught men. Farid ad-Din Attar (1145–1221) remarked that since Muhammad said we gain two-thirds of our religion from Ayesha, we could also learn from her handmaiden, Rabia (Smith 2001, p. 21).

Raudvere's work explores a modern circle of Sufi women who in 1995 established a foundation in honor of Gönenli Mehmet Efendi. He obtained permission in 1924 from the newly formed Directorate of Religious Affairs to lead public prayer meetings. Unaffiliated to a traditional Sufi order, he preached an open, inclusive message that especially appealed to women. Unable to wear the traditional cloak and turban of office, he wore a suit and carried a walking stick instead (p. 148). The women run a pastry shop, a library and lead *dhikr* for other women (p. 107). They challenge images of Muslim women as passive, says Raudvere, who calls them "activists." It was as such that she interviewed them, not as "daughters, wives, students or professionals" (p. 82). Their leadership may be of women, not of men and women, but they act in the public arena, running their center.

Some of Arat's interviewees defended the traditional division of labor between men and women (2005, p. 95). Others saw "ideal Islam" as validating their "autonomy in the public realm" (p. 97). Women helped Refah win its large vote share in 1995 (p. 90). Some women expressed regret that they had little say in party decision making (p. 97). This changed with the Virtue Party, which sent three women to parliament in 1999. One, Merve Kavakci, wore *hijab*. Holding a dual Turkey–US citizenship, she was stripped of the former, prosecuted and removed from parliament. In 2002, all Islamic parties fielded women candidates.

Minister for religious affairs, Mehmet Aydid, has expressed the idea that a gender-equal-friendly version of Islam has emerged in Turkey. "Critical of Pakistan (and Iran and Saudi Arabia) for their un-Islamic treatment of women," he appointed two women vice-*mufti* (Muslim judges) in 2005 and a woman deputy director of religious affairs to "drive home the point" (Cohen, p. 275). All legal inequalities have been removed from Turkish law, subsequent to Çiller's term. Her use of Islamic language and symbol has been dismissed as opportunism. Raudvere characterizes her attempt to "promote a pro-Islamic attitude" by wearing a "chic head scarf" when visiting mosques as "feeble" (p. 44). Cizre implies that she wrapped herself in Islam, shifting from the center to the right, blending nationalist elements of "flag," "blood" and "sacrifice for the state" with "religious terms such as *ezen* (call to prayer)," "Allah," and the notion of "being Muslim" and "secular" (p. 211). Yet if the alliance was based on her secular credentials, why would Çiller need to play the Muslim card? In an interview with Daniel Pipes, she stressed her commitment to secularism, calling it an "indispensable principle" (p. 77). She spoke of Turkey's role as an East–West bridge in assisting Arab–Israeli peace (Turkey recognized Israel) and in championing human rights, democracy and secularism in the Middle East as proof that such values can coexist with Islam (p. 79). The sincerity of anyone's faith-commitment is a matter for God. However, in shifting toward Islam and her alliance with Refah, Çiller may have discerned the political trend, given the AKP's ascendancy at the time.

What role did culture play?

There were precedents for women's success outside the domestic sphere. Halide Edibe, for example, was a "public figure" throughout her life (p. 41). She divorced her first husband in 1910 when he married a second wife (p. 38) and broke with Atatürk when he accused her and her second husband of treason. Edibe and her husband advocated an American mandate for Turkey, to protect Turkey from predatory European ambition (p. 41). Edibe was a pupil at the American College for Girls (p. 37), which Çiller attended. Edibe also had instructions from an Imam, arranged by her father, a senior palace official. She lived in exile from 1929–39. In the first multi-party election (1950), she won a seat, although she resigned in 1954. Her *Memoirs* (1926) challenged Atatürk's self-aggrandizing account of his single-handed creation of Turkey. Understandably, then, it was difficult to find any copies of this book in Turkey until the end of single-party rule (p. 41). Elements of popular culture remain patriarchal but counter-trends exist, dating from at least the early twentieth century.

What role did dynastic ties play?

Çiller had none. Like most Turkish women politicians, she grew up in a politicized home. Her mentor, Demirel, was an experienced and senior politician. Yet since he did not support her for party chair, refusing to back any candidate, she won on merit, regardless of any tactics used to encourage media attention.

Did gender play a significant role in Çiller's rise to power?

Gender was a major factor. Supporters saw this as an asset, part of the new beginning after the 1983 democratic restoration.

Did gender play any role in Çiller's exercise of power?

Cizre says that Çiller used her gender to "gain advantage over male rivals" (p. 207). She cultivated the image of "motherhood," "identifying with the mothers of the soldiers who died" in the anti-PPK struggle (pp. 206–7). Yet she also wanted to give the impression that she possessed "man-like atributes" such as "courage, endurance, determination and militarism" (p. 207). She liked to publicize traits borrowed from the "male domain," aiming to outshine male rivals" (p. 207). Dubbed an "iron lady," she "imposed decisions," acting sultan-like (p. 209). Army chief Doğan Güreş called her a "tiger" (p. 202).

Women leaders, it seems, attract criticism for behaving like monarchs, whereas men, when they do so, tend to be called decisive. Çiller's Council of World Women Leaders' entry states that her main achievement was modernizing the military, which we might think of as masculine. Such gender-biased presuppositions are dubious. According to Heper, she took "patronage and nepotism" to a new level (p. 225). Her candidates' list for 1995 was supposed to represent a new, young, dynamic cadre but was full of former police chiefs, governors and well-known personalities (Cizre, p. 203). Yet perhaps she was merely following a well-established system. Demirel alienated many by "selective use of patronage," favoring only supporters. Commenting that this "bordered on nepotism," Arat adds that Demirel's brothers and nephews actually did become wealthy (Arat 2002, pp. 93–4).

Is there any particular relationship between Çiller's gender and her strengthening of democracy in Turkey?

Çiller may not have strengthened democracy. She was, like many politicians, ambitious. However, the tactics she used have a long history in Turkey. Her failure was that she did not achieve a higher standard than men. Perhaps gender-based expectations are naive.

Does the post-colonial context have any bearing on Çiller's career?

The military's role has roots in what Apostolov describes as the "defining feature" of the Ottoman policy, that Turkey was a "frontier state" (p. 30). Atatürk's ban on religion in the public sphere, part of his determination to differentiate Turkey from Ottoman imperialism, invited later secular–religion tensions. To some degree, this has dominated politics since 1950. Kurdish insurgency might have been prevented if, during the transition from empire to republic, plans for an autonomous or independent state, which would have included territory in today's Iraq, had succeeded. Ataturk's ideas about the integrity of Turkey's Anatolian borders made that impossible.

Did Çiller promote women's issues and rights?

In 1995, there were 8 out of 450 women in parliament, including Çiller, 1.5 percent. This was lower than the 4.5 percent high during one-party rule.

Today, there are 50 out of 550 (9.1 percent), so progress has occurred (the size of the Assembly increased in 1998). Moghadam says that Çiller did "not show much sensitivity to the gender issue, unless it had instrumental value" (p. 93). For example, during the 1995 campaign she targeted "secular upper middle class" women," emphasizing the "contemporary" woman of Turkey. She "promised to increase the number of female deputies" and introduced a 10 percent quota (p. 89). Unfortunately, the party lost all seats in 2002. Establishing a direct cause–effect between Çiller's tenure and increased women's participation is problematic. Yet the fact that she was her nation's first female prime minister and foreign minister may have encouraged other women to enter politics, contributing to the rise to 9.1 percent. Clearly, barriers still exist. Pakistan's 22.5 percent includes 60 reserved seats. Perhaps Turkey would increase representation dramatically if special measures were taken, given that other factors are present, such as high female literacy and employment in certain professions, economic prosperity, and relative freedoms.

Conclusion

Corruption allegations involving her husband and herself, although unproven, cast a shadow over Çiller's career. As with Benazir and the two Bangladeshis, in contexts where corruption allegations are tools of confrontation they can be dismissed as politically motivated. Gultekin refers to several corruption scandals in Turkey involving "eminent political figures," resulting in "loss of credibility" (p. 195). However, no charges led to conviction. Çiller's rival, Yilmaz, was also cleared.

Çiller's failure to proactively support women's empowerment, or to exhibit the conciliatory, selfless qualities her supporters hoped for, may disappoint us. Yet conciliation and generosity are not exclusive to either gender: Demirel is praised for mediation skills. "Women," says Cizre, are "equally motivated by power" (p. 207). We should not expect women to adopt certain agendas or possess particular attributes *merely because of gender*.

Chapter 5

Sheikh Hasina and Bangladesh

Image 5: Sheikh Hasina.
Source: public domain.

Bangladesh's second female leader, Sheikha Hasina, was the fourth woman to head a government in a modern Muslim state. Prime minister from 1996–2001, she started her second term in January 2009, having won an absolute majority. After collaborating with Khaleda Zia against their common foe, General Ershad, they alternated in power. Their parties, personalities and policies diverge, although fiscal policies are similar. For some, dynastic ties to slain male leaders and pragmatic appeal explain their careers. This was true for Benazir. Some question whether their careers, seen as atypical, benefit non-elite women. This chapter agrees that dynasty *was* the main factor behind Hasina's choice as party leader, *although the choice was* also expedient and pragmatic.

Once in progress, Hasina's career could not be *reduced* to dynastic ties, being best understood within *political realities*. The polarization of *secular* versus *Islamic identity*, pitting Hasina against Khaleda, is a *false dichotomy*, fueling extreme forms of radical Islam. Fed by an *ancient current of openness*, the "secular" view of Bengali nationalism is misnamed.

This current exists in Bangladesh today, predisposing people toward a gender-equal, human-rights-affirming and pluralist worldview. It has deep sources in Islam, especially Sufi Islam. The resulting combination of cultural and religious components represents a "spiritual" tradition, which is why the term "secular" is problematic and polarizing. Muslims often think "secular" means "profane" but a Muslim-majority state inevitably takes "on a religious hue," as has Turkey (Soroush 2000, p. 61).

Mujib's ideas about "secularism" as "non-communitarian" were closer to what Jinnah had in mind for Pakistan and to Sukarno's ideas for Indonesia. The spiritual tradition identified below is *an authentic version of Islam*, not *un-Islamic*, opposed to true, BNP Islam. The post-colonial legacy is relevant to debate about whether Khaleda and Hasina, as the "battling Begums," strengthen or weaken democracy. Neither record is perfect. On balance, they have achieved much, more or less establishing a stable, two-party system. Addressing weaknesses of the parliamentary system as currently practiced must be a *priority for the nation*. The two women are partly responsible for these short-comings. However, many others share blame. On the other hand, if the two woman had transcended current practices, *democracy would be healthier*.

After a brief survey of the literature, we will discuss the political context, avoiding overlap whenever possible with previous chapters. Throughout this section and the following, which focuses on Hasina's career, the culture–religion matrix, or perhaps nexus, is a central motif. Identifying a preference for *harmonious religious coexistence*, we explore consequences for gender, democracy and human rights.

Are there lessons here for other Muslim spaces? Given the right combination of factors, neglected, suppressed, forgotten and dormant resources in Islam, based on Qur'anic verses, can rise to the surface. This is happening for example, in Morocco (which I have visited) and in Jordan, which I have not. My wife has visited it though, and I know several leading Jordanian Muslim scholars. Where this current is strong, it changes human lives of both sexes *for the better*.

We will return to issues surrounding Hasina and Khaleda's *media images*, looking at dress, language, use of symbolism and the interplay between image, symbol and party-political message. In addition to honorary doctorates, Hasina has received awards for combating poverty, humanitarianism, promoting peace, freedom and human rights, issues about which she is passionate. Like Benazir, she speaks of her "destiny," taking up what her father could not finish. Akin to Benazir again, her father's legacy was ambiguous. Restoring Mujib's memory emerges as a major motif. How does his memory support her commitment to democratic, multi-party politics?

Literature Survey

Biographical information is from the *Encyclopædia Britannica* online and the Awami League website. Among monographs on Hasina, I consulted Abdul Matin (1997) and Āhameda (1998). Matin is a brief, party-partisan study. Āhameda is a longer treatment. Hasina has authored several Bengali books, which I unsuccessfully tried to obtain. Several sources cite her words. I again used Thompson (2004), Karlekar (2005), Begum (2006) Shehabuddin (2008), case study material and Mitra *et al.*

Mitra's chapters depict each party in favorable light. Content, though uncritical, includes electoral data, party histories and other relevant information. Amin (1996) on women in colonial Bengal opened my eyes to new possibilities. Her starting point is 1876, when the first book by a Bengali Muslim woman was published in Dhaka. She finishes with the Dissolution of Muslim Marriage Act in 1939. This fascinating study has a lot to say about patriarchy and limitations on women's lives. It shows that elite Muslim women spoke in the public square, creating change that led to legislation, educational initiatives, even "to jobs and careers" (p. 270). As elite women, their lives were atypical. However, they trod a "widening platform for *political activity*" (my italics) that in the end benefited non-elites as well (p. 277). Amin argues that distance between the private and the public spheres receded for these women, as it did for Victorian-Edwardian women in Britain. Due to cultural differences between "the two disparate groups of women" she offers comment cautiously. Yet these women – who were publishing books, and running schools and even estates – were not *oppressed by men*, although many non-elite and some elite women were. Taking part in "first-wave feminism" over a hundred years ago (p. 277), they laid foundations on which Khaleda and Hasina later trod.

I argue that tendencies and seeds favoring women's empowerment lie deep in Bangladeshi culture. Given the right conditions, they grow and blossom. Eden College, Hasina's *Alma Mater*, was founded in 1873, part of the awakening of feminism in colonial Bengal. Later, the Raj assumed responsibility for running the college but it was started – only a quarter of a century after England's first women's college, Bedford (founded in London in 1849) – not by English "doing good" in their colony but by Indians.

Abbas (2002), on women's participation in Sufi ritual, is a pioneer text: "Almost nothing has been published in English about men and women in South Asian Sufism" (p. xv) yet women make major contributions to Sufi ceremony.

This chapter draws on personal experience while visiting and living in Bangladesh. As a result, not every observation I make is sourced. I have also spent time in West Bengal.

Political Background

The nature of Bengali Islam: syncretistic or humanitarian Islam?
Bengali Islam is frequently described as eclectic or syncretistic. This refers to a blurring of the boundary between Hinduism and Islam. I prefer to identify Bengali Islam as a broad spiritual tradition or current to which members of various religions belong: Muslim, Hindu, Buddhist and Christian. There are only small numbers of Buddhists (0.7 percent) and Christians (0.3 percent) but they are equally proud of and participate in wider Bengali culture.

As a small girl, my wife would visit whichever village or *para* (neighborhood) was having a festival, whether Hindu, Muslim or Christian, and she was always welcomed. No one turned her away. The wandering Baul singers of Bengal are Sufis who praise Vishnu. Bengalis love their poets, Hindu, Muslim and Christian, singing all their songs, playing all their tunes; Bengali poetry is often set to music. How did this spiritual tradition begin? To answer this, we need to briefly sketch the pre-colonial history of Bengal, tracing how Islam reached the Ganges delta. Then we pick up Mujib's narrative, tracing how Hasina came to lead the Awami League in opposition to military rule, how her policies differ from Khaleda's, and what caused mutual animosity. Evidence is examined that women played public roles from British times, before contributing significantly to the independence struggle. Media attention focuses on two women. However, their careers are not quite the special case or cultural aberration some suggest. There is a long tradition of strong Bengali women who allow no one to dominate them. This does not deny the horrific instances of wife beating and violence toward women. It does question the degree to which patriarchy permeates Bangladeshi society, as many claim.

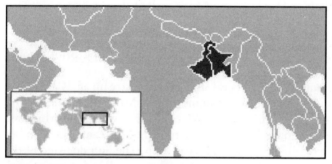

Map 9: The Bengal region. Approximately the size of France, this comprises Bangladesh (East) and West Bengal state (India) (West). Communities in Orissa, Tripura, Bihar, Assam and in diaspora, about 250 million people worldwide, also speak Bangla.

The area or region of Bengal, during the British Raj, was roughly the size of France. Bengali speakers today number approximately 250 million worldwide. In addition to West Bengal, the Indian state that borders on Bangladesh, and Bangladesh itself, sizeable communities speak Bengali in Tripura, Assam, Orissa, Bihar and elsewhere, including in diaspora. Bangla (Bengali) is the world's fifth or sixth most widely spoken language. During 2009, the governments of Bangladesh and West Bengal endorsed a request for the United Nations to declare Bengali an official language.

Before becoming part of the Mughal Empire, several political entities existed in Bengal. Immediately prior to Mughal rule, the area was under the Delhi sultanate. The Hindu–Buddhist Pala dynasty ruled Bengal from the mid-eighth to almost the end of the twelfth century. This empire had dominated much of the subcontinent. The Sena dynasty that succeeded did not rule as large a territory but oversaw a period of literary excellence. It was during this period that Sufi preachers first reached Bengal, so before any Muslim army came many people were Muslim. Sufis were open, inclusive of elements of local belief and practice that harmonized with their teaching. Some were happy with Hindus if they recited the *Kilimah* and changed their names (Karlekar, p. 27). Sufi shrines were built near existing sacred sites, *pobitro bhumi*. Such practices as offering garlands of flowers continued. Allah was another name for the Divine, Sufi saints were gurus teaching love of God and of others, that devotion (*bhakti*) leads to *samadhi*, realization of oneness with God. Later, Sufi saints attracted Hindu devotees. Some Muslims followed Hindu gurus. I have visited shrines where pilgrims from many faiths offer prayer. Karlekar says, "One finds instances of Muslims worshipping Hindu deities" (p. 27). Many families crossed religious boundaries, so local and clan loyalties took priority over religion (p. 27).

Karlekar refers to a "liberal and creative stream in Islam" that flowed in India since the "beginning of the Muslim conquest" (pp. 26–7). Episodes of intolerance and violence toward non-Muslims, including desecration of holy sites, interrupted this stream or current but in Bengal especially it never totally dried up. The Sufi doctrine of the unity of being allows for openness to the varied and diverse, even paradoxical ways, that God speaks to humanity. If all are one, apparent differences can be reconciled. A Muslim general conquered the Sena in 1205, after which a series of Muslim rulers governed under the Delhi sultans. In 1508, a Mughal general took Bengal, becoming the first Governor of Dhaka. After this, semi-independent Nawabs ruled, nominally subject to the Mughals. They maintained a splendid court, to which Begum refers in describing how Khaleda cultivates the image of "Muslim royalty": "the very regal Nawabs" were "subservient to the Mughals" but "retain the splendor of royalty in the collective memory" (p. 276).

In 1757, the British defeated Nawab Siraj ud-daulah at the Battle of Plassey, obtaining a Mughal *firman* (decree) granting them tax-collecting rights and *de facto* rule. Until 1880, they left a puppet Nawab in place. This dynasty, the Najafi, was descended from Muhammad. The last heir died in 1989. With Calcutta as capital of the Raj until 1911, Bengalis were close to the center of British India. Graduating from universities, they entered the civil service. Several led Hindu reforms. Many became involved in the self-rule movement. Muslims and Hindus contributed equally to a literary renaissance. Bengali women, Muslim and Hindu, wore the sari, which in West Pakistan would be seen as unpatriotic. Many Muslim women also wore the *teep* as cosmetic decoration, which West Pakistanis saw as syncretistic (Shehabuddin, p. 64). Hashmi points out that seclusion was not widely practiced (p. 194), neither was head-to-foot covering, although I have noticed more women in *chador* over recent years. Due to working in the garments industry, more women now wear *shalwar-qameez*, which used to be despised as Pakistani (p. 188).

All communities commemorate *Noboborsho*, Bengali New Year, which West Pakistanis regards as non-Muslim. For some Muslims, the popularity of music and singing alone made Bengali Islam's orthodoxy suspect. In Sufi Islam, women's circles are common. A video available at the time of writing on several websites showed Bangladeshi women offering *dhikr*.

Abbas (2002) did extensive fieldwork for her book on women's participation in Sufi ritual, mainly in Pakistan. She grew up in Bangladesh, where she developed a love of music (p. xxv). She shows how women take part in worship at Sufi shrines on a daily basis. Not only do Sufi women worship apart from men, they also worship with them (p. xiv). Another video on the internet shows Sufi men and women dancing together in Egypt. In the Indian subcontinent, women who sing at Sufi shrines often support themselves (p. 1). Abbas' research also looked at women in Sufi ritual among the diaspora, including Arab states where migrants from the subcontinent work, as well as in Europe.

Sufi women have a long history of teaching. Tradition associates the highest levels of spiritual states with them, including miracles. Even sultans have built shrines to honor women saints. Men acknowledge their wisdom. Some men had women teachers, including Ibn Arabi. Nurbakhsh (1983) tells stories associated with 124 Sufi women, whose lives impacted men and women.

There are exceptions to gender-equal-friendly versions of Sufi Islam. Ershad follows a popular Pir who opposes female leadership. He stipulates that his wife, "a former member of parliament," wears *hijab* when attending ceremonies (Riaz, p. 44). Ershad, though, increased the number of reserved seats and gave women responsibility in his administration. His sister-in-law, Mumta Wahab, was deputy health minister. In Bhakti Hindu practice, women play and sing alongside men. Rekha and I took part in such worship, when she sang and I spoke at a local Krishna temple near her parents' village, run by distant Hindu relatives. Visiting a Hindu temple at Cox's Bazaar, we saw a Hindu lady washing and changing Gopal's dress (infant Krishna), then removing and returning the *murti* (image) to the inner chamber, which is usually reserved for Brahman males.

Even Ibn Taymiyyah (d. 1328), who denounced Sufi practices and beliefs, had a woman teacher, an acknowledged expert on *hadith*, and a large number of women admirers. Muslims, he said, should purify Islam by abandoning Sufi practice. They must desist from taking part in Christian festivities. This is similar to the criticism that celebrating the *Noboborsho* is non-Muslim, involving song and music. Ibn Taymayyah demanded total dissimilitude between Muslims and others: they should wear different clothes, distancing themselves from non-Muslims. Through Wahhabi influence (Al-Wahhab read Taymayyah), anti-Sufi teaching impacted Bengal (Karlekar, p. 29). Shah Waliullah (1703–64) was also influential. He "felt that only a revival of pure Islam could save the Mughal Empire ... Islam had to be cleansed of the influence of Hindus" (p. 24).

Yet Sufi Islam's openness to truth, wherever encountered – including the possibility that people outside ritual or legal Islam, who live moral lives and adore God, may also be "muslim" – can be regarded as a *bone fide* expression of Islam. Despite political distancing between Bengali Hindus and Muslims, exacerbated by financial disparity, a result of British *divide et impera*, the two communities remained culturally close. West Pakistanis reacted to Tagore's popularity among Bengali Muslims, banning his songs. Tagore's *Amar Shonar Bangla* (My Golden Bengal) became Bangladesh's National Anthem. Tagore also penned India's anthem. Nazrul Islam (1925–75), the Muslim poet, an intimate friend of Tagore, regarded him as his mentor. Both were committed to universal values and to human solidarity. Nazrul drew on Hinduism as much as he did on Islam. Michael Madhusudan Datta (1824–73), a Christian, almost equally honored, believed that literature bridges religious differences.

This spiritual tradition, inherently open to the universal nature of religious experience, generally informs positive interreligious relations, minimizing the male tendency to regard women as subordinate. In Sufi ritual, women and men are spiritually and liturgically equal. By the late nineteenth century, some Bengali women, with their Hindu peers, were entering the public sphere. Eden College, founded in 1873 by members of the Hindu Brahmo Samaj, within which the Tagore family were leaders, has educated many Bengali women leaders. Originally a high school, the college was added in 1926 (Amin, p. 153).

In her investigation of women's empowerment in Bengal, Amin shows how Hindus and Muslims took part in a single movement. These women were elite but others, less privileged, followed the precedent they set (p. 277). Women began to publish. Women, not men, exercised "domain over the private" sphere, where women often had greater influence and more say in household affairs than men (p. 75). With increased access to education, women gained awareness of rights, making education the "mediator between public and private spheres, between home and the world" (p. xvi). Some women inherited estates, ran their own business, exercising "power in both the public and private spheres" (p. 73). In 1897, a *madrassa* for girls opened in Calcutta (p. 143). Another criticism of Bengali Islam was that women marched in demonstrations, suggesting that women's empowerment was well underway by the early 1950s (Shehabuddin, p. 64). Women took part in the independence struggle. Several, with no dynastic ties, had political careers before Hasina or Khaleda entered the arena.

Mujib and the birth of Bangladesh

Chapter 3 saw how, denied the option of an independent Bengal, and faced instead with the choice of remaining in India or acceding to Pakistan, the majority of Bengali Muslims voted to take the whole province into Pakistan. Significantly, Huseyn Shaheed Suhrawardy, who led the first ML ministry, also led this campaign. When rioting broke out in Calcutta in 1947, he appealed to Gandhi to help restore order, calling for Hindu–Muslim harmony (Gupta, p. 955). Fazlul Haq, known as *sher-e-bangla*, "tiger of Bengal," former chief minister, left the League complaining that Jinnah ran it like his "personal fiefdom" (Karlekar, p. 41). He was so opposed to partition that he thought it best that the British remain. Very soon after Pakistan was created, the League's support in East Pakistan declined. It was regarded as dominated nationally by West Pakistan, in the east by "upper Muslim landlords, businessmen and intellectuals" (Molla, p. 216). In June 1949, dissatisfied ML elements met to form the East Pakistan Awami Muslim League.

Fortuitously, the League was in place to lead the language issue. Mujib was a joint secretary. Jinnah had indicated that Urdu ought to be the sole state language. Many in the west thought Bengali too "Hindu." One solution was to substitute the script with Arabic, deeply offensive to Bengalis, as was the "attempt to ... ban Tagore's songs in the state-controlled media" (Riaz, p. 25). The language issue began with Jinnah's preference for Urdu, then developed when the central legislature voted for English and Urdu as its official languages, on February 23, 1948. In 1950, a report recommended Urdu as the state language. In 1951, Prime Minister Nazimuddin labeled as "enemies" those who wanted Bangla as an official language (Karlekar, p. 42). Anyone familiar with Bengali's pride in their language could anticipate a negative response. Demonstrations and strikes followed. On February 21, 1952 (*Shaheed Dibosh*) "police fired on students of Dhaka University, who were at the forefront of the language movement" "killing four," giving us the language martyrs (p. 43). More strikes were met with "severe repression." Finally, on April 19, 1954, Bangla was recognized as an official language.

However, West and East Pakistan were already alienated. In addition to language, economic disparity and inequality in distribution of government jobs and military posts drove West and East apart. Many District Officers were from West Pakistan. In fact, the administrative system was largely carried over from the Raj. To put it bluntly, West Pakistan rigged the system to run East Pakistan as a colony. In addition, many West Pakistanis adopted a racist attitude. Ayub Khan dismissed Bengalis as a "down-trodden race" full of "suspicion" (Ahmed 1997, p. 236). East Bengali Islam was heterodox. Bengalis were deemed racially inferior. There were exceptions. Rekha and I have a British Pakistani friend, whose wife is Bengali, who speaks such perfect Bangla that one of her nephews calls him "Bengali uncle."

Bengalis have a reputation for intelligence, and some of the ethnicities in the west such as Rajputs and Pathans are renowned for their martial characteristics, although ethnic profiling is dubious if not sinister. Yet could Bengalis value feminine qualities alongside masculine, perhaps a result of Kali's popularity as mother, who defends her consort, Shiva, from demons while he mediates, preserving cosmic harmony? Kali and Shiva are co-equal, co-dependent. Their sexuality is flexible. Kali is also Parvati, the feminine patron of arts. As Kali, she is masculine, ferocious, the destroyer of ignorance. Shiva is Nataraj, Lord of the Dance, a more feminine manifestation, but Shiva is male. "I bow to thee, Mother" (*Bande Mataram*) set to music by Tagore, written in adoration of Kali, became the song of the self-rule movement during opposition to the 1906–11 partition. Armed insurgents dedicated their weapons to Kali (Metcalf and Metcalf, p. 85).

Does Sufi Islam's doctrine of the unity of being help open minds to the feminine and masculine nature of God? "Allah" is grammatically masculine but this does not mean that God is sexually male. Given the structure of many Muslim societies, God is probably imaged as "male," despite the fact that imaging God in human terms is problematic. Yet positing that, within God's ultimately mysterious, unknowable nature, female and masculine qualities coexist is within the bounds of acceptable speculation.

As a result of the language issue, Bengalis identified even more markedly with their "rich, eclectic, liberal, humanist culture" (Karlekar, p. 43). The AL claims that the word "Muslim" in their original name was pragmatic; in 1949 no one was ready for a "secular" party. The "cataclysmic events" of 1952 changed this. When the United Front, with the League as largest member, won the 1954 election for provincial assembly, a more secular atmosphere emerged (AL website 2010). I would argue that this was not exactly "secular" but a preference for the spiritual current outlined above. In fact, the party adopted a non-communal policy and identity, known as the Murree Pact (1955). Muslim was dropped from the name and Fazlul Haq became chief minister. East Pakistan's exclusion from power sharing contributed to the state's inability to agree a constitution until 1956 (Shehabuddin, p. 62). The question of whether Pakistan was a state for Muslims, or a Muslim state, delayed the process, as did asking, "If it is a Muslim state, what does this actually mean?"

Issues about the nature of the state and Islam's role inevitably resurfaced in Bangladesh. In 1956, Suhrawardy became prime minister, an effort to placate the west. He and President Mirza had a plan to unite the west's four provinces into one, which failed. Suhrawardy tried to "ease economic difference between east and west," which sadly generated "more political friction" (Gupta, p. 956). Threatened with dismissal, he resigned (1957).

In 1958, when Ayub Khan declared martial law, all political parties were banned. Mujib, already jailed several times for political activities, succeeded Suhrawardy as AL leader in 1963, following its revival. The 1965 India–Pakistan war exposed the east's vulnerability. India blocked "transport between" Pakistan's "two wings" (Molla, p. 219). Mujib demanded greater autonomy, publishing his Six-Point Formula. No progress took place under military regimes. To Ayub, Mujib was a "secessionist" (Molla, p. 220). Mawdudi, for whom the idea of dismembering Pakistan was anathema, vehemently opposed him (Shehabuddin, p. 63). In return, Mujib taunted Mawdudi that he would only be permitted to enter East Bengal if he, "the Sheikh," wished him to (Ahmed 1997, p. 240). Mujib did not want secession, although his Six-Point Formula denuded the center of power.

In 1970, in Pakistan's first national poll, Mujib won the largest block of seats, so should have formed the government. When this proved unlikely, he called for an independence struggle (March 7, 1971). On midnight, March 26 he declared Bangladesh's independence in a radio broadcast, sending a telegram to Dhaka. A politically active woman, Manjula Anwar, translated the content. On March 27, Major Zia ur-Rahman (there were few senior Bengali officers) read an independence declaration. The war began. Later, the existence of Mujib's telegram was denied, serving to downplay his role and that of civilians, in contrast to Zia's role. Part of AL–BNP rivalry, this dispute about who issued the declaration of indpendence revolves around competing concepts of national identity (see AL *Newsletter*, Vol. 3, No. 15, August 14, 2004, disputing the BNP version).

Atrocities committed during the war, pitting a well-trained army against mainly irregular freedom fighters, have been well chronicled. *Razakars*, paramilitary killing squads recruited by JI collaborators, aided the Pakistanis against the *Mukti Bahini* (freedom fighters) (Riaz, p. 96). India helped form the *Mujib Bahini* under the sheikh's nephew, Sheikh Fazlul Haque Moni. Loyal to Mujib, this answered neither to the provisional government nor to the *Mukti Bahini* command. Ten million people became refugees. Homes, crops and infrastructure were destroyed. My wife recalls how Pakistani soldiers killed all local monkeys, including a semi-tame pet, to prevent them giving their positions away when attacking. Ahmed cites rumors that Martial Law Administrator General Niazi encouraged soldiers to impregnate Bengali women, since this would improve the gene pool (p. 238). Few thought Bengalis capable of armed resistance, seeing them as effeminate: "They will run when the first shot is fired" (p. 238).

Women as well as men fought the Pakistani army. Two were decorated. Syeda Begum Sajeda Chowdhury, an Eden graduate and Mujib protégé, "mobilized 500 women" in 1964 against Ayub, giving her first public speech (Commonwealth Secretariat, p. 30). During the war, she ran women's training camps. In 1973, she was given one of parliament's 15 reserved seats. In 1977, she became Awami League General Secretary, remaining in office for 11 years. In 1979, she ran unsuccessfully for an open seat (p. 31). In 1991, she gained a seat. Of eight others who did so, two were Khaleda and Hasina. She won again in 1996, serving in Hasina's cabinet.

Manjula Anwar, elected to the Pakistani assembly in 1954 and 1970 and to Bangladesh's parliament in 1973, played an organizing role in the war. She was Minister of Health (1972–3) and Minister of Social Affairs (1973–5) under Mujib, in whose cabinet Badrunessa Ahmed also served. Under Zia and Ershad, women ran the Ministry of Women's

Affairs and held several deputies' posts. Ershad's sister-in-law was Deputy Health Minister (1985–6). Rabia Bhuiyan, the first woman barrister, was an MP from 1986–8 serving as Minister of Social Welfare and Women's Affairs. She was re-elected in 1996.

The first civilian period and both military periods saw women in government. Eden graduate Jahan Ara Begum, vice-president of BNP's executive committee, groomed Khaleda for the party leadership. She became a minister of state in 1991. Motia Chowdhury, known as "daughter of fire," another Eden graduate, joined the Awami League in 1971 as "a member of its working committee." During the war, she nursed the wounded, travelling up and down the country. Under military rule, she spent time in jail (Commonwealth Secretariat, p. 37). Winning a non-reserved seat, she was Minister for Agriculture, Food and Disaster Relief, a "major portfolio" in Bangladesh "not traditionally associated with women" from 1996 to 2001 (p. 37). She is currently third in seniority in Hasina's cabinet, one of five women (counting Hasina) in a 31-member cabinet, the largest number yet. The thousands of rape victims from the war were declared *Birangona* (war heroines). Mujib said it would be patriotic for men to marry them.

Mujib's Downfall: Hasina's Political Baptism

Known as *bangabandhu* (friend of Bengali, or father of the nation), Mujib was initially president, becoming prime minister when prime-ministerial governance was adopted. The 1972 constitution embodied socialism and secularism as principles of state. Secularism is widely said to have respected non-Muslim contributions during the independence struggle. However, it alienated some, not least of all JI members. They had opposed separation, collaborating with Pakistan. Others were unhappy to lose the Islamic elements of national identity, expressed in the Objectives Resolution and the 1956 constitution. Although few steps had been taken to translate specific Islamic ideas into law, many Bangladeshis were unprepared for secularism, which is why some greeted Mujib's assassination with the cry that now an Islamic state could be established. My view is that Mujib did not intend to establish a Turkish-style "secularism" that relegates religion to the private sphere. Atatürk once declared that he had "no religion" (Mango, p. 17). Mujib, who led *salat* (prayer) straight after the Constitutional Bill passed, meant non-communalism. The constitution spoke of ending "communalism" and religious discrimination (Riaz, pp. 32–3). Non-communalism gives religion space in the public sphere. Some think Bangladeshi secularism failed because, as a top-down imposition, it was an apolitical "abstraction," unrooted in "society" (Riaz, p. 21). It did exist, however, represented by the spiritual current identified above. It was misnamed. As articulated, it differed from "its Western variant" so "cannot be labelled as an alien and imported phenomenon" (Riaz, p. 21). Nonetheless, it helped Zia's political agenda.

The commitment to socialism was pragmatic. There were leftist elements in the League that wanted a full-blown communist system. Mujib resisted this. However, he compromised, embracing a broad socialist commitment to wealth distribution, welfare provision and a centrally controlled economy. Some represented the war as a class struggle between the proletariat of East Pakistan and the bourgeoisie of West Pakistan, between capitalist oppressors and the "oppressed" (Riaz, p. 27). The concept of "Sonar Bangla" (Golden Bengal) as a classless society was popularized. Bangladesh faced serious food shortages and economic meltdown, later exacerbated by flood. Refugees had to be rehoused. Paramilitary groups retained arms. Some engaged in illegal cross-border smuggling. Others stole from and terrorized the population. Blackmail and hoarding was endemic. In addition, political factions pulled in different directions. Armed militants threatened the state's stability (Molla, p. 224). AW leaders contributed to the "economic crises" by patronizing supporters (p. 225).

In the 1973 election, the League won an absolute majority, 293 seats out of 300. Chowdhury (2003) thinks that some malpractice took place, although not on the scale of subsequent elections during military rule (p. 37). The large majority reflected the party's popularity but also heralded democracy's eclipse for almost two decades. The opposition Nationalist Socialist Party claimed that the League killed and arrested thousands of members; Mujib claimed thousands of League fatalities (Chowdhury 2003, p. 46). In response to criticism, oppressive measures were taken. The State of Emergency, called December 28, 1974, suspended political pluralism and many civil rights. Government-controlled media replaced the free press (p. 46). A constitutional amendment, passed in eleven minutes on January 25, 1975, restored the presidential system, making Mujib's "position lifelong" (p. 30). His assassins claimed that he was establishing a monarchy (*Daily Star*). Effectively, with only seven non-League seats in parliament, there was no opposition, so Mujib thought he had a mandate to end the pluralist system, at least for the time being (Chowdhury 2003, p. 46; Riaz, p. 93). Formally, BAKSAL, uniting left-wing parties into a single entity, governed. Dubbed "the second revolution," the aim was to set up "multi-purpose cooperatives as economic units in every village," implementing a grass-roots type of socialism (Molla, p. 225). Industries were nationalized (Chowdhury 2003 p. 25). Foreign investors had to collaborate with the public sector. The problem was that socialism lacked wide support, while Bangladesh lacked "the economic resources to carry out a socialist ... policy" (p. 26). Chowdhury suggests that although Mujib led the independence struggle, he had no experience of government (p. 27). Riaz says that Mujib "subordinated civil society to his own needs" (p. 92).

Mujib's legacy, then, is ambiguous. Having established democratic institutions, he did not appear to have a strong "commitment to democracy." He refused to allow "the government institutions to grow with autonomy beyond the sphere of his overwhelming authority" (Chowdhury 2003, p. 30). Chowdhury regrets that Bangladesh's founding father, unlike India's Nehru or the US' Washington, failed to establish solid democratic foundations. Benazir mourned the early loss of Pakistan's founder, Jinnah, suggesting that had he lived longer, democracy might have taken firmer root (2008, p. 167). In the "case of Pakistan," this was compounded by wars with India. Cohen (2004) suggests that if India and Pakistan had enjoyed better relations, Bangladesh might not have seceded (p. 296). What held the "two wings" together was "opposition to India." India wanted "Pakistan to fail," so did nothing to cooperate and help her neighbour cope with the difficult geo-political situation (p. 298). Easier transportation, cross-border trade and travel would have helped. A possible future for a Pakistan that does not fail, or subdivide into smaller states, might see the former wings reunited within a larger confederation. This could include Kashmir, and other regions that prefer separate statehood within an EU-type form of "political and economic cooperation" (pp. 291–2). In Europe, Slovakia and the Czech Republic parted company, amicably in their case. Both then acceded to the EU, thus no real border exists between them for purposes of travel and work.

The backlash was brutal. On August 15, 1975, Mujib, his wife and almost every member of their family were killed, followed by the entire senior leadership of the League on November 3. Aware of the danger that the Bangladeshi military might imitate their Pakistani counterpart and intervene in governance, Mujib had tried to minimize this risk. Reducing military expenditure (60 percent under Pakistan) he had formed the JRB (Jatiyo Rakshi Bahini, the National Security Force) as an alternative. His bodyguard, the JRB, also dealt with security, disarming bandits and bringing hoarders to justice. It also broke strikes. In January 1974, it received immunity from prosecution. This annoyed the police and the military, becoming a factor behind Mujib's vicious assassination. JRB members were former *Mujib Bahini*, with some

152   Muslim Women of Power

Mukti Bahini. After the coup, the Awami League was suspended. Zia lifted the ban in 1978, having formed his own party. Sajeda Chowdhury became General Secretary. The 1979 elections saw Zia's National Party win 207 out of 300 seats. The AL had the second largest number (p. 39). The League campaigned for a return to parliamentary government (Molla, p. 227).

When Hasina, the oldest of Mujib's two surviving daughters, became party leader in 1981, this was the situation she faced. Zia was not part of the August coup but may have known about the plot, which he did not stop. Zia benefited from the chaos, emerging as the strong man who restored order. He did not attempt to bring the officers who committed the crime to justice, granting them indemnity. When Hasina returned to Bangladesh on May 17, 1982, Zia was the "self-appointed President" (Matin, p. 14). He denounced her as a collaborator with foreign forces who intended to "re-establish one party rule" (p. 14). She says she was the first voice of protest against dictatorship. Then Zia was assassinated. After Ershad toppled Zia's democratically elected successor, Hasina opposed his military regime, with the same object of restoring democracy. Regardless of Mujib's ambiguous legacy, this was the task, similar to Benazir's, to which she committed herself. Ershad continued his former boss's "anti-Awami League policy" (p. 14). A period of cooperation with Khaleda, head of Zia's BNP, followed, united againt Ershad, a common foe. Their parties had little reason to collaborate, with competing visions of Bangladeshi identity, although little now separates their fiscal policies and legislative programs.

AL's alliance with the Soviets ended when the Cold War finished, resulting in a policy shift. Those adopted by the BNP, a free market economy responding to IMF and World Bank requirements, replaced socialist policies (Riaz, p. 40). The AL is possibly more committed to wealth sharing. Reacting to the Islamization process, the League retreated from the language of secularism. This had been "borrowed from the outside." Instead, the current of Bengali Islam that I have identified was emphasized. This locates religious openness in the "traditions of Bengal," seeking to "reclaim the land already occupied by the Islamists" (Riaz, p. 40). Riaz thinks this backfired, "implicitly" legitimizing Islamists' "existence and arguments." It could be insincere, an "inclination to return to power at any cost" (p. 40). Or, it could represent the League's "non-communal" stance, which attracted and still attracts cross-community support (Molla, p. 232).

A Christian, Pramod Mankhin, an ethnic Garo, was elected to parliament in 1991, 2001 and 2008. In 2009, he became the first Christian cabinet member, with the portfolio for cultural affairs. He also chairs the Bangladesh Christian Association. No candidate can win without substantial Muslim support. A retired Catholic head teacher and an attorney, he headed the Chittagong Hill Tracts committee during Hasina's first term, when she concluded the Peace Accord. Hasina promoted a Christian army officer whom Khaleda had sacked. Continued commitment to spreading wealth is also consistent with Islamic ideals, building on traditional Bengali Muslim identity. This combines Islam's ideal of social and economic egalitarianism with "Bengali culture and language" (Riaz, p. 19). Today, the AL and BNP's main differences lie in ideas about nationalism, the role of religion and culture, debate about Bengali and Bangladeshi identity, and foreign relations.

Sheikh Hasina: Elected Awami League Leader

Born in 1947, Hasina attended Eden College, where she chaired the Union. She was elected to various other student leadership posts. She earned her bachelor's degree in 1973, having married a nuclear physicist, Dr M. A. Wazeed Miah in 1968. Distinguished in his own right, he stayed outside politics. They have a son and a daughter, who live in the USA with, so far, despite speculation, no sign of political ambition. Visiting Germany when her father was killed, Hasina remained overseas until 1981. Some point to lack of previous political experience, describing her as a housewife one day, party leader the next. However, Hasina says that politics was "in her blood" (Matin, p. 9). She took a leading role in several anti-Ayub protests, and was briefly detained during the war. Her first public speech was at a London rally on August 15, 1980, marking Mujib's death. The following year, the AL elected her president *in absentia*. Mujib used "Sheikh" as a title, although it may be a traditional given name in his family. In the subcontinent, sheikh can denote membership of the landed gentry, or indicate ancestry. It is also used for Sufi teachers. Some Arab rulers are sheikhs. All Mujib's children had the title.

The party was "fractured" and "fearful to continue … activities due to intimidation, repression and occasional imprisonment." Most middle-level leaders had emigrated (Molla, p. 236). Historically, the party's support base was strong, represented by students, women, workers and other wings. Hasina helped rebuild the AL from the bottom up. Like Khaleda, she was in and out of prison during Ershad's regime. The BNP boycotted Ershad's 1986 election. The AL was skeptical about entering the contest but decided to do so. Ershad won, 153 seats to the AL's 73. The year 1986 saw the first general election in which women won open seats (some had won by-elections); Hasina won a seat from three constituencies. The AL had been "allowed to win" these seats. It would have won a majority, if the election had been free. Ershad was a "thug, a liar and a dacoit (bandit)" (p. 16). Hasina said, "since we do not have guns, we can only try the ballot box" (p. 15). Such language is rhetoric, expressing cynicism. Chowdhury sees her later desire to topple the BNP as a willingness to illegally overthrow a democratically elected government, citing a statement referring to "launching a violent movement" (p. 84). This would undermine or contradict any peacemaking credentials. Even though she was named official leader of the opposition, detentions continued.

The anti-Ershad struggle, narrated in Chapter 3, ended with the 1991 election, which Khaleda won. Several reasons can be identified. The Awami League faced a tough challenge reviving support and rebuilding networks. The fact that the BNP was the democratic government that Ershad had overthrown favored Khaleda. Many thought justice demanded a BNP return to power. Khaleda's personal loss was the more recent, too. She did not constantly refer to her status but her widow-image definitely attracted sympathy, which she used effectively (Begum, p. 277). Zia was still popular, while anger at Mujib had not altogether disappeared.

How did Hasina address the democratic aspect of her father's legacy? She said that her "father's legacy would strengthen" her party's cause. The nation had a great deal of love and respect for him. She hoped she would "be able to complete his work" (Matin, p. 10). She consistently called for a return to the 1972 constitution, including its "secular" spirit. She stressed that strong leadership was needed after the war, during the early years of freedom. Mujib's BAKSAL had responded to crises. One-party rule was not meant to be permanent. Neither had her father, as accused, "mortgage[d] Bangladesh to India" (p. 13). Hasina stood "steadfastly for the restoration of democracy and the rule of law" (p. 14). Frequently citing her father's sacrifice, she was willing to face death for her nation's sake (p. 9). His picture, not hers, continues to be everywhere. However, she has admitted that Mujib made mistakes (Chowdhury 2009).

There have been several attempts on Hasina's life. Matin, invoking Benazir's self-image, calls her Bangladesh's "woman of destiny," just as Mujib was the "man of destiny" (p. 27). Zia made similar claims after the chaos of 1975, namely that strong leadership was required to establish stability. By adopting Bangladeshi rather than Bengali nationalism and emphasizing his own role in the war, minimizing Mujib's, Zia positioned himself as the true "father" of the nation. He did not explicitly claim this honor but hinted that Bangladesh's real birthday was August 1975. Mujib had spent the war in jail, so his role could be downplayed. Hasina described the 1988 parliament, after both the AL and BNP boycotted the elections, as "so-called," and derided Ershad's eighth amendment, making Islam the state religion, as "playing politics with religion" (p. 18). When Hindus in Bangladesh were attacked following the destruction of the mosque in Ayodhia, she accused Ershad of hiring "gangsters to create fear and mistrust" (p. 19).

Most analysts regard the introduction of Islam into Bangladeshi politics as a legitimizing tactic; military rulers need to justify their regime. It is not clear how Islam does this, although authoritarian regimes elsewhere use state-formatted Islam to discourage alternative discourse. Presumably, by proclaiming that the state is Islamic, that Islamic laws are being introduced, autocratic rule somehow derives legitimacy from this fact without need for *bone fide* elections.

Muslim rulers asserted power by various means. Legitimacy derived from *ruling according to Islam* rather than from how *power was obtained*. Yet in Bangladesh, little has changed legally. Most lawyers qualify, as my brother-in-law did, in England, which is considered prestigious. Analysts hint that Zia and Ershad used Islam as a tool, hinting at insincerity. They did attract petro-dollars, but perhaps they were nonetheless genuine. Many Bangladeshis wanted constitutional recognition of their Muslim heritage.

Hasina: Opposition to Khaleda

The year 1991 saw Hasina as official opposition leader, for the second time. After her first term in office, 1996 to 2001, she began her third period in opposition; then, after winning the 2008 election, she started her second administration.

Chapter 3 touched on the behaviour of both Hasina and Khaleda in opposition. Chowdhury describes a regrettable record of boycotting parliament, even when a budget was being debated. Both women complain that the other side continues to refuse them sufficient time to speak. According to Hasina, Khaleda "adopted an autocratic style," denying the opposition a "legitimate role." She broke "electoral promises" (Matin, p. 20). Equally, Hasina has been accused of having an authoritarian style, spending more time dealing with the opposition than improving law and order and the state's situation (Chowdhury 2004, p. 94).

In opposition, both women have vowed to bring the government down, calling strikes and demonstrations. In June 2002, AL activists prevented Khaleda from attending a scheduled meeting (Chowdhury 2004, p. 95). The AL refers to BNP activists attempting to shoot Hasina in 1991, and to bomb attacks on political meetings during March 1994. Before the 1991 election, Khaleda agreed to restore parliamentary governance but then "prevaricated" (Matin, p. 19), preferring the presidential system. In the end, she passed the twelfth amendment (1993). She also agreed to create independent corporations for state-owned media. In July 1994 the AL whip accused the government of plotting to transfer power to "evil forces" (Chowdhury, p. 85). Opposition MPs resigned *en masse* (December 1994). The government took legal action to compel attendance, based on members' oaths of office. The first 1996 election led to sustained extra-parliamentary protest, resulting in Amendment 13, the provision for caretaker governments. At this point, Hasina was collaborating with JI, despite traditional animosity toward the AL.

On some issues, Hasina successfully impacted policy from the opposition benches, although not without resorting to extra-parliamentary tactics. I visited Bangladesh during each woman's administrations, watching parliament on television and witnessing empty seats on one side of the house.

Despite their label as "warring Begums," the two rarely meet, inside or outside parliament. In September 2009, they met at an *iftar* (breaking of the daily fast). Hasina is reported to have asked Khaleda to attend parliament, where her voice would be heard. Photographs of the two women together, taken at that rare meeting, provide an opportunity to confirm Begum (2006) on how their dress expresses different ideas about national identity. Earlier – on May 9, 2009 – Khaleda had visited Hasina to express condolences on the death of her husband (he had remained outside politics, uncontaminated by allegations of corruption or cronyism – unlike the husbands of Benazir, Çiller and Megawati).

Both women's democratic legacy would be healthier if they had worked out a way to involve the opposition in governance. Chowhdury thinks that a more effective committee system, perhaps learning lessons from the US, would help (p. 94). Perhaps it might, although the US system is adversarial and polarized. He calls for a "culture of power sharing" (p. 94). Unfortunately, the legacy the two women inherited habitually resorts to extra-parliamentary tactics. Opposition to British rule in India was almost entirely outside parliament. The language movement, the struggle for autonomy and then for independence, were conducted on the streets, eventually with the gun. Boycotting elections and parliament is well established as a method of politics. Sometimes, street action is necessary in any democracy. However, in Bangladesh, mass support for one party one day and then another the next tells us little about either party's real popularity. My in-laws joke about "rent-a-crowd" politics; poor people paid to demonstrate are anti-BNP one day, anti-AL the next. Neither of the leaders can be wholly blamed for this adversarial system, or for the lack of a concept of a "loyal opposition" in traditional Bengali culture. It is, though, regrettable that neither has yet set a higher standard. During the 2006–8 caretaker regime, Hasina was arrested for corruption before going into voluntary exile, returning when allowed to contest the December 2008 election. There were no convictions. The AL site says she "wages war against corruption" (AL, p. 5).

Hasina's Administrations

In government, Hasina makes efforts at conciliation, appointing – to a limited degree – a rainbow cabinet, with two BNP members, during her first administration. However, this has not resulted in opposition members attending parliament. Probably only a government with both women in the cabinet would achieve that. The Jatiya Party had a ministry in 1996, but later left the coalition. It is represented again in her current administration. Some see cooperation with Ershad's party as hypocritical. On the other hand, his party wins seats and he served time in jail, admitting guilt publicly. Cooperation may be sincere conciliation.

Hasina's and Khaleda's economic policies are similar. Both comply with the IMF, encourage inward investment and micro-credit, minimize inflation and maximize tax revenues. Hasina's first term saw an average GDP growth of 5.5 percent. Inflation was 1.5 percent, a better record than Reagan's, whose fiscal achievements are generally highly regarded. His average annual GDP growth was 3.4 percent, inflation 3.9 percent (Carroll, p. 65). Committed to making Bangladesh a middle-income country by 2010, Hasina has initiated a raft of social programs aimed at providing a safety net. One rural project offers shelter and training, benefiting 33,000 families. In 1996, Bangladesh was a "food deficit" county. In 2002, it had a surplus.

In her first term, Hasina launched a National Policy for the Advancement of Women, approved by parliament during 1998 in "keeping with the requirements of the Beijing Platform for Action." The plan provided "greater coordination," and the government was consulted before ratification. Six years later, "important changes were made" without consultation, which would have taken place during Khaleda's second term (Shehabuddin, p. 122). Several gender-related laws were passed, including the Violence against Women and Children Act (1998) and Repression of Cruelty to Women and Children Act (2000). In 1996, the Permanent Law Commission was mandated to review all laws concerning women. In 1997, elections took place under a new system that gives women 3 out of every 11 seats on union councils. 13,000 women gained council seats, 63 became municipal commissioners, although the latter have been "restricted from performing some duties" such as marriage and birth registration (Rai, p. 179). Interest in competing for general rather than reserved seats has increased (p. 180). Most women elected, according to Rai, are "elite" (p. 181).

Actually, most male politicians are or become elite. At issue is what elite means? Any politician needs to have some name recognition, record of achievement or that *je ne sais quoi* that attracts notice and votes. Bengalis like leaders who possess inherent qualities that command allegiance. Non-elites as well as elites possess these. Yet ordinary women are showing increased interest in the "democratic process" (Shehabuddin, p. 157). More take part in politics at every level (p. 181). In 1988, when there were no reserved seats, only "three women sat on union and sub-district councils." In 1973, there was one female chair, four in 1977 and 1984. A pre-1989 study says that 60 percent of women in local politics were under the age of 30, while only 4 percent had college degrees (Heitzman and Worden). They cannot be called elite. Hasina promises to increase reserved seats to 100, one-third of the total.

The "best managed women's organization" in Bangladesh, the *Mahila Parishad* (founded 1970) opposes reserved seats but works hard to implement the promised 10 percent "quota for women in the job market" (Hashmi, p. 187). A "major force," the *Parishad* stands for "secularism" and "an exploitation-free society" (Chowdhury 1994, p. 104). The Bangladesh Women Lawyers' Association is another important body.

Hasina's 2009 cabinet, which saw a lot of new faces, appointed the first female ministers of home and foreign affairs, Sahara Khatun and Dipu Mono, both senior posts. Women were first appointed to equivalent posts in Britain in 2007, so Bangladesh is close behind. In foreign relations, Hasina signed a treaty with India on December 12, 1996 over the long-disputed sharing of water. She worked hard to repair relations with India, strained since Mujib's death. The BNP has a pro-Pakistani, anti-Indian policy. Border disputes and cross-border traffic strain Bangladesh–India relations, and there have been several violent exchanges (Jayapalan, p. 135). Large-scale illegal traffic of people and produce occurs. Bangladesh is the largest supplier of illegal weapons in South Asia, risking Talibanization (Karlekar, p. 275). Khaleda accuses Hasina of compromising Bangladesh's security and sovereignty. The AL stresses Bengali identity in linguistic-cultural terms: what Bengalis share across faiths. Its website always refers to "Bengali nationalism," whereas the BNP stresses Bangladeshi's Muslim identity. "Bangladeshi" situates national identity within the state's political boundaries; Bengali extends this across Bengali geographical space.

The BNP claims that the Chittagong Hill Tracts Accord appeased India, where the *Shanti Bahini* took refuge, ending illegally border crossing. The accord ended decades of violence, restoring land or giving compensation to indigenous Hill Tract people, mainly Buddhist and animist. Greater autonomy was granted through a regional council. Peace fighters received money for surrendering weapons. Minorities habitually support the AL although some prefer "Bangladeshi" to "Bengali." A Chakma said in 1972, when Bengali nationality was added to the constitution, that no one had ever asked him to be "Bengali." His nationality was Chakma, his citizenship Bangladeshi (Riaz, p. 32). Some, but not him, were Bangladeshi and Bengali.

Hasina has received peace and humanitarian prizes, in addition to honorary doctorates. Citations honor her commitment to human rights, democracy, freedom and peace. The BBC called her an "iron lady" for her stance on these issues (AL, p. 2). Awards include the Houphouet-Boigny Peace Prize and the Indira Gandhi Prize for Peace. Internationally, she champions the Culture of Peace. Hasina negotiated a bilateral trade agreement with Bhutan. Immediately after India and Pakistan tested nuclear bombs, she visited both states, trying to reduce regional tension. She acceded to various international conventions, including the Land Mines Treaty and the Economic, Social and Cultural Rights Covenant, and established a Human Rights Commission. She was the first South Asian leader invited to attend a G8 summit, in July 2001 (by then in opposition). This recognized Bangladesh's economic potential. In 1997, she co-chaired the micro-credit summit. At a non-aligned movement summit (which she currently co-chairs) in 1998, she proposed a Convention on the Right to Development. She sees good relations with India as pragmatic, and has no wish to undermine Bangladeshi sovereignty. Her father solved several border disputes, signing a 25-year Treaty of Cooperation, Friendship and Peace with India (March 19, 1972) (Jayapalan, p. 131). Ahmed, a subdivisional officer in East Pakistan in 1970, described Mujib's "Indian style waistcoat," implying a pro-Indian, non-Pakistani identity (1997, p. 240).

The Issues

What role did Islam play?
Hasina's selection as party leader had no specific Islamic aspect. After the first 1996 election, she allied with JI against the BNP. She later allied with Ershad's Jatiya, which is Islamically oriented (Hashmi, p. 191). Although "position one" voices exist in Bangladesh, many Islamists support women's participation in parliament.

Mujib and Hasina have been accused of using Islam for political gain. Unlike Khaleda, Hasina did not at the start of her career habitually wear *hijab* but began doing so more often, especially after first visiting Mecca. Begum describes this as "overtures to Islamic signifiers," suggesting some insincerity (p. 279). Some people expressed concern about Mujib's "personal piety," questioning whether he would qualify for a Muslim funeral (Shehabuddin, p. 88). Mujib "peppered his speech with Islamic expressions" (Shehabuddin, p. 69). He took pride in "being Muslim," and in his nation being the second largest Muslim state (Riaz, p. 5). In 1974, Mujib took Bangladesh into the Organization of Islamic Conference, negotiating Pakistani recognition at the Lahore Summit. He was emphatic that "secularism" did not mean the absence of religion; "the people of Bengal will have the right to religion," he said. He certainly did not want to ban religion. Muslims, Hindus, Buddhists and Christians would each "observe their respective religions" (Shehabuddin, p. 68). Under Mujib, parliament opened with a reading from the Qur'an. This was followed by one from the holy books of Hindus, Buddhists and Christians, "four times, twice and once a week" respectively, reflecting the size of the three communities (p. 67). Since Zia, only the Qur'an is read. State media gave time to all four religions. Visiting Bangladesh, I notice that this practice continues. Now though, the call to prayer is always broadcast. Under Hasina, the AL presented itself as a safe guardian of Islam (Riaz, p. 6). Cynics see this as political expediency, but it could be sincere. Around 85 percent of Bangladeshis are Muslim, and they appreciate state recognition of this. However, in 2008, they overwhelmingly supported the AL's "non-communal" policy. If they wanted an Islamic state, they could have voted for this option, offered by numerous parties.

Hasina takes care to dress as people expect, which some see as an effort to "shed" her "pro-India and secularist image." Again, this could be regarded as insincere, but equally it could simply be to avoid causing unnecessary offense. Others criticize both women for failing to do their Islamic duty, namely to tell all women to veil (Shehabuddin, p. 171). Many rural women, targeted by secularist and Islamist agencies, navigate a middle path, neither spurning the former nor fully embracing the latter. Bangladesh would only Talibanize if law and order breaks down. Militants target non-Muslims, accusing them of spying, and NGOs as agents of Christian or secular hegemony. The 2008 election result indicates minimal support for JI, leaving the party too weak to exercise any veto power (Karlekar, p. 264). The controversial Vested Property Act (1974), used to confiscate Hindu land by declaring those who owned it state enemies, was finally repealed under Hasina in 2001, perhaps too hastily (Riaz, p. 8). The opposition was absent. Compensation was made available, although little has been paid.

Hasina's commitment to "economic development" based on "love of all and malice to none" (Āhameda, p. 255) sounds very much like Sufi *suhl-i-kul*, "peace with all." Hasina has visited the shrine at Ajmeer in India, where Hindus and Muslims pray. In 2003, my wife Rekha and I befriended the Minister of Religious Affairs in Khaleda's second government at a New York conference. His commitment to religious harmony was beyond question. What is developing in Bangladesh is a little like the English situation, where the established Church, which does have a special status, first gave other Christians space in the public square, then shared this with other faiths too.

What role did culture play?

Bengali, as opposed to Bangladeshi nationalism, sees Islam and culture as inseparable. The AL "values Islam as an integral part of culture" (Riaz, p. 6). That culture has a history of openness. Women entered the political domain in the nineteenth century, playing major roles in the language and independence struggles. They served in cabinets before Khaleda or Hasina were elected. At the very least, this laid a foundation for gender-equal developments.

Hasina's body is "a recovery effort, recovery of a secular, cultural, linguistic identity" (p. 279). Hasina usually wears cotton saris; Khaleda wears silk, never cotton. Hasina occasionally wears silk, but only the type that looks like woven cotton (local handicraft). Her saris are patterned, "rural scenes, angular ferns, wild flowers, birds in flight, fish Bangladeshis like to eat, and sometimes even her party's symbol." These are "folksy" images. Some of her saris have Bengali letters. All celebrate "secular, linguistic, Bengali nationalism" (p. 279). Khaleda's mode of dress stresses Muslim – possibly Arab or Persian – ancestry, purer Muslim heritage than Bengal's. Hasina's image is solidly Bengali. Yet as such, like Tagore and Nazrul, she embraces universal values (AL, p. 3).

What role did a dynastic tie play?

Hasina's family tie led to her choice as party leader. Senior leaders had been killed so few alternative candidates were available. Once elected, she set about restoring her father's legacy. Like Benazir, this has obsessed her. She finally saw trials begin in 1996 for the 1975 murders. Although the process faltered during Khaleda's second term, convictions eventually followed. Five of the killers were executed on January 28, 2010 after their appeal failed. This seems fair. Most of us would want to see our relatives' killers brought to justice. Hasina constantly refers to Mujib's sacrifice. As he did, she is willing to die for her country. In fact, people remain ambivalent regarding Mujib, which might suggest that her career does not depend on his legacy.

Once elected to office, she proved herself a savvy, astute political operator, making it puerile to reduce her career to "dynastic ties." Hasina's choice of designation, though, references her father, not her husband. She is "Sheikh Hasina," not "Begum Hasina Wajed"; a deliberate, political choice (Begum, pp. 277–8).

Does the post-colonial context have any bearing on Hasina's career?
Bias toward extra-parliamentary politics, border issues with India, separation from Pakistan, and the issue of Bengali versus Bangladeshi identity, have roots in the colonial past. So likewise does military intervention, carried over from the constant threat of force that backed civilian power during the Raj. The Raj was also authoritarian, offering little consultation until toward the very end. Bangladesh is a weak state, not yet a failed one. Border areas do, however, harbor militants (Karlekar, p. 199). Failing at the ballot box, Hasina needs to ensure that militancy does not succeed with the bullet.

Did gender play a significant role in Hasina's rise to power?
In Hasina's case, there was no male relative who could have taken power in her place. Gaining sympathy as one of Mujib's two surviving children certainly played a role in her own rise. As a woman, she could "soft sell" Mujib's image, playing on her survivor status, suffering for the nation that her father had founded (Thompson 2004, p. 38). In fact, as hinted earlier, people probably judge her on her record, not on who her father was. When she became PM, gender was less significant. Khaleda had preceded her. Female leadership was no longer a novelty. The choice was between two women.

Did gender play any role in Hasina's exercise of power?
The AL calls Hasina "daughter of democracy" (p. 4). Her peace and human-rights agenda and declared concern for consensus (AL, p. 2) fit what some expect from female leaders. Begum, though, describes her "rhetoric" as "combative." Khaleda's, by contrast, is "calm," her remarks less personal (p. 276). Hasina likes to be addressed as sir" (Thompson, p. 48). Having lost all, she has nothing to lose. Her vision is her father's, of a "*sonar bangla.*" By focusing on "grief and injustice," she sidesteps "her party's failure" (Begum, p. 274). Her commitment to women's empowerment is gender related. Her record speaks for itself. Bangladesh has moved toward eliminating all legal discrimination against women. Most of Ayub's liberal 1961 Ordinance remains in place. That had actually removed many inequalities. Men still divorce at will and without reason but grounds for wife-initiated divorce were extended. All divorces require court approval (derived

from Qur'an 4:35), though a man's cannot be revoked (Hossain 2003, p. 101). Law requires *one witness*, male or female (p. 99). Men must have prior permission from their existing wife or wives and from the Arbitration Council to marry polygynously. Spousal rape is a weak area. A woman's marriage to a non-Muslim is irregular, not illegal (p. 99). Judicial rulings permit a woman to remarry a former husband "without an interim marriage with a third party" and established entitlement to "maintenance for life" or until remarriage, rather than a one-off payment (p. 106). The law is close to "position two." The Law Commission decided against a common family law, based on vastly different religious traditions on marriage and divorce (Office of the Law Commission 2005). Problems associated with women's empowerment "are more social than legal ... inequalities in the law are hardly found" (Hossain 2003, p. 96). *Mahila Parishad*, the left-leaning women's organization, strongly supports a uniform code. Non-Muslim communities have their own Family Law.

Did Hasina promote women's issues and rights?
Hasina's career has significantly impacted women's rights. More women have entered politics, thousands at the local level.

Conclusion

Three times leader of the opposition, thus far, and winner of prizes and awards for peace, human rights, humanitarianism and democratic commitment, Hasina presides over her second government. She has already earned her place in history. As she attempts to move beyond adversarial politics, hopefully with the cooperation of opposition members, further democratic consolidation will help secure her legacy.

Chapter 6

Megawati Sukarnoputri and Indonesia

Image 6: Megawati Sukarnoputri.
Source: public domain.

Megawati gained her first parliamentary seat in 1987, the year after Hasina won hers. Like Çiller, she served in parliament before becoming party leader. Megawati was elected leader of the Indonesian Democratic Party (PDI) in 1993, the year Çiller became prime minister. Ousted as party leader by President Suharto, who manipulated all three legal parties in 1996, she was prevented from standing in the 1997 elections. Reforming her party after Suharto's resignation, she added "struggle" to the name (PDI-P), then won the largest block of seats in the 1999 election. Her opposition to Suharto was personal as well as political; he had overthrown her father, Sukarno, the state's founder.

From independence in 1945 until 1998, two men ruled Indonesia: her father until 1967, then Suharto. Her father's legacy was mixed. His China-inspired "guided democracy" concentrated autocratic authority in his hands, leaving the legislature to rubber stamp decrees. Megawati had a strong sense of destiny, as have others discussed in this book. Sukarno's memory was profoundly involved, linked with her mystical beliefs, derived from Indonesia's spiritual tradition. She had less need to vindicate her father's memory, since Suharto had started to do this himself, initially encouraging her political career. Nonetheless, she used her father's memory, whose image was less tarnished than Suharto's, to challenge the latter's leadership, a move he had not anticipated. In 1999, she failed to secure the presidency by a narrow margin, becoming vice-president instead. Abdurrahman Wahid, previously Megawati's ally, who won, was a last-minute candidate. Some Muslims voiced objection to a woman head of state. Wahid, by contrast, led the largest Muslim organization in the country.

In 2001, Wahid was impeached. Although a vice-president automatically succeeded in the event of a mid-term vacancy, Megawati was definitely parliament's choice, serving until October 20, 2004. She was the first and so far only Muslim woman to become head of a modern Muslim state, as opposed to head of government. Islamic objections to a woman leader expressed in 1999 were dropped. Re-election bids in 2004 and 2009, however, were unsuccessful, making her a one-term president. At the time of writing, she remains party leader but a return to office appears unlikely. Megawati's single term does not necessarily denote failure. The perception is that she made relatively few mistakes but did not do enough to earn re-election. Her performance did not meet expectations, a perception that may not be altogether accurate. In politics, though, perception is sometimes more important.

Many of the issues Megawati had to deal with, both in opposition to the previous regime and as president, are similar to those faced by the other four women in this study. As did three others, she opposed a dictatorship. Her party was one of only two allowed to contest seats against the governing Golkar, which up until 1999 always won an absolute majority, re-electing Suharto. Indonesia's military was closely allied with the government, so much so that while Suharto's was not technically a military regime, the distinction between this and a civilian one is dubious. The military had a built-in say in governance, more than in Turkey.

Like Benazir in Pakistan and Çiller in Turkey, Megawati had to deal with civilian control of the military. Separatism, closely linked with the role of the military, was also a major concern, again resembling Pakistan and Turkey. Foreign relations emerged as a dominant theme, especially relations with the USA, Australia and response to the "war on terror" following 9/11. Indonesia became center stage after October 12, 2002, the day of the Bali bombing.

The role of Islam and the emergence of Islamist parties in the wake of democratization resemble situations in other contexts discussed. In Bangladesh, where *Jamaat* had almost single-handedly represented political Islam before Ershad's resignation, there are now numerous Islamist parties. None enjoy electoral success. They do cause civil strife and instability. Some threaten state security. This is similar in Indonesia. The most successful religious parties, though, are more like Turkey's AKP, supporting the existing nature of the state but wanting greater recognition of Islamic values.

Indonesia is often described as "secular," which is inaccurate, since religious belief is enshrined in the constitution. When formed in 1973, the PDI brought together five non-Islamic parties, two of which had Christian affiliations. Approximately 9–10 percent of Indonesians are Christian. Indonesia is best thought of as a state that officially embraces religious pluralism, inviting parallels with Bangladesh's 1972 constitution and with Awami League philosophy. This understanding of religion's role evolved within the developing notion of Indonesian nationalism, which some say had to be invented. Benedict Anderson's comment that, "Indonesia" was "imagined" in the early twentieth century (p. 11, n4) was cited earlier. Each of the contexts has had to develop national identities in the post-colonial space. In tracing the political background to Megawati's political debut, discussion focuses on the origin of the idea of Indonesia, on religion's role, the relationship between religion and culture, and whether gender-equal-friendly currents exist. This section, following the literature review, begins with a table of military–civilian periods, complicated by the military's constitutional role.

Literature Survey

Biographical information is mainly from the *Encyclopædia Britannica* online and McIntyre (2005). McIntyre was especially useful for Megawati's relationship with her father and for her early political career, as well as events surrounding her presidency. He wrote a small monograph on Megawati in

1997, the year after she was ousted as party chair. Also, on her rise to the vice-presidency followed by the presidency, much data was found in Soesastro *et al.* (2003) and Fic (2003). The former was written a few months into her presidency. Contributors considered the challenges she faced and likely directions and actions she might take. In addition to the economy (suffering from the 1997 East Asian crises), militant Islam, foreign affairs, separatism, constitutional reform and asserting civilian authority over the military were among issues discussed. Already called the "do-nothing president," the consensus was that she would last her term but would probably not earn another, which proved to be the case.

Fic also covers the circumstances surrounding Megawati's election in some detail but sets her career in a broader historical context: the history of Indonesia as a space that traditionally embraced religious and cultural pluralism. He discusses how this fared under the first two post-independence regimes. Fic was one of my main sources for reconstructing this narrative. I also refer to Geertz's anthropological research.

On the role of the military, I consulted several experts including Sudarsono (2007) and Kingsbury (2003). Kingsbury tracks the role of the "military" in Indonesian space back to earlier imperial entities, suggesting a similar historical role to that of the Ottoman Empire. Like the Ottomans, the empires that pre-existed Indonesia depended on the military for their existence, and to maintain control across Indonesia's culturally diverse and geographically fragmented space. Kingsbury argues that this remains true for the modern nation-state. Of course, the name "Indonesia" was coined in the early twentieth century, so the space that Indonesia now occupies had different names.

On gender, I consulted Blackburn. As Shehabuddin did in her book on gender in Bangladesh, Blackburn surveys progress since independence, with some data on the pre-independence situation. She ends with Megawati's presidency. An interesting similarity emerges between Indonesia and Turkey. Both entered their modern periods granting women legal equality but they also developed a state-formatted gender ideology that discouraged women's political participation. Arguably, ideology rather than cultural and religious aspects hindered women's empowerment. Indonesia, with the world's nineteenth highest GDP, is the only one of the four states to score "free" on the freedom index. As in Turkey's case, the percentage of women in parliament should be higher, given these factors. Yet, in the context of the four states, Indonesia is third. On the other hand, women's representation has risen, as shall be seen. Megawati, like Çiller, did not prioritize gender. However, the fact that she was president appears to have positively impacted gender equality.

Finally, the case study on Indonesia by Parawansa in the 2005 IDEA handbook, *Women in Parliament*, supplemented some of the above material.

Political Background

Alternating Civilian and Military Rule in Indonesia

Civilian Rule and Military Interventions
First president, Sukarno 1945–67
1949 end of "union" with the Netherlands
1945–57 limited presidential power; first general election, 1955; president elected by MPR every five years; until 1999, this was by acclamation – 1999 was the first CONTESTED election
Attempted coups 1948, 1956, 1965

Martial Law declared March 14, 1957; ended May 19, 1963; modified form of martial law renewed September 1964, giving regional military commanders power to impose emergency measures, abolished 1967

Guided democracy (1957–65) (limited civilian governance)

1960 – military allocated 75 seats in the People's Representative Council (DPR), plus 155 in the MPR (People's Consultative Assembly) where the 75 also sat

Military-backed coup: March 11, 1966
Second president, Suharto 1967–87
Limited civilian political participation; government GOLKAR Party plus two opposition parties; military seats in parliament and cabinet
Martial Law in Aceh, 1989–98

Interim Regime
Third president, Habibie 1998–9 (former vice-president; resigned when the MPR rejected the annual accountability report

Democratic Restoration, 1999
(Multi-party politics; new constitution restricts presidency to two terms, directly elected from 2004; military seats reduced to 38; from 2004, no appointed MPR members)

Fourth president, Abdurrahman Wahid 1999–2001; impeached

Fifth president, Megawati 2001–4

Martial Law in Aceh, May 2003–May 2004; State of Emergency May 2004–May 2005

Sixth president, Susilo Bambang Susilo 2004–9; 2009 end of military seats

The modern nation-state of Indonesia covers over 17, 000 islands in an archipelago stretching southeast from the tip of Malaysia. Spice attracted traders to the islands, which became places where peoples and cultures met and mingled. Buddhist and Hindu elements encountered indigenous nature-based religious beliefs, producing a local synthesis. The Tantric forms of Hinduism and Buddhism took root between the seventh and thirteenth centuries when the Srivijaya dynasty ruled much of the archipelago. The Srvijaya, who enjoyed exclusive trading rights with China, held loose sway over their territory, more by cooperation than force. Toward the end of this period, Muslims began to arrive, spreading their faith. They did so by preaching Sufi beliefs, much as Sufis had evangelized Bengal before any Muslim conqueror arrived. Like Malaysia, Muslims never invaded Indonesia from elsewhere, although local dynasties did expand territorially.

Map 10: Indonesia – comprising over 17,000 islands.

From the thirteenth century to the beginning of the sixteenth, the Majapahit ruled a large empire. The rise of independent sultanates and the arrival of Europeans ended their rule. Under the Majapahit, a conscious effort to create harmony saw regional religions and cultures represented in court ritual (Fic, p. 148). The Portuguese came first (1512) but the Dutch emerged as the dominant power, after competing with the British in the early seventeenth century. From 1603, the Dutch East India Company's rule gradually spread across the archipelago, although it took until the early twentieth century for the colony's borders to resemble those of modern Indonesia. East Timor remained Portuguese until 1975. The Dutch East India Company was wound up in 1800, after which Holland ruled directly.

It took 200 years after the end of the Majapahit Empire in the sixteenth century for Islam to establish itself as the majority religion (Fic, p. 149). Just as Buddhism and Hinduism meshed in with pre-existing beliefs, so did Islam. Many Sufi preachers came from India. Espousing "life in poverty," they taught "a complex syncretic theosophy" that was "already familiar to the Indonesians." Their "magical, charismatic authority" enabled them to marry daughters of Indonesian nobility, giving their children the "prestige of royal blood" (p. 151). Tradition names eight saints (walis) among early evangelists. Fic and others describe a process that saw Muslims trying to Islamize Indonesia, while Indonesia, especially Java, tried to absorb and subordinate Islam to itself. Fic argues that a tradition of pluralism and tolerance of diversity developed. Honoring all faiths, this tended to find common ground, rather than elevate one tradition at the cost of others.

Anthropologist Clifford Geertz, based on fieldwork in the early 1950s, described three strands of religion in Indonesia: one, santri, represents an attempt to establish the Islam of the Prophet and the early caliphs (1968, p. 69). Often encountered in coastal areas, this feeds off contact with the Arab world. Geertz described another strand as "prijari," a synthesis of Islam with Indic beliefs strong among the traditional elite, many of whom entered the civil service under the Dutch. The third strand, "abangan,". is more interested in ritual and "well-being" than belief. It flourished among rural non-elites.

Majority Indonesian Islam is a form of adat, or local tradition compatible with Islam. This emphasizes such positive aspects as dispute resolution and consensus, avoiding unnecessary conflict. Adat involves "social obligations, etiquette and rituals" that "create then perpetuate harmony and order," which is "valued above all else" (Forshee, p. 37). Santrinization is happening but has more to do with ritual than politics

(Azra, p. 63). "Islamic belief and ritual is one thing," says Azra, "political behavior is another" (p. 64). The majority of Indonesians are often described – as are Bangladeshi and Turkish Muslims – as *cultural* Muslims.

For many, Islam is viewed as a *din* (religion), which does not depend on the state for vitality and existence. There are "no convincing signs that the majority of Muslims support the idea of formal Islamic politics" (p. 64). Fic refers to the belief that religion in Indonesia is part of a wheel of change (*kolomongso*), so that Islam is not the final form but a stage in a process (p. 213). This could leave scope for the type of evolved Islam preached by M. M Ṭāhā, whose idea of an Islamic state would make no distinction between Muslims and other "believers." Law would be wholly consistent with international human rights, derived from the ethical spirit and "intent" of the Qur'an. Or, as Muhammad Iqbal taught, the finality of the Prophet's message can be seen as potential, residing in its eternal validity, which should not be confused with current understanding. When we refuse to change, which is one of God's "greatest signs," we "immobilize what is essentially mobile" (1998, p. 256). So-called "cultural" Muslims do not, however, polarize *din* and *dunya* (world) into separate spiritual and mundane realms. They want the former to permeate the latter, informing every aspect of life, but do not think that a state's Islamic *bone fides* depends on implementing ninth-century interpretations of law.

The Independence Movement: Sukarno's Leadership

Sukarno (1901–70) emerged as a leader of the independence movement, forming the Indonesian National Party (PNI) in 1927. A year later, a National Women's Federation was formed. The membership was mainly ex-patriot but some elite Indonesian women also joined (Blackburn, p. 89). Initially, this was part of the wider suffragette movement. Dutch women had gained the vote in 1919. Some in the colony promoted female education, taking steps to protect Indonesian women, but most Dutch placed economic interests over any other concerns (Blackburn, p. 17). As the nationalist movement developed, the Women's Federation shifted focus from rights to aiding the independence struggle (p. 18). Since elected bodies had little power under colonial rule, many women saw no reason to dissipate their energy, giving the independence struggle priority (p. 91). Some conservative religious groups did argue that women were not yet ready for a "role in public life" but, in 1938, four women were elected to municipal councils. At the time, they could stand but could not vote. The vote was granted in 1941 (p. 91). Publications at this time stressed an "idealized version of Indonesian womanhood, influenced by modernist Islam and Western, middle-class modernity" (p. 19).

From 1942 to 1945, the Japanese occupied Indonesia. Under occupation, "women's organizations were unable to make any demands on the state or to organize independently" (p. 22). A tradition developed of subordinating everything to the nationalist struggle. Sukarno collaborated with the Japanese, who promised independence. They helped set up a Provisional Committee to write a constitution. In 1945, Sukarno declared Indonesia's independence, becoming president, acclaimed by the Provisional Committee.

Refusing to recognize this, the Dutch set about attempting to reclaim their colony. Allied forces under Admiral Mountbatten landed to oversee Japanese withdrawal. An armed struggle for control of the islands began. Initially, the Indonesian militia confronted British and Dutch troops. The British then supported Indonesia's independence, calling for a diplomatic resolution, strongly advocated by the UN. In 1949, the Dutch yielded, recognizing Indonesia's sovereignty as the UN's 60th member. For a year, Indonesia was a federation of 16 states. In 1950, this was replaced by a unitary state. The first elections took place in 1955, with no single party achieving a majority. The PNI and an Islamic party, the Masyumi, both won 57 seats in the 257-seat People's Representative Assembly (DPR). Next largest was the Nahdatul Ulema (NU) with 45, followed by the Communist Party (PKI) with 39. The NU, founded in 1926, supported Sukarno during the independence struggle. With a membership of approximately 40 million, it is now one of the largest Muslim organizations in the world. On December 1, 1956, Mohammad Hatta (1902–80) resigned as vice-president, protesting Sukarno's increasing authoritarianism. There was no vice-president until 1973, when Suharto appointed the ninth Sultan of Jogyakarta, who remained in office until 1978.

Islam and the Indonesian State

When the 1945 constitution was written, some Muslims wanted to insert, after the principle of belief in Allah, that Muslims would be governed by *Shari'ah*. Sukarno and his deputy, Mohammad Hatta, rejected this in favor of placing all religions "on an equal footing" while prohibiting "atheism" (Fic, p. 159). Hatta preferred the federal system as a way to preserve regional religious and cultural identity. Sukarno preferred a "strongly centralized government." Fic suggests that although Pancasila, the state ideology, embraced pluralism in theory, in practice the state was too centralized, too anxious to create a single Indonesian identity, to permit genuine pluralism. All political parties had to accept Pancasila in order to operate. Some Islamic parties, such as the NU, stood – as in Turkey – for Islamic values and space for Islam in the public sphere without calling for an Islamic state. Masyumi was more inclined to argue for a full-blown Islamic system, campaigning for this in the 1950s. From the late 1950s, the militant Darul Islam controlled large areas of Aceh, demanding an Islamic state. It was defeated in 1965. Aceh was given greater autonomy in 1962, including permission to implement aspects of *Shari'ah*. Separatist activities continued in Aceh, where Megawati declared martial law in 2003.

Sukarno and Suharto took harsh measures against individuals and organizations that wanted to establish an Islamic state (Azra, p. 59). Their centralizing policies "grossly violated the multifaceted pluralistic heritage of the country" and the principles of "representative government" (Fic, p. 177). Late in his regime, Suharto adopted a "more conciliatory tone" toward Islam, setting up the Indonesian Association of Muslim Intellectuals (ICMI) under Habibie in 1989. This recognized Islam as a "cultural" rather than "political phenomenon." Habibie had a reputation for "personal piety," and what Azra calls a "honeymoon" period followed between the state and political Islam. This saw an increase in the number of Muslims at the expense of Christians in the cabinet (p. 61). Islamic banking was permitted. Fic describes this as a "re-confessionalization" of national life, further compromising traditional pluralism (p. 176).

Sukarno was anti-colonial, pro-Marxist and authoritarian. Increasingly, he looked to the Communist Party and the military for allies. Inspiration and aid were mainly from China, although the Soviets extended a substantial line of credit. To some degree, Cold War realities impacted all four states. Pakistan lurched from a China orientation under Bhutto to a Western one under Zia. Bangladesh leaned toward the Soviets under Mujib before aligning with the West and with the Arab world under subsequent leaders. Rivalry between the left and right in Turkey led to military intervention. On March 14, 1957, Sukarno declared martial law. By then, newspapers were being censured, critics removed from office and dissidents jailed (Blackburn, p. 24). In November 1958, General Nasution articulated the concept of *dwi-fungsi* (dual function): that as well as defending the state, the military is an active component of the nation's social life. Since it played a crucial role in establishing the state, it was entitled to "a role in its political life" (Sudarsono, p. 151). Sudarsono dates this conviction from the formation of the state. Kingsbury sees antecedents in pre-colonial times, arguing that Indonesia, like the Majapahit, cannot "maintain territorial integrity" without military-imposed unity (p. 12).

Both the Srvijaya and the Majapahit have been called "mandala empires." Strong at the center, they were weaker at the periphery, lacking fixed borders, which defines modern states. According to Kingsbury, these earlier imperial entities differ from contemporary Indonesia, which is a unitary state, because they were "fluid and expansionist" (p. 17). This type of state had "some legitimacy" at the time, since it was the "commonly recognized order," but it does not work with modern states.

The political system in place from 1957 until 1966 was called "guided democracy." Like Atatürk in Turkey, Sukarno did not think Indonesia ready for full-blown democracy, requiring nation building first. Indonesia lacked direction. Sukarno would steer it along the right path. The large number of parties, none of which had a parliamentary majority, was a problem. To give direction, Sukarno centered power in his own hands, ruling by decree. In 1959, he dissolved the elected Assembly, replacing this by two appointed bodies. The Peoples Consultative Assembly (MPR) became the highest authority, charged with formulating policy and appointing the president. The MPR is a "sovereign body" (Kingsbury 2002, p. 59). In theory, there was no party, but the military sponsored its own "functional group," later known as Golkar, which was represented in the MPR. About 25 percent of seats went to the PKI. The military soon divided into pro- and anti-communist factions, creating friction. Military personnel were appointed regional governors as well as to diplomatic and other important posts. One-third of Sukarno's new cabinet was military. This trend continued until democratic restoration.

In July 1963, the MPR declared Sukarno president for life. With the provisions of September 1964 (known as the Pepelrada regulations), the military gained extensive emergency power in the regions, enabling them to impose curfews, detain citizens and implement other restrictions. Sukarno, who told the USA to "go to hell with its aid," regarded the UN and its specialist agencies as stooges of neo-colonialism. He withdrew from the UN in 1965, after Malaysia's election to the Security Council. In response, China increased aid (Reynolds, p. 269).

Sukarno's Fall, Suharto's Rise

On October 1, 1965 a series of events led to Sukarno's overthrow. First, a group of officers calling themselves the 30th of September Movement, claiming to have Sukarno under their protection, assassinated six generals. This was denounced as a communist coup. In riots that followed, thousands of communists were killed. Suharto, then a major general, responded. Taking command of loyal troops, he secured authority from Sukarno to restore law and order. By October 2, he was in control. By March 1966, he was effectively running the country, having removed General Nasution, a rival, from the cabinet, then a year later placing Sukarno under house arrest. Initially, Suharto was reluctant to remove Sukarno from office, content to exercise authority with Sukarno as a ceremonial figure. Finally, he charged Sukarno with complicity in the so-called communist coup. Under house arrest, Sukarno died in 1970.

Suharto's New Order was all about development. Sukarno might be father of the nation; but Suharto would "father" its development. He looked to "development" to legitimize his rule, to what can be called "performance" (Soesastro, p. 5). In the end, it was lack of performance that brought his regime down. He was not wholly responsible for this, since the East Asian economic meltdown of 1997 led to rampant inflation and negative GDP. Initially, he lowered inflation, denationalized industries and attracted foreign investment. Anti-communist, he banned the PKI and shifted toward rapport with the West, receiving aid from the USA and other governments. Various governments were sympathetic to the military's political role, convinced that "Indonesia's civilian political parties could not be relied on to guarantee stability in politics or for foreign investors" (Sudarsono, p. 152). Successive US administrations supported Suharto, although officially Indonesia was non-aligned. He did improve Indonesia's strained relations with the United Nations, rejoining as early as April 1966, when Sukarno was still nominally president. He was instrumental in forming ASEAN (Association of South East Asian Nations) in 1967. Following the return to the UN, Indonesia served on the Security Council for the first time from 1975–6. Stress on state unity and centralization led to repressive measures against separatism – a factor in seven regions – and to widespread human-rights abuses. There is little doubt that, like Pakistan under Zia, aid money was used to repress and oppress, even to weaken democracy.

Toward the end of Suharto's regime, revelations about the extent of corruption and the manipulation of statistics on poverty reduction shed new light on his alleged positive performance. From 1973, he allowed three parties: GOLKAR, the party of government, and two in opposition, formed by amalgamation of all other parties. One opposition party was the Indonesian Democratic Party (PDI) (including the PNI); the other was the United Development Party (PPP), the more Islamic of the two. Fic describes the PDI as standing in continuity with the ancient tradition of openness and pluralism, what he calls Indonesia's "primordial values," to which Megawati is committed. "Inspired by the heritage of pluralism," the PDI "tries to bring into a broad national coalition the diverse components of Indonesian society today – religious, ethnic, cultural and regional" (p. 193). Golkar never won less than 62 percent of the vote in all five elections (1971–97). It was in this context that Megawati made her political debut, during the 1987 election, April 23.

Although elections were held in 1971, then every five years, Suharto did little more than preserve the "trappings of constitutional democracy" (Vatikiotis, p. 27). He later wrote about the need to balance democracy with stability. In his view, keeping up an appearance of democracy was sufficient. One commentator wrote, "In the strictly defined sense in which the term is employed in Indonesia" democracy "was respected" (p. 26). He stood unopposed for election as president – by acclamation – every five years.

The Military and Government in Indonesia

In 1966, the military were awarded 75 seats in the legislature (DPR) and 155 in the MPR (where all DPR members also sat). By 1973, 34 percent of cabinet ministers were from the military, while governors and ambassadors were 70 percent and 44.4 percent respectively (Rinakit, p. 45). Before long, it was difficult to distinguish between the military's role as "guarantor of state security" and as "protector of the Suharto family and crony businesses" (Sudarsono, p. 156)). The military was allowed to operate within the commercial sector, depending less and less on government. When Suharto resigned, only 25–30 percent of the military's budget came from government (Sudarsono, p. 156). This degree of independence made it difficult for government to exercise real control over officers or soldiers serving under them, which has parallels with the military's business involvement in Pakistan. Prussia, it was said, was not so much a state with an army but an army with a state; similarly, the military's entanglement in Indonesia's politics raises questions about the state's civilian or military nature (Kingsbury 2003,

p. 6). The size of the MPR fluctuated over the years, from 700 to 1,000 and back again. The military became Suharto's "praetorian guard," although its power peaked in the period 1967–78 (Wanandi, p. 93). Advancement in the military was only possible for those close to Suharto, or to his son-in-law, a general.

Gender under Sukarno and Suharto

The 1945 constitution granted equal rights for women and men. Culturally, Indonesia has an interesting gender history. Some areas, such as West Sumatra, have matrilineal systems, where husbands are "guests" in their wives' homes and women inherit property (Blackburn, p. 8). Some areas do not clearly distinguish between "male and female" and have "fluid notions of sexuality." In southwest Sulawesi, transvestite priests (*bisso*) form a third gender (p. 9). While Islam imposed "rules relating to how men and women should behave," in practice "compromises" were reached and matrilineal practices continued (p. 9). Whether women were treated as equal depended on the ethnic and religious group to which they belonged (p. 85). Sukarno developed a state-formatted gender ideology, as Atatürk did in Turkey. This was part of inventing the concept of "Indonesian-ness," since the country had not previously existed (p. 85). Sukarno's gender ideology subordinated women's issues to the cause of national unity, the fight against neo-colonial forces. During guided democracy, "almost all notions of the rights of citizens ended." The "pendulum swung" toward "citizen's obligations" (p. 98). Women were to work for the state's goals.

In the 1955 election, 7 percent of successful candidates were women but none served in any cabinets during the 1950s (p. 23). Women were drawn into nationalist activities, such as taking part in "military style drills" to prepare for defending the state against "neo-colonial oppressors, especially connected with the struggle for Irian Jaya and against the formation of Malaysia" (p. 98). War was waged with Malaysia over Borneo from 1962–5. Holland retained Western New Guinea until 1962. After a brief spell of independence, it was occupied by Indonesia, becoming Irian Jaya. Cynics might see this as colonial oppression. A separatist movement quickly emerged. East Timor was also occupied after Portugal's withdrawal (1972). Women's role was to maintain social stability as mothers and wives (p. 25).

Under Suharto, the concept of "*ibuism*" developed. Mother (*ibu*) and Father (*bapak*) were central concepts, vested with the responsibility of caring for the population. The former were tasked with practical functions, "without any prospect of reward except through their husbands," the latter "enjoyed access to power and privilege" (p. 25). During the International Decade for Women (1975–85), a Ministry for Women was created (1978). A junior post, this saw the first woman minister, although outside the cabinet until 1983. After that, the post still "lacked a department" (p. 26). Wives' organizations began to dominate the Women's Federation (p. 25), an elite organization, made up of "wives and daughters" of members of the regime (p. 101). At the village level, women had "hazy notions" about the state they were meant to serve. Elite women had civil pride but directed this toward the local community and family, not the nation (p. 98). Under the New Order, women were defined as citizens with "gendered responsibilities." The nuclear family was the model, the "foundation stone of the larger state" (pp. 25; 99). The Marriage Law of 1974 allowed co-wives and easier divorce for men (p. 87). Islamic law was restricted to domestic matters, disregarded in areas regarded as "public," such as criminal law (p. 87).

Constitutionally, men and women were declared equal. Ideologically, women were seen as a "subordinate group," which undermined their rights. The New Order purged the women's movement of leftists, eliminating "critical elements" (p. 101). Suharto's daughter, Siti Hardiyanti Rukmana was vice-president of GOLKAR from 1993 and a cabinet minister during 1998. Under the system of controlled elections, women comprised 7.8 percent of parliament from 1977–82, 6.3 percent from 1982–7, then 13 percent from 1987–92 and 12.5 percent from 1992–7. Megawati was a member of parliament from 1987 until 1997, when she was prevented from standing. From 1997 until the end of Suharto's regime, the percentage was 10.8 percent. During this period, those nominated by parties to stand for the legislature, men and women, were first vetted by the government. With the stress on development, women's best contribution was seen as having fewer children (Blackburn, p. 166).

Indonesia is quite often described as a patriarchal culture. After the independence struggle, during which "women played a major role ... patriarchal values broadly reemerged, as did the perception that the role of women was to manage the household" (Parawansa, p. 82). However, the actual situation is multifaceted and complex. In the 1980s, a large number of male and female homosexuals "came out" (Blackburn, p. 139). Alongside patriarchal attitudes and definite ideas about male–female roles, some more fluid attitudes exist, "avoiding a strict categorization into male/female, heterosexual/homosexual." There is a tradition of male transvestitism in "religion, the arts and prostitution" in Java and South Sumatra (p. 139). Pre-colonial history saw female village heads and regnant queens. Mernissi (in Mernissi and Lakeland 1993) mentions four who succeeded each other in "the state of Atjeh between 1641 and 1699" (North Sumatra) (p. 109). The NU, which has a women's section, supports reproductive rights as "compatible with Islam" (p. 166).

Blackburn describes domestic violence as an issue, one that did not get much exposure until recently. Often, wife beating and even rape is regarded as a "personal" problem, not "to be resolved at a public level." In addition, women distrust the "police and judiciary." Some even see male sexual excess as natural (p. 195). This is similar to comments by a prominent Bangladeshi woman *Jamaat* member, Begum Rokaya Ansar, for whom men are "under constant visual assault from immodestly clad women." In this view, rape would not happen if women did not tempt men (Shehabuddin, p. 105). In the 1998 riots, there was large-scale gang rape of Chinese women. Chinese have been victimized in Indonesia since independence, despite the national motto *"Bhinneka Tunggal Ika"* (Unity in Diversity). Public acknowledgement of these rapes led to wider debate about "all kinds of violence against women" (p. 195).

Due to the authoritarian nature of the state between 1949 and 1999, neither men nor women had much opportunity to take part in genuine democracy (Shehabuddin, p. 222). As in Turkey, currents in the culture conducive to women's empowerment can be identified. The independence movement granted women legal equality in many areas. The state-formatted ideology then channeled women's energies away from politics toward nation building. Fic refers to belief in the mythical Ratu Kidul as "holding sway over all leaders," anointing their succession. She protects the nation's "destiny from eternity to eternity" (p. 213). This interesting tradition pictures ultimate authority in female guise.

Megawati: Political Debut

Megawati is usually described as a reluctant politician, a housewife until her debut in 1987. Like Hasina, she had some involvement in student politics. Sukarnoputri means "daughter of Sukarno." She was born in 1947, Sukarno's second child. McIntyre's investigation of her upbringing questions, to a degree, the "reluctant" hypothesis. He describes her as having had a closer relationship with her father than did her brother Guntur (born 1944), who was his "mother's son," which Suharto understood. Guntur, who bore a striking resemblance to his father, was popular with the PDI. However, the role of "symbolizing and vindicating" his father did not attract him, so he "stayed out of the public eye." In 1954, his mother left Sukarno after he married another wife (p. 142), Guntur went with her and had nothing to do with any of his father's other wives. Megawati's sister, Rachmawati, rebuked her for joining the PDI, arguing that Sukarno's legacy was above politics. Megawati, she said, was wrong to exploit Sukarno's name by identifying with a single party (p. 153). It was perhaps because Megawati wore the "mantle of family loyalty" lightly that she gave it "more flexible expression." Guruh (born 1953), a popular musician, expressed leftist sympathies, saying that he followed his father's politics and wanted to serve the poor. In 1992, when he agreed to stand for election, he indicated a willingness to challenge for the presidency.

When Megawati chose to study agriculture at college, Sukarno said she had decided to help him with the crises that faced the country resulting from a poor rice harvest the previous year (p. 145). Sukarno appears to have anticipated an active role for her in "adult life" (p. 145). He took pleasure in women's prominence in "traditional society," which he saw as superior to colonial times: "before the Dutch came here, we had a large number of female village heads, brothers and sisters" as well as "Queens and female heroes." South Sulawesi had queens before the Dutch arrived, he said, as did other regions. Mernissi refers, as cited above, to four queens of North Sumatra in the early seventeenth century.

Returning home one day from university, Megawati saw her belongings being loaded onto a truck outside the presidential palace (p. 146). Her father had been ousted. Her social circumstances changed dramatically. She and Guntur both discontinued university. Because of Sukarno's second wife's presence, Guntur was reluctant to visit Suharto, who was increasingly ill and under house arrest. Sukarno described him as "not as close as he could be" (p. 159). In contrast, one story suggests that Megawati was closer to her father yet also had an ability to distance herself from aspects of his legacy. When Suharto told her that the Assembly wanted to declare him president for life, since the people wanted this, she counseled that perhaps, given his age, it would be prudent to consider other candidates. Had he not trained cadres for just this purpose (p. 181)?

In 1970, Megawati returned to higher education but left before completing her course. That year, she married an air force officer, Mas Pacul, for whom she bore two children. She was at Suharto's bedside when he died (p. 147). On January 22, 1971 her husband died in a plane crash. Already, she had a reputation for keeping silent, so little is known of her feelings. However, erratic behavior followed. A year later, she eloped with an Egyptian diplomat. After "one and a half hours" of marriage, she was "somehow reclaimed by her family" and again did not "say much at the time" (p. 148). In March 1973 she married Taufiq Kiemas, who owned several gas stations. He had been active in the PNI (p. 151). From 1979, she ran a flower shop with some friends. Otherwise, she settled down to life as a homemaker.

In 1987, Megawati and Taufiq agreed to stand for seats under the PDI banner. She was approached by the PDI, which was interested in using Sukarno's "name to attract support." Guntur, Megawati, her husband and Guruh were invited to run. Only Megawati and Taufiq agreed (Eklöf, p. 88). Guruh followed in 1992, winning seats in subsequent elections. Party General Secretary, Nico Daryanto, said that the PDI wanted them not because "they were Sukarno's children" but for other capacities, such as their ability to speak to the masses (pp. 148–9). The possibility of a Sukarno relative standing was first explored for the 1982 election (Eklöf, p. 88). That year, the PDI was permitted to use Sukarno symbols, although no family members stood. Then, only Sugmawati (Megawati's sister) approved the idea. Later, she withdrew support, arguing that the PDI was insufficiently radical, "too unwilling to challenge the government" to fly Sukarno's banner (Eklöf, p. 89).

Although Megawati and her husband stood as opposition candidates, they had Suharto's support. He thought it good publicity for Sukarno's daughter to run, presumably as a token of political openness (East and Thomas, p. 233). In October 1986, a few weeks after sanctioning Megawati and her husband as candidates, he declared Sukarno and Hatta "Heroes of the Revolution." This honored Sukarno's role *until 1945* but did not endorse his *later conduct*. On the one hand, Suharto sanctioned the PDI's "use of Sakarno's image in its election campaign." On the other, he "tried to control and co-opt the Sukarno symbol" (Eklöf, p. 89). Earlier, he gave the Sukarno family several businesses, understanding that in return they would stay out of politics (Schmetzer 2001). The rehabilitation process had actually started even earlier, in 1978, when Suharto renovated Sukarno's tomb. Critics suggest this was to divert attention from his even more grandiose scheme to construct a lavish mausoleum for himself (Eklöf, p. 100). He may have wanted to strengthen the PDI as the main opposition, as opposed to the Islamic-oriented PPP (p. 87).

Megawati and her husband were both elected. Critics point to lack of political experience. Later, she said, "I say to those people who belittle housewives, it doesn't mean a housewife does not understand politics" (Schmetzer 2001). Very soon, she developed a reputation for silent protest against Suharto's regime; as Wahid said: "She expresses her protest in a silent way ... she leads by not doing anything." It was enough that she was not "being co-opted by the government" (McIntyre 2005, p. 163). Her growing opposition to Suharto was expressed more by what she *did not say* than by outspoken criticism. She "took little part in public debates and was often absent from legislative sittings" (Aspinall, p. 145).

In 1992, Megawati won re-election. Guruh, who stood for and won a seat that year, was much more vocal and critical of the government. Posters of Sukarno, allowed in 1982 and 1987, were disallowed in 1992. People, though, saw Sukarno's image through his children. The ban underscored the "impression that Sukarno was a symbol of opposition to the government" (Eklöf, p. 151). Suharto may have regretted his decision to allow their entry into politics.

In July 1993, the government refused to accept Soerjadi as PDI Chair, which led to a second leadership election that December. Megawati was persuaded to stand in a three-way contest. Her emergence as candidate is something of a puzzle. Suddenly, she was at the center of a "hysterical campaign." Hundreds of supporters lined the streets outside, praying and fasting for her success, even sleeping there (Aspinall, p. 145). It was "clear that she had the overwhelming support of the PDI grass roots." Some explain this sudden popularity as a return of enthusiasm for Sukarno. McIntyre thinks that her gender played a role, comparing her with Aung San Suu Kyi, Sheikh Hasina and Benazir Bhutto, who also appeared more or less from nowhere as "avenging nemesis" to "protect or redeem" their father's legacies (pp. 139–40).

Megawati owes much to her ability to "symbolize her much-loved father" (p. 140). With other female leaders, she also symbolized "purity." She was not the head of the family, of "a gang" or of a "conglomerate" (Aspinall, p. 141, citing Benedict Anderson). Nor was she a general. When she entered the hall or rose to speak, she was "mobbed." If an opponent tried to "obstruct proceedings they were jeered" (Aspinall, p. 146). Guruh, more charismatic than Megawati, intended to stand for leader, then withdrew, supporting his sister instead, saying that she symbolized their father's spirit (McIntyre 2005, p. 140). "Despite a wooden speaking style," her "statements on social issues, economic reform and an end to political and political bullying touched a deep chord in the nationalist public." People saw "in her sweet suffering a symbol of their own isolation" (Hefner, p. 175).

Rather as Benazir did, Megawati positioned herself as champion of the oppressed against a corrupt ruler. Supporters referred to her as "mother earth" (Thompson 2004, p. 42), which might draw on deep mythical notions about the feminine nature of Indonesia's protector spirit. After she failed to secure the presidency in 1999, supporters threatened to rampage around Jakarta. She appealed to them, saying, "I am your mother. You are my children. I want you to go home" (Gouda, p. 204). Believing that *karma* would lead her to the presidency, she was unwilling to act against Wahid in any way that might attract karmic penalty. Suharto had suffered from ousting her father; she was not about to repeat this error (Soesastro, pp. 4–5).

Challenging Suharto

In October 1995, "seven PDI branches in central Java" issued a statement calling on Megawati to stand for the presidency at the earliest opportunity. Until now, Suharto probably had little real reason to see her challenge as very serious. No one had yet stood against him. Now, not only was Megawati possibly a rival but Habibie was also known to be thinking about a challenge. Golkar had the majority of seats, while Suharto personally appointed many members, including the military contingent. Yet seeking a sixth term, he might not survive a contest. By not rejecting the branches' call for her candidacy, Megawati tacitly indicated acceptance. Suharto engineered a way to prevent her candidacy: Habibie would get the vice-presidency.

In May 1996, Suharto caused a PDI congress to be convened. Attended by anti-Megawati elements, they obediently re-elected Soerjadi, now acceptable. Megawati refused to recognize this, continuing to occupy party HQ. To "roars of approval" from the assembled crowd, she declared that she was the party's chair and would fight to restore democracy (McIntyre 2005, p. 166). She took out a phalanx of law suits against the government. A mass students' movement began to organize. Suharto, though, managed to win back, at this point, one Megawati ally, Wahid, who had known Megawati since her youth. Grandson of the NU's founder and a descendant of a "legendary Sultan of Pajang," Wahid now led the movement (Fic, p. 203). A scholar, teacher and politician, millions of Indonesians saw him as a saint (*wali*). In that capacity, he was known as *Gus Dur*. Although Wahid had earlier supported Suharto, since 1993 he had identified himself with the opposition. Consequently, Suharto now fomented rivalry in the NU, which he promised to end if Wahid persuaded Megawati to drop some suits. He agreed, endorsing Suharto's presidency (McIntyre 2005, p. 172).

On July 27, police (then part of the military) raided PDI HQ, killing five Megawati supporters. She still submitted a list of candidates for approval, which was rejected. Unable to stand in 1997, she could not contest the presidency. Suharto won a sixth term, with Habibie as vice-president. Hundreds of PDI members, including Taufiq, were accused of having had PKI ties (McIntyre 2005, p. 161). Human Rights Watch called for a moratorium on aid to Indonesia. Popular opposition to Suharto gained momentum. As the economy faltered, dissatisfaction increased. The type of people's movement that brought communist-bloc dictators down finally toppled Suharto. On May 12, 1998 four teenage demonstrators were shot. On May 17, students occupied parliament, forcing Suharto's resignation on the 21st (Hadiwinata, p. 78). Article 8 of the constitution provided for a vice-president's succession after a mid-term vacancy, so although many people did not want Habibie, he was inaugurated as president. Some saw him as an acting president, expecting a fresh election.

Democratic Restoration

Dissatisfaction continued under Habibie, so much so that Fic speaks of a yearning for "divine intervention" (p. 183). Habibie, however, lifted restrictions on political parties, set a date for democratic elections and began the process of asserting civilian control over the military, reducing their seats to 38. He did not acknowledge Megawati as leader of the PDI, which resulted in her gathering supporters under the banner of the PDI-P. Habibie did not consult widely, taking some controversial decisions, such as buying new military equipment (Hadiwinata, pp. 78–9). The election took place on June 7, 1999. The PDI-P won the largest number of seats (153) followed by Golkar (120) and Wahid's National Awakening Party (PKP) with 51. Both the PDI-P and Golkar included non-Muslim MPs, 57 and 13 respectively, indicative of their broad appeal (Suryadinata, p. 142). The Soerjadi-led PDI faction won two seats, insufficient to contest the 2004 election (below the 2 percent threshold).

Openly supported by Wahid during the election, Megawati expected to win the presidential vote in the MPR, since some Golkar members also indicated support. Her main opponent was Amien Rais, whose National Mandate Party won 34 seats. With support from other Muslims, he was elected Chair of the MPR. During the campaign, his "loquaciousness," stinging criticism of Megawati and specific policy statements contrasted sharply with her silence, adding to her appeal (Thompson 2004, p. 44). Perhaps, people thought, she would consult more widely and consider a range of options before acting, instead of dogmatically pursuing preconceived policy.

The MPR had decided to meet annually, instead of every five years after elections. The president was required to deliver an accountability speech. On October 19, Habibie's speech was rejected by a vote of 355 to 322. When he withdrew from the presidential election, Golkar decided not to nominate a candidate. The PPI-P nominated Megawati. The PBB – The Crescent Star Party – (13 seats) nominated Yusril Mahendra. Rais, who had already floated the idea of Wahid's candidacy, nominated him on behalf of a coalition of Muslim parties. Rais opposed Megawati as insufficiently reformist (Suryadinata, p. 143). The PBB, radical parties such as *hizb-ut-tahrir*, *Laskar Jihad* and Islamic Defender Front, together with some individual politicians, objected to Megawati on gender grounds. Both the NU and the second largest Muslim organization, the Muhammadiyah, formerly led by Rais, said that gender was no barrier (Smith, p. 308).

When Yusril withdrew, Megawati, who had expected Wahid's support, found that they were rivals for the presidency. Wahid believed he could pick up Muslim votes that Megawati would lose, so could govern with broader support (Fic, p. 198). The vote was close. Initially, Megawati led but the final result saw a Wahid victory, 373 to 313. Regarding him as a brother, Megawati felt that he had stabbed her in the back (Gorjäo, p. 37). However, when supporters began violent protest, she called for calm. Some may have thought a Wahid–Megawati team would be the ideal combination (Hadiwinata, p. 80). Wahid persuaded Megawati, having failed to win the presidency, to stand for the vice-presidency, which she won, nominated by Wahid's PKP. Several candidates withdrew. The final vote was 396 for Megawati, 284 for Hamzah Haz. Hamzah, later her vice-president, had opposed her on "position one" grounds. Hamzah's critics call him an Islamic fundamentalist (Suryadinata, pp. 196–7). Megawati attracted moderate Muslim support. Describing her election as "to pacify the masses, who supported PDI-P" is to belittle the fact that her party had the largest single vote share (Abdulgani-Knapp, p. 8).

Wahid owed widely for his presidency, since his party held only a handful of seats. He began by appointing a "rainbow" cabinet with members from across the main parties and several retired generals. Hamzah was appointed minister for welfare. However, reshuffles and dismissals soon led to the charge that he was rewarding cronies (Suryadinata, p. 182). Dismissals and resignations then began to cause concern, in addition to his governing style. His instinctive "ad hoc" decisions did not "contribute to a stable government" (Gorjäo, p. 38). Having "purified" the palace before he entered, he seemed to distance himself from day-to-day politics in favor of somehow mystically embodying national unity. He went on the *hajj* with a large following. His supporters believed him divinely inspired (Fic, p. 202). To NU members, he was their "*satria piningit*" (knight and savior). What had seemed to be the "dream team" became the "dreaming team" (Soesastro, p. 3).

When Wahid presented his accountability speech to the MPR in August 2000, it met a hostile response. Most of his speech was read for him, due to his poor eyesight and failing health. He apologized for his mistakes and promised to delegate greater responsibility to Megawati, who would chair the cabinet. He dozed off during the session but in the end came through better than expected (Barton, p. 324). There was a real possibility, nonetheless, that the MPR would try to remove him. Fear of violent response from NU supporters – not that Wahid approved of this – encouraged a compromise. Specific issues included his poor relations with the IMF and with some ASEAN states, which he alienated by floating the idea of a West Pacific Forum, including some but not all members. He was especially critical of Singapore (Anwar, p. 78). He annoyed the US by visiting Cuba (p. 77). It soon became apparent that Wahid did not intend to let Megawati govern, claiming to have delegated "tasks" not "authority" (McIntyre 2005, p. 226).

On gender, however, he appointed a "strongly feminist (and Islamic) minister," Khofifah Indar Parawansa, author of the IDEA case study, who changed the ministry's name to the Ministry for Women's Empowerment" (Blackburn, p. 29). The Family Planning Coordination Board was moved into the ministry, which now enjoyed a higher status. With the old Women's Federation largely discredited, new organizations mushroomed, including Islamic groups and those campaigning for voter education and against violence (p. 29). As elsewhere, women who identify with and vote for Islamic parties do not necessarily share "position one" opinions. New labor laws were passed and a human-rights chapter added to the constitution (second amendment). The national police were separated from the military.

However, although 2004 was set to be the date when all military representation would end, military seats in the MPR were extended until 2009. East Timor held a UN-supervised referendum on August 30, 1999, choosing independence. Wahid ordered the demilitarization of Aceh, indicating that the Acehnese might also vote on independence, and he adopted a conciliatory stance on Irian Jaya. He agreed the name change to "Papua," admitted "past abuses" and said that "independence" was an "allowable topic" (Barton, p. 293).

By late August, two corruption scandals allegedly involving Wahid led to the DPR appointing a special committee of enquiry. The committee reported irregularities. Summoned to explain his conduct, Wahid eventually attended the commission, saying it was illegal and that he was not accountable to the DPR. NU members said it was treason for Muslims to depose a legitimate ruler (Fic, p. 206). Two censure measures were passed, criticizing "ineffectiveness" and "failure to eradicate corruption" (Fic, p. 207). Calling the DPR a "kindergarten" did little to improve relations (Gorjäo, p. 38). As talk of impeachment gathered momentum, Wahid categorically stated that "he would not resign," nor could parliament remove him. In fact, the constitution was vague on impeachment. Since the MPR appoints the president, it could presumably remove him, having "power to establish the legality of its own actions" (Lubis, p. 110). Megawati was characteristically silent. On May 30, the DPR voted 365 to 4 with 39 abstentions, to impeach Wahid, convening a special MPR session. The PKB walked out. At this stage, the military members abstained, having voted for Wahid in 1999 (three voted for Megawati, three abstained). Wahid threatened to dissolve the DPR and MPR and to declare martial law. The military, however, began to switch support. Wahid had interfered in their internal affairs, removing senior officers and sacking several generals from his cabinet. Supporters declared willingness to die for him. For them, he "could do no wrong" (Fic, p. 204).

Wahid claimed that if he were removed, seven provinces would secede (Fic, p. 209). When he dismissed the police chief on June 2 without parliamentary approval, the chief refused to comply, as did officers ordered to arrest him. On July 13, Wahid announced that a national emergency would be declared on July 20 if no political settlement were reached. On the morning of July 23, having postponed this, he dissolved parliament and instructed Susilo, tasked with depoliti-cizing the army, to declare martial law. He refused. Instead, the police surrounded parliament, protecting members as they gathered, later that day, to unanimously impeach Wahid and install Megawati. Again, the PKB did not attend. At first, Wahid refused to acknowledge his removal or to leave the palace. Megawati was careful to allow him time to leave with dignity, not wanting a repetition of her father's humiliating exit.

Now, voices that had opposed a woman head of state lifted objec-tions. All Muslim members and parties supported her, apart from the PKB. Hamzah Haz won the vice-presidential election with strong PDI-P support, defeating four candidates in a three-round contest. He no longer objected to a woman leader. Hamzah had resigned from Wahid's cabinet after two months, either due to foreign policy disagreements or because of corruption allegations.

Megawati's Administration

Megawati was soon referred to as the "do nothing" president (Soesastro, p. 3). If being president was her "destiny," then legitimacy did not depend on "performance." It is incorrect, though, to say she did not achieve anything. She pursued allegations of human-rights abuses against separatists in East Timor, using her first presidential decree to establish a tribunal (Fic, p. 219), although few prosecutions followed due to various immunities enjoyed by the military. She established anti-corruption and judicial commissions, various auditing bodies and a constitutional court. Impeachment powers were vested in the court, not in the MPR, removing a constitutional lacuna. Additional reform is still needed, to clarify separation of powers, also unclear. Overlap between the DPR and MPR, for example, causes confusion, as does the president's role versus parliament's (Lubis, p. 110).

Megawati failed to pass proposed laws on whistle blowing and freedom of information (Lindsey, p. 17, n17) but "deserves praise for supporting a culture of openness in government" (p. 19). Under the third constitutional amendment, November 9, 2001, all MPR members will be elected, those elected to the DPR joining those elected to the new Regional Representative Council (DPD). In August 2003, the MPR approved direct presidential elections from 2004, with a two-term limit. In July 2003, Megawati abolished the military-dominated Supreme Advisory Council, which had exercised considerable power and influence. She tried to govern by consensus, appointing ministers from all parties. She called her cabinet "*Gotong Royong*" (Fic, p. 219), named for the village practice of mutual help. Although she did not prioritize gender, a 2003 act required parties to consider a 30 percent female quota. Megawati had reservations about this, saying that it could "reduce women's standing" (Parawansa, p. 89).

Megawati improved relations with the IMF and ASEAN but snubbed Australian politicians several times. Indonesian–Australian relations have been strained since 1975, when five Australian journalists were killed in East Timor. Relations continued to deteriorate over human-rights issues. Megawati also criticized Australia for depicting the Bali bombing as an attack on its citizens (88 out of 152, the largest single nationality), when people from many countries had died (21 including Indonesia, excluding unidentified fatalities). Prime Minister Howard's attendance at a 2003 service was seen as disrespectful to Hindus, who do not hold annual memorials for the dead.

Post 9/11, Australia was seen as aligning itself too closely with the US in what Indonesians increasingly feared was a war against Islam, not terror (Seneviratne). On the other hand, Megawati improved Indonesian–US relations by visiting Washington soon after 9/11, negotiating a trade-aid deal worth millions of dollars. Individuals' acts, she told Bush, do not justify invading a country (Anwar, p. 86); "violence should not be answered with violence" (Azra, p. 53). However, she condemned terrorism.

The US-led invasion of Afghanistan was immensely unpopular in Indonesia, expressed by street demonstrations, "sweeping" for Americans – rounding up and detaining of any foreigner – and calls for an armed *jihad* against the West. The NU and Muhammadiyah denounced this "sweeping" as illegal. They also encouraged humanitarian action instead of joining a foreign conflict (Azra, p. 51). At home, Megawati argued that Indonesia simply could not afford to lose US aid and trade (Anwar, p. 85). Public anti-American sentiment, though, gave the impression that Indonesia was embracing radical Islam (Anwar, p. 86). Hamzah, who downplayed the threat of radical Islam before October 2002, was openly contemptuous of US foreign policy, which some saw as a sign of the government's pro-Islamist sympathy (Smith, p. 314). Hamzah seemed to give a "green light" to demonstrations. Later, he urged restraint (Azra, p. 54). Azra does not think that Megawati was slow or hesitant in responding to 9/11, saying she was quick and "firm" (p. 53). When she went on the *hajj*, it was seen, though, as a gesture toward Muslim allies (McIntyre 2005, p. 226).

Her belief in *karma,* in ancestral spirits and guidance is *abangan,* not *santri.*

Fiscally, Megawati may have had more success than critics allow. Lindsey describes her as "reviving the economy" (p. 19). From negative growth in 2000, she achieved 4.8% in 2001, ending with 4.1% in 2004. Inflation "declined from 10.03% in 2002 to 5.06% in 2003," although unemployment rose from less than 4 percent to 9.1 percent (Prasetyawan). Unfortunately, the perception was that the economy performed badly, since she was "unable to communicate" its "strength." Susilo, who promised to create jobs, was somehow convincing. His "media image" depicted him as an agent of change for the better. Megawati, who saw herself as the champion of ordinary people (*wong cilik*), found that her opponent skillfully usurped this ground (Prasetyawan). Perception may be more important than performance. Reagan, who tripled the national debt, is remembered as an economically successful president. Susilo, who took growth to over 6 percent by 2009, may have built on Megawati's legacy.

Indonesia: GDP 2000–9

Year	GDP – real growth rate (%)
2000	Wahid (inherited from Suharto/Habibie) 0
2001	Wahid until July 23/Megawati 4.8
2002	Megawati 3.3
2003	Megawati 3.5
2004	Megawati until October 20/Susilo 4.1
2005	Susilo 4.9
2006	Susilo 5.6
2007	Susilo 5.5
2008	Susilo 6.3
2009	Susilo 6.1

Source: Adapted from CIA World Factbook (public domain).

Megawati's government successfully supervised direct presidential, vice-presidential and parliamentary elections in 2004. She lost the presidency in the second round, 60.62 percent to 39.38 percent, handing over power on October 20. Golkar won the largest single block of seats. Susilo also defeated her in 2009 by 60.8 percent to 26.79 percent. In 2009, her husband was elected MPR speaker. Described as a "wheeler-dealer," obtaining "political favors" for relatives and friends (Kingsbury 2002, p. 114), he may have played a similar role to Benazir and Çiller's husband's, who profited from their spouses' careers. Unlike Zardari, he did not enter politics on his wife's coat-tails, nor does his reputation seem to cloud Megawati's. Her perceived "do nothing" style, rather than Taufiq's cronyism, resulted in electoral defeat. He repudiates the charge of masterminding her career, saying that he would never have married a "political idiot" and cannot "push her around" (Schmetzer).

The Issues

What role did Islam play?

Islam did not hinder Megawati's rise to power, despite some initial opposition. MPR members if not everyone outside parliament withdrew this opposition. Support for parties aiming to make Indonesia an Islamic state or to establish a single caliphate has declined. In 1955, Muslim parties, both those supporting Pancasila and those demanding an Islamic state, won 44 percent of the vote. This vote share dropped to 37 percent in 1999, rose by a percentage point in 2004, before dropping again in 2009 (29 percent). Many Islamist parties, including the PBB, failed to pass the 2 percent threshold required to stand in 2014. In 2002, a move to introduce *Shari'ah* law failed to reach the floor of the MPR, attracting insufficient support (Smith, p. 368). Most Muslims have reconciled Pancasila with Islam (Azra, p. 56), rather as Turks have with their secular constitution. Pancasila-supporting parties won 72.89 percent of votes in 1999 (Fic, p. 187).

Wahid, who I heard speak on several occasions, was fully committed to a secular, pluralist state as well as to a progressive interpretation of Islam, arguing that political Islam would divide Indonesians, who shared values across faith traditions. He tried especially hard to "promote rapport" with the often-persecuted Chinese community, appointing a Chinese man as a minister and another, a former opponent of Sukarno, to Chair the National Business Development Council (Fic, p. 196). The state should not promote one religion above others. It should be "above religion" (Fic, p. 176). Wahid visited Israel, wanting to open up trade and other relations. Upholding the universality of human rights – as codified by the UN – he supported their "application in Indonesia" (Fic, p. 196). Members of all faiths mourned his death, on September 30, 2009.

The claim that Megawati encouraged radical Islam, at which Riaz hints, is unjustified (pp. 143, 174). Electoral support for all religious parties, Christian too, has fallen, so no floodgate was opened. Susilo's Democratic

Party (formed 2001), currently the largest in the DPR, is based on Pancasila. Only violence and state collapse could lead to Indonesia's Talibanization, as in Pakistan and Bangladesh, which is hardly likely to earn enduring popularity. Although Islamism is far from a "coherent force" (Blackburn, p. 229), Fic thinks that unless infiltration by radical Islamists is halted, Indonesia could Balkanize (p. 224). Pancasila as "just and civilized" is seen as fully compatible with Islam (Azra, p. 59). Indonesia's constitution calls for participation in establishing and maintaining "abiding peace and social justice, and equitably shared prosperity" (Anwar, p. 77). These are values that Muslims share with all people.

What role did culture play?
Although often described as "patriarchal," social traditions on gender in Indonesian are variegated and complex. Women did exercise power and authority in the past, while traditional belief sees a female spirit as the guardian of "authority." Men derive legitimacy from her. This represents a positive foundation for gender equality. Allied with "position one" Muslim views, it has seen noteworthy progress on gender issues in Indonesia.

What role did dynastic ties play?
Dynasty played a crucial role in Megawati's career. The PDI wanted to recruit members of Sukarno's family. Several declined. She was one of three (counting her husband) who accepted nomination for election. On the one hand, she may not have embarked on a political path without this encouragement. On the other hand, she is described as wanting to vindicate Sukarno's legacy. It should be said, though, that his memory had not been neglected in the way that Bhutto's and Mujib's had, nor did it require the same degree of reviving.

Did gender play a significant role in Megawati's rise to power?
Gender did play a role, although had a brother stood for the party leadership Megawati might have stayed in the background. Her gender may have appeared less threatening, although the whole idea was to challenge the government. Yet, despite habitual silence, she regarded becoming president as destiny. She neither said nor did anything to discourage supporters from propelling her into leadership. Once ousted, she clung to her position, confronting the government. She had her own ideas about reviving her father's legacy, accompanied by a sense of personal mission to pursue this. Her supporters' use of "mother" imagery suggests that her gender was seen as politically significant.

Did gender play any role in Megawati's exercise of power?

Some suggest that Megawati saw herself as an avenging nemesis, toppling the "Bad King" who had ousted her father, the "Good King" then reigning rather than ruling as the "Good Queen" or "Queen of Justice" (see Kingsbury 2002, p. 252). Her supporters saw her as "mother earth," perhaps as an incarnation of the feminine principle that validates all Indonesia rulers. She liked to be seen as "mother of the nation," comforting her people (Abdulgani-Knapp, p. 8). She was not proactive in empowering women, although her attempt to pursue human rights fits preconceptions about women's priorities. Her patience with negotiation ran out in Aceh, however, where she turned to a military solution.

Is there any particular relationship between Megawati's gender and her strengthening of democracy in the state?

Few if any question Megawati's commitment to democracy. She established several "institutions that will continue to promote the democratic rule of law" (Lindsey, p. 19). The transition of power was "achieved peacefully and entirely within the constitutional framework," as was the 2004 handover (Fic, p. 224). Her style was certainly not authoritarian; Wahid's critics called him more autocratic than Suharto (Fic, p. 209). Her record is less ambiguous than her father's in terms of democratic legitimacy. On the other hand, she was lukewarm in pursuing depoliticization of the military, with which she had a close relationship (Wanandi, p. 105). The military saw her as an ally on state unity and stability (Wanandi, p. 99). It had covertly supported the PDI in the 1982 election, irked by Sukarno's tight control (Vatikiotis, p. 82). There is some similarity to Çiller's relations with the military. Using them in Kurdistan, Çiller said this was counter-terrorism, not counter-insurgency (Pipes, pp. 73–4).

Despite the military's role in Sukarno's ousting and in the 1996 raid, Megawati inclined toward military solutions. After initially negotiating a peace in Aceh, she declared military rule, subsequently changed to a state of emergency, when problems arose. In a 1993 pamphlet, she indicated that *dwifungsi* was acceptable, provided the military serve the people (Suryadinata, p. 154). Her loss to Susilo was partly because people thought he would lead more effectively; it also reflected the view that, as a former general, he might be better able to exert civilian control.

Although the military's political representation ended in 2009, it has yet to divest itself of many business interests, which it was supposed to achieve by the same deadline (Vaswani). Some junior officers want depoliticization, suggesting that their oath should be to the constitution and flag, not to the president as "supreme commander," a somewhat "vague notion" (Vatikiotis, p. 82).

Does the post-colonial context have any bearing on Megawati's career?
Dealing with separatism and the role of the military are part of the post-colonial legacy. This resulted in an artificial state, requiring "force" to maintain unity. A federal solution, as in Pakistan, briefly in place from 1949–50, has been suggested. Indonesia may be too geographically dispersed for a unitary state, which Megawati supports (Lubis, p. 110). Fic observes that resources need to be better shared across provinces and regions, or fragmentation is possible (p. 225).

Did Megawati promote women's issues and rights?
Megawati did not prioritize women's issues. However, subsequent to her term, the percentage of women in parliament increased, from 8.8 percent in 1999 to 11.3 percent in 2004 to 18.2 percent in 2009, the third highest of the four states. Perhaps she did help to create an atmosphere that looks more favorably on women's political participation. The 2003 Election Act, too, although not a "special measure" as such, has had some effect. Violence against women is more widely acknowledged and discussed.

Conclusion

Despite her one-term presidency, having served as the first Muslim woman head of a modern state Megawati has a place in history. Other men and women have served single terms. Failure to gain re-election does not necessarily devalue their record. Her "silence" was arguably appropriate during opposition to Suharto, even on the 1999 campaign trail. In office, she failed to highlight achievements, such as relative fiscal success. Reagan, whose performance in office was similar in terms of GDP growth, attracted praise; he projected a "feel good" factor that transcended actual accomplishments.

Megawati was not overthrown, forced out or impeached, instead playing a significant role in Indonesia's democratic transition. Sukarno was ousted, Suharto and Habibie resigned, Wahid was impeached. No one tried to remove Megawati or compel her resignation. She oversaw significant human rights and constitutional reform. Subsequent administrations followed each other smoothly. So far, international observers have judged elections free and fair. Corruption remains a major issue and civilian control of the military is not yet secure. Transparency needs improving. However, Indonesia outranks Turkey, a prospective EU member, on the freedom index. Megawati merits some credit for helping to restore democracy and for progress made since the end of Suharto's repressive rule.

Conclusion

Gender, Politics and Culture in Islam

This chapter summarizes what can be said, in conclusion, under each of the eight questions posed and explored throughout this book.

What Role did Islam Play?

Since all five women came into office through constitutional mechanisms, which varied across four Muslim-majority states, Islam cannot be said to have hindered their careers. No legal impediments existed in any of these states. When religious objections were raised, they represented opinions and attitudes, not constitutional obstacles. As a matter of fact, women had the vote and the constitutional right to stand for election in Turkey long before they did in many European countries. There, too, women gained the franchise without the type of long, hard struggle against male bigotry that preceded the female vote elsewhere. In the other three states, women were granted the vote, with little or no debate, at independence.

Historically, too, Muslims have hardly monopolized the idea that "a woman's place is in the home." "Position one" attitudes existed and exist in all four contexts. However, they did not enjoy enough support to prevent women achieving power. This was true on two occasions in Pakistan and, so far, four in Bangladesh. "Position one" is perhaps less evident in Turkey, although some of those interviewed by Arat (1989) saw the public domain as men's sphere, the domestic as women's (p. 46). Pakistan's *Shari'ah* Supreme Court ruled that Benazir could be prime minister as long as the president was male, suggesting that a barrier remains in place that could prevent a woman from becoming head of state. In Indonesia, objections were raised against Megawati in 1999 but when the MRP voted for her to succeed Wahid in 2001, no Muslim MP objected. Wahid's party boycotted the session. It did not object to Megawati on gender grounds, though. Rather, it rejected Wahid's impeachment. In Bangladesh, JI publications and some individuals, such as Delwar Hossain Saidi, oppose women's leadership yet the party allied itself with Khaleda and was a coalition partner in her second administration. JI also collaborated with Hasina during the 1996 campaign for a caretaker government to supervise elections. In practice, by collaborating with women, JI has affirmed their leadership role. Çiller formed an alliance with an Islamic Party, serving as deputy prime minister. Megawati's cabinet included members of Islamic parties, one led by her vice-president. Jatiya, an Islam-oriented party, is a coalition partner with Hasina's government, even though the founder, former president Ershad, follows a Sufi sheikh who disapproves of women leaders.

Benazir, Çiller, Hasina and Megawati are said to have made some type of accommodation with Islamists, such as performing the *hajj* or starting to cover their heads when this was not habitual for them. Khaleda, for her part, appears to have had a reputation for piety. She has not attracted the same type of comment about changing or adjusting her habits. Given that wearing a head cover has become more common in Turkey and Bangladesh especially, it could be that Çiller and Hasina changed their personal practice out of respect for others, or that they have become more pious. We should not assume insincerity or political opportunism – to improve their standing – without allowing for other possibilities.

Women's involvement in Islamist and Islamic parties is a factor in all four states, showing that some Muslim women want Islam to have more public recognition. However, not all "Islamic" women – those who think Islam should speak in the public square – vote for Islamic parties, or agree with "position one" attitudes. Many subscribe to reformist ideas. In Bangladesh, for example, Muslim women speak of *hijab* as a mental state, devising their own forms of acceptable dress. The women are said to have strengthened the role of Islam in the public square because they collaborated with Islamist or with Islamic parties. This flies in the face of the claim that Islam hinders women's political leadership.

All four states have wrestled, to different degrees, with issues of national identity and Islam–state relations. Islamist parties – that is, those aiming to radically alter the nature of the state – have minimal chance of electoral success. However, it can be said that all have become more conscious of Islamic identity. This has taken place at exactly the same time that at least one of the states repeatedly chose female leaders.

What Role did Culture Play?

Currents were identified in all four states, drawing on Sufi heritages and traditions of tolerance and diversity, that may have prepared the ground for gender equality to grow. In Turkey, the governing AKP responded to criticism that women had been excluded from the central council of its predecessor when it appointed them to its own. The AKP now has several women MPs. Wahhabi Islam, dominant in some Arab contexts, disapproves of Sufi Islam, probably because the popularity of sheikhs and of visits to their shrines challenges the centralization of power in the king and Mecca's exclusive role. Arab contexts have seen less progress. Combined with Sufi and other currents of Islamic thought, cultural seeds may exist in the four states that aid women's empowerment and greater gender equality. Kemalists in Turkey pointed back to the role played by pre-Islamic women in Anatolia, while others suggest that Ottoman women were not quite as docile and powerless as they have been depicted, at least at an elite level.

Bengali women, again at least at an elite level, emerged into the public domain in the late nineteenth century. Some played important roles in the language and independence struggles. During the latter, there was hardly a single Bengali woman who did not make some contribution to the war effort. Sukarno pointed out how some women took part in village leadership in partnership with their brothers, while queens ruled several pre-colonial states, in Indonesian space. These cultural antecedents, combined with Sufi influence, may predispose people toward a "position two" understanding of Islam.

On the other hand, in Turkey and Indonesia, state-formatted gender ideologies unrelated to Islam may actually have hindered gender equality, regardless of cultural seeds that favored this.

In Arab contexts, a patriarchal form of leadership reasserted itself after the early period of Islamic history, when women and men had both collected *hadith* and took part in decision making. As military expansion and governance of a large territory began to characterize the caliphate, women played less central roles. Men claimed a monopoly on political leadership, often linked with military experience. They perpetuated male-centered readings of the Qur'an, insisting that "position one" interpretations were correct, that this had to be imitated (*taqlid*). Alternative interpretations were denounced as *bida* (innovation). Perhaps the fact that Islamic rule – although it took centuries before the majority adopted Islam – came through conquest resulted in less tolerance of other faiths.

In Bangladesh, Islam preceded conquest. Indonesia never fell to Muslim invaders. In both pre-Islamic contexts, feminine ideas of the divine existed.

Of course, pre-Islamic Arabs revered female deities. However, the Qur'an so roundly condemned their worship that Arab Muslims may be less prepared to speculate about God's gender. That "Allah" is masculine grammatically does not make God a man. Perhaps south and southeast Asians found it easier to associate female notions of divinity from their pre-Islamic pasts with the single but multifaceted God of the Qur'an that came to them from Arabia. This condemns the notion of multiple deities, including female ones, but does not preclude belief in a God with limitless attributes and qualities, just as Brahman manifests through many forms, some male, some female, some androgynous. Perhaps, if the desert climate produces an ethos that values uniformity (Geertz 1968, p. 16), this finds ambiguity, mystery, God as ultimately unknowable, complex, multifaceted, not as a simplistic unity, problematic. South and southeast Asian cultures may be more comfortable with flexible notions of divine reality.

The "number one" position on gender is often represented as non-negotiable, as identical with an Islamic view. If culture is Islam and Islam culture, just as Islam is society, politics and economics, "culture" has no independent existence and women would be treated identically across the Muslim world. This, though, is not the case. Saudi Arabia is actually the only context where "position one" remains in place without any adjustment. As an attitude, it is still popular elsewhere, mainly in the Arab world. The Taliban, some of the political parties operating in Pakistan, Bangladesh and Indonesia, would legally establish "position one" if they ever achieved power. They lack anything like enough electoral support to have a chance at forming a government. Their only hope is to bomb their way to power. They oppose women's emancipation, targeting NGOs that empower women. They hate the pluralist ethos of South Asia, so destabilize society by targeting non-Muslims and Muslims who associate with them. In Bangladesh and Pakistan, they represent them as fifth columnists for India or the West, demonizing them. The seeds of doubt sown can disrupt long histories of coexistence. However, all Arab countries except Saudi Arabia have enfranchised women, even though participation in politics remains minimal. Yet where democracy is increasing in strength, women are becoming empowered, even in Arab space where "position one" views are strongest.

Anthropological studies show us that Islam does in fact adapt to different cultural contexts, that it has a capacity to live comfortably with local customs and practices as long as these do not explicitly clash with core Islamic values or beliefs. Geertz (1968) describes Indonesian Islam as "adaptive, absorbent, pragmatic," Moroccan as stressing uniformity and unity (p. 16).

Much of Akbar Ahmed's writing also depicts how Islam has adapted to different contexts. In his 1992 BBC series, *Living Islam,* we see examples of

Muslim sensitivity to cultural practices not deemed incompatible with Islamic values, especially when he visits Africa. He begins by identifying the Islamic ideal, located in the life and teachings of Muhammad, and in what Muslims consider to have been the perfect or near-perfect society over which he ruled. He then explores how, in different contexts, Muslims try to approximate that ideal. Since contexts differ, so do Muslim responses, yet Muslims as such are not different but the same; "what is different is the emphasis each culture places on universal aspects of life" (2002, p. 7). The argument that Islam dishonors any culture other than Arab culture, insisting on arabizing all cultures it encounters, does not fit the facts. In this view, arabism is Islam, and Islam is arabism and all other "cultures" are redundant.

V. S. Naipaul (1998) argued that Islam requires non-Arabs to embrace Islam so totally that it displaces not only any pre-existing culture but pre-Islamic history as well; "nothing is required but the purest faith," which means they "must strip themselves of their past," become "empty vessels." This effectively turns their territories into "cultural deserts ... with glory of every kind elsewhere," that is, in Arabia (pp. 311, 318).

Mernissi (1992) regards all things Arab as so intertwined with Islam that she uses "Arab" and "Islam" interchangeably, explaining that this is not meant to denigrate other cultures' contributions to "the mosaic that is Islam." Things Arabic and Islam, she says, "are intimately linked" (p. 176, n4). She was, though, speaking of her native Morocco, which in many respects is as much part of the Arab world as Egypt. Pakistan has positioned itself closer to Arab culture than Bangladesh has, which is one reason why some Pakistanis claim that Pakistani Islam is purer.

I argue that the spirit of Bangladeshi and Indonesian Islam, for example, may be closer to Muhammad's Islam than Saudi Islam, due to the re-emergence of gender-biased readings of Islam in the latter. The cultural contexts of Bangladesh and Indonesia, where religions have historically coexisted harmoniously and where pluralism has flourished, allowed gender-equal-friendly versions of Islam to emerge. The Muslim claim that culture and Islam are interchangeable is not actually compromised by the fact of cultural and religious diversity, since the culture from which Islam is insep-arable varies across contexts. Islam may be inseparable from both Arab and Pakistani culture, for example, yet these two cultures are not identical, neither is Islam practiced identically in these contexts. However, there is a great deal of overlap in many, perhaps in most, areas of faith and practice. My visits to Morocco, Egypt, Turkey, Malaysia, Bangladesh and Indonesia, for example, left me in no doubt that Islam was the majority faith and impacted enormously on the reality that surrounded me, yet I was also aware of subtle differences. Morocco was somehow not Egypt, Bangladesh was very similar to Indonesia yet it was not identical. Islam spread outward from Arabia. Perhaps South Asian Islam, renowned for flexibility and openness, can help Arab Islam return to the spirit that flourished in Muhammad's time, when women as well as men offered advice and counsel.

What Role did Dynastic Ties Play?

Four of the five women in this study had dynastic ties with dead male leaders. A senior male politician, who had led his country several times, mentored one of the five, who had no tie to any previous leader. Can their careers be reduced to or explained away with reference to these ties, as some hint or suggest? On the one hand, dynastic ties are not uncommon in politics. It may well be true, too, that none of the women would have become party leaders, with the possibility of electoral success, without a dynastic link or mentor. On the other hand, this is also speculation. We cannot actually know for sure that they *would not have become* successful politicians without any of these relationships. Nor should we use dynasty to explain their careers away, any more than George W. Bush, whose father certainly kick-started his career, should be seen only as a surrogate for his father. All politicians need some name recognition, some distinctive achievement or attribute, to enter the arena and attract votes. In the case of four of the five women, this special attribute was a family member who had led their states. Çiller may have merited a place on Demirel's cabinet for her academic work in economics. On the other hand, she was untried and unknown in the political arena, so it is more likely that she owed her senior post, as a novice MP, to his patronage. Certainly, had she not served in the cabinet, her chances of gaining the party leadership after Demirel stepped down to become president would have been minimal. People turned to her because she had established a name for herself. This proved sufficient, especially so since Demirel decided on neutrality.

Thompson (2004) says that the South Asian women leaders, with the exception of Benazir, were reluctant politicians, who had to be cajoled by "party leaders and the demands of public opinion" (p. 43). I am not sure if this was true for Hasina either. Her claim that politics runs in her blood and constant references to student activism belies the idea of reluctance. Khaleda may well have lacked ambition yet there is no real evidence that it took much effort to convince her. Certainly, once appointed party chair, she has proved to be a consummate politician. Megawati responded to a sudden, even unexpected, popular movement in her favor yet she also had a strong belief in her destiny, which does not sound like reluctance. Why did the PDI turn to a relative at all? Interestingly, Suharto was himself keen on strengthening the PDI, one of two legal opposition parties within the carefully controlled political system, because it suited his policies to do so. He thought that the secular PDI was a more appropriate opposition than the Islam-orientated PPP. He began rehabilitating the man he had ousted, encouraging the PDI to approach members of the Sukarno family. "Destiny" is a feature in three of the five stories. Çiller, whom Thompson does not discuss, was strongly motivated.

How true is it that, once in power, some of the women spent too much time furthering dynastic interests, as Thompson suggests; "once praised for leading a moral cause against tyranny, they were accused (not always unfairly) of governing in the interests of their family dynasties" (p. 50)? There is little if any evidence that Benazir was grooming Bilawal for leadership before her assassination. Her death catapulted him into party leadership, although exactly why this happened raises questions. Yet another Bhutto family leader does make the PPP look like a personal fiefdom. Khaleda seems to have groomed Tarek for leadership, although of the four with dynastic ties she plays least on this. On the other hand, she chooses to keep Zia's name (Begum, p. 277). Given the various ways in which she could be known, retaining "Zia" was probably a deliberate choice. When Hasina's son, Sajeeb, visited Bangladesh in 2004, Tarek wrote to him congratulating him on his entry into politics. However, he returned to the USA, where he has pursued a successful career in technology. His father had no political involvement. Bringing her family's killers to justice was certainly a preoccupation for Hasina. However, this did not take up so much time that she neglected everything else. Megawati is said to have been obsessed with Sukarno's legacy, yet in many respects she had less work to do here, since his rehabilitation had already begun.

Did Gender Play a Significant Role in the Women's Rise to Power?

Yes, in each case, gender was a significant factor. In Hasina's case, there was no live male relative who could carry the mantle. Many senior party leaders were also dead or exiled, which left few other candidates. Undoubtedly, by choosing her, the party wanted to capitalize on her image as victim. Her relationship with the nation's and the party's founder had a strong appeal. A lot of work had to be done to rebuild the party. Choosing her was pragmatic. Despite ambiguous aspects of Mujib's legacy, the hope was that people would remember positive aspects of what he had accomplished, forgiving later mistakes. Mujib had been elected, while those who followed him seized power. Any elections they held were far from fair. As women, all five covered by this book were less threatening than men might have been to the governments they opposed. Also, in at least four cases, they more readily evoked ideas of suffering on behalf of the nation. Their experience of personal tragedy enabled them to symbolize their nation's struggle against adversity, poverty and other problems.

Benazir became party leader, her brother being unable to do so due to the violent nature of his opposition to the government. Her gender, for many, was seen as more suitable for leading peaceful resistance. By representing her father as a democrat, ousted and executed by a tyrant, she hoped people would overlook his authoritarian tendencies. If the 1977 election was dubious, the 1970 one had been fair.

Megawati's brothers supported her leadership, apparently seeing her as somehow representing their father's spirit, perhaps because, as a woman, her suffering was more poignant. One brother was a popular musician. The other was not close to Sukarno, so could hardly claim to be his champion.

The BNP turned to Khaleda when rival candidates could not agree on a leader. Again, her tie to the slain founder was an advantage. Regardless of how he gained power, Zia was a popular president. As his widow, she could play effectively on the "mystique" and "tragedy" associated with widowhood, suggesting self-sacrifice for the nation, which draws "men and women to her" (Begum, p. 277).

When Çiller stood for the DYP leadership, which would automatically give her the prime ministership, what was called the "Çiller factor" was gendered. People thought a woman would represent a break from the discredited politics of the past. Her physical attractiveness, together with the fact that she had enjoyed a successful career outside of politics and was married with a family, translated into a positive media image as the modern Turkish woman. With two children, she was a "working mom." Part of the message that a woman leader could signal was the desire of the nation to be seen as a progressive, liberal society ready to join the EU.

Did Gender Play any Role in the Women's Exercise of Power?

Gender played a role in how all five women exercised power. This impacted how they represented themselves as "mother" and "sister." Two have been described as "queen-like." Mujib's killers accused him of having kingly ambition, meaning that he wanted to rule for life, and to do so autocratically. In Megawati's case, the "queen-like" criticism is more because she is said to have "done nothing" – leaving the business of government to others, as a ceremonial queen does. In Khaleda's case, her "queenly" style may refer to authoritarian tendencies. Choosing to wear the headscarf attracted notice, given the Muslim context. Discussion of how Hasina and Khaleda dress, too, is gendered. Ahmed's comment on Mujib's "Indian" style shows that how men dress can have political significance but it is less easy to imagine a similar discussion about how male politicians' dress symbolizes their political agendas, although wearing a "tie" and a "suit" is seen as pro-Western (1997, p. 240).

The role of husbands and their conduct may be another gendered issue. Male politicians' wives do make news for negative reasons. However, the degree of attention focused on how three of the husbands may have "cashed in" on their wives' careers raises questions about whether male spouses are *more likely* to be guilty of this type of conduct. Benazir and Megawati's spouses have, in each case, been called the real "leader." Then again, a great woman often stands behind a mediocre male. The type of barbed comment that being beautiful and changing her clothes frequently did not qualify Çiller to be prime minister is less easy to imagine being made about a man. Comments and discussion generally about what a woman leader wears are more common than reference to male attire. To some degree, these women's "clean images" suffered from their spouses' conduct, or in Khaleda's case, from her son's, since her husband was killed. With reference to allegations of corruption, it has to be said that few if any politicians escape this in these contexts. Ershad, found guilty and jailed, remains a significant political player.

Aspects of the five's careers support the idea that women leaders will attempt to rule by consensus, taking particular interest in such issues as conflict resolution, human rights, healthcare and education. This is less true for Çiller, whose focus was on the economy. Benazir, Hasina and Khaleda – Megawati to some degree – prioritized some or all of the above. Actually, they did not do too badly in the economics area either, whereas Çiller failed to meet expectations. Hasina and Megawati are known as consensus politicians, perhaps more in their intent than practice. Yet accusations of authoritarianism also exist, with Khaleda and Çiller being especially targeted. Inevitably, surrounded by men wishing them to fail, accusing them of being too potentially "soft" on state security, some women leaders out-male men in taking a "tough" or "hawkish" stance. Here, Megawati and Çiller's close relationship with the military and their use of military solutions to counter separatism contrasts with Hasina's success in negotiating peace in the Chittagong Hill Tracts. Benazir failed in her efforts to control the military, remaining vulnerable to the possibility of a military coup. The tendency to appoint women politicians to what are called "soft" jobs, such as welfare, education and health rather than to defense, security and foreign relations means that women leaders feel compelled to show that they can handle the latter as well as the former. A woman who does this is likely to get dubbed an "iron lady." A man is simply living up to his gendered expectations. On the other hand, a man might be called too feminine for preferring a "soft" approach to security or defense issues. Obama has been criticized for suggesting that he might talk to certain regimes. Hasina's "iron lady" label, though, was given for her commitment to human rights.

Is there any Particular Relationship between the Women's Gender and Strengthening Democracy in the Four States?

All five women came to power either at the beginning or near the beginning of democratic restorations, having in four cases helped end dictatorships. Women are perceived to be more naturally democratic than men, or at least less inclined to be tyrannical. Their gender was seen as an advantage in challenging male tyranny. Most tyrants have been men. There is the view "out there" that if more women were in charge, there would be fewer wars, more non-violent conflict resolution, a greater stress on fairness and justice. This might be the case. So far, the record of women in power is mixed *vis-à-vis* preference for peaceful resolution of conflict. Two of the five turned to military solutions, although Megawati did so after giving diplomacy a try. This mixed record is in part due to the perceived need, identified above, for women to prove that they are as reliable as men in defending national security or maintaining unity when threatened by separatism or insurgency. In Bangladesh, the two women leaders have taken part in four peaceful transitions of power, although not without hiccups. Khaleda's first 1996 election was overturned and the military stepped in after her second term ended. However, it supervised a successful 2009 election. Hasina and Khaleda can be credited with making a military coup all but unthinkable in Bangladesh.

Benazir's democratic legacy in Pakistan is difficult to evaluate. She won two elections. Neither administration completed its term, which no government in Pakistan has yet achieved. Despite the most recent return to democracy following her death, democracy remains fragile. Her legacy, which is strongly associated with democracy, will no doubt be used to support this in coming years. Megawati helped to overthrow a dictatorial regime, reformed electoral law and handed on power to her successor. Although she did not win a second term, her commitment to democracy was unquestioned. It was her perceived failure to improve the economy that cost her re-election, although her record was actually not bad. Her closeness to the military may have been a handicap in asserting civilian control. The retired general who succeeded her may be better placed to depoliticize the army than she was.

The hope in Turkey was that a woman leader would set a higher standard, placing the people's interests above ambition and self-interest. Çiller's critics accuse her of compromising any higher standard for the sake of power, making deals, appointing cronies, misusing her office to line her own pockets, shifting policy for political expediency. She is accused of weakening democracy, not of strengthening it. She shows that women can be "equally motivated by power" (Cizre, p. 207). We should not expect women to adopt certain agendas or possess particular attributes *merely because of gender*. Yet Çiller did not do anything that Turkish male politicians had not done for years. She was heavily criticized for allying with Erbakan, yet he had taken part in three earlier coalitions, two with her party's founder. Erbakan's critics accuse him of using democracy as a means to gain power, so that he could dismantle democracy to establish an Islamic state. Yet there is minimal evidence that he really intended to do this. Turkey's democracy did not suffer as a result of Çiller's actions. The successor party to the one she entered into a coalition with has won two subsequent elections. It governs as a pro-European yet Muslim-oriented party committed to the state's secular constitution. In their particular contexts, Hasina and Megawati were or are seen to be more supportive of minorities, committed to their nation's pluralist legacies.

Does the Post-colonial Context have any Bearing on the Women's Careers?

All four states continue to deal with aspects of the colonial legacy. In two cases especially, Pakistan and Indonesia, borders and ethnic and cultural compositions of the state present issues related to national unity. This is also relevant in Turkey *vis-à-vis* Kurdish separatism. In Pakistan and Indonesia, a federal system might be advantageous. The former could include other political units, such as Bangladesh and a sovereign Kashmir. However, successive administrations remain committed to the unitary state. This leads to the role of the military, perceived as essential for maintaining unity and suppressing separatism. All four states have had interludes, longer or shorter, of military rule. In all four, the military can be described as politicized. In Pakistan, disputes with India have similarly strengthened the military's role, which is independently wealthy. This is also the case in Indonesia, where it has agreed to extricate itself from commerce. It has not yet done so. Military rulers have ousted civilian politicians, claiming corruption and incompetence. They have more often than not accumulated wealth for themselves.

Post-independence, "socialist" and "left" solutions seemed more attractive than those traditionally associated with former colonial powers, leading to a "left"–"right" divide and to rivalry. The Sino–Soviet split complicated this situation. India leant toward the Soviets, so Pakistan chose China. Mujib leant towards the Soviets. Indonesia was pro-communist under Sukarno, anti-communist under Suharto. Turkey's military intervened due to left–right rivalry.

In several states, World Bank and IMF requirements have led to changes in policy directions, even in foreign relations. The need to attract Arab aid impacted how several states define their relationship with Islam. Islamist parties argue that neither capitalism nor communism has solved national problems so Islamic solutions should be tried. Existing systems, seen as imposed by the departing colonial powers, are declared non-Islamic. Turkey, which was not formally colonized, adopted European-style democracy (with which the Ottomans had experimented) and aligned itself with Europe through NATO and other European institutions. It hopes to accede to the EU. There, however, Islam has re-entered the political arena. Some would prefer to see closer relations with other Muslim countries, rather than with Europe, perhaps within an alternative EU-type organization.

Under colonial rule – or in the case of Turkey, under the Ottomans – democracy barely existed. Imperial regimes were autocratic. A relatively small number of civilians governed British India and the Dutch East Indies but military support was never far off. The pre-independence political systems were almost entirely authoritarian. Democracy does not "happen" instantaneously. Democratic institutions and the civil societies that nourish them take decades to develop. Military men regard themselves as loyal patriots and as effective leaders. Within the military, they give orders, which subordinates obey or face punishment for not doing so. Fearing state collapse, the military intervene, thinking that if they do not protect borders, suppress separatism, and respond to humanitarian crises such as earthquakes in Pakistan and floods in Bangladesh, the state would fail anyway, therefore they might as well govern.

Hasina and Khaleda's habit of boycotting parliament in opposition and of resorting to strikes and demonstrations instead of debate is an aspect of the colonial legacy. During the anti-British, pro-independence movement there were few opportunities for dialogue around a table. This was also true for the language movement and eventually for the Bangladeshi liberation struggle, both of which were extra-parliamentary. The adversarial nature of multi-party politics, too, is based on systems that do not always work elsewhere as well as they might. Chowdhury (2003) suggests that Bangladesh can adapt lessons from the US system, yet politics there are deeply polarized. Aspects of the committee system are admirable and worth adapting but copying the filibuster would bring the opposition back into parliament in an unhealthy way. Problems associated with a "loyal opposition" in Bangladesh may be a less positive aspect of local culture, which recognizes a single person as charismatic leader, leaving little scope for anyone else.

Did these Five Women Promote Women's Issues and Rights?

Three of the five women in this study prioritized women's issues although two did not. In all states, however, the percentage of women in parliament increased *after a woman or women had held office*. The two women who did not do very much for gender actually did make some effort. Çiller targeted women voters in her 1996 campaign and introduced a limited party-candidate quota. Megawati signed into law an act requiring parties to consider a 30 percent candidate quota, despite personal reservations about special measures.

Finally

There are Muslim women who suffer brutality and abuse at the hands of Muslim men. There are Muslim men who believe that Islam sanctions this conduct. There are too many instances of "honor" killings in Muslim contexts, too much violence against women. Islam does not permit self-help justice, although some women have decided that Islam, not an incorrect interpretation of Islam, is the problem. They have chosen to abandon Islam. Comments by one such woman, Taslima Nasrin, whose education places her in a strong position to work for reform, have alienated Muslim women so that that her voice no longer speaks to their situations. Hashmi cites her suggestion that as men take shirts off on a hot day, women should be able to do so too (p. 196). Certainly, in Bangladesh, men often dress very scantily at work in the fields or in construction, while a much stricter dress code restricts what women wear. Islam can be understood in a way that brackets Muslims from the rest of humanity, raising a psychological barrier, claiming that democracy, human-rights – including those of minorities – and gender equality have no place in Islamic societies. Or, Islam can be understood in

208 Muslim Women of Power

a way that affirms human solidarity: God created tribes and nations so that we can know one another (Qur'an 49:13). *Mu'minun*, believers, those who "enjoin what is right and refrain from what is wrong, and hasten in emulation in all good works" (3:114) may be Muslim or muslim. Some Muslims see no reason why international human-rights standards and Muslim law should not perfectly match.

The five women whose careers this book has explored were or are Muslim. In different ways, they are women of faith, even though several were criticized for acting "piously" for reasons of political expediency. Yet there is no good reason to think that they are less than good Muslims. Several could be described as secular. However "secular" here does not mean anti-religious or profane. It means advocating equal rights for all people of faith. A Muslim-majority state will, though, want to see certain Muslim values, values that people of all faiths share, enshrined in its laws.

Five Muslim women have led (one currently leads) four states. This, at the very least, regardless of how every detail of their legacies is evaluated, flies in the face of the notion that Muslim women are universally subordinate to men. Other Muslims states have a lot further to go. Some – Jordan, Morocco and several others – have made a good start. "Position two," as a credible interpretation of Islam, did much to make the five careers possible, which in turn has helped to make "position two" more plausible as an alternative to "position one." Much needs to be done in the four states that have had women leaders and elsewhere, both in Muslim and non-Muslim space. Many countries with stable democracies, more freedoms and greater prosperity have achieved less on gender equality than the four Muslim states. Representations of gender relations in Islam that leave "our superiority" versus "their inferiority" unchallenged merit serious critique.

References

Abadan-Unat, Nermin and Oya Tokgöz (1994), "Turkish Women as Agents of Social Change in a Pluralist Democracy," in Nelson and Chowdhury (eds), *Women and Politics Worldwide*, pp. 705–20.

Abbas, Shemeem Burney (2002), *The Female Voice in Sufi Ritual: Devotional Practices of Pakistan and India.* Austin: University of Texas Press.

Abdulgani-Knapp, Retnowati (2003), *A Fading Dream: The Story of Roeslan Abdulgani and Indonesia.* New York: Times Books International.

Acar, Feride (2002), "Turhut Özal: Pious Agent of Liberal Transformation," in Heper and Sayari (eds), *Political Leaders and Democracy in Turkey*, pp. 181–98.

Adams, Charles (1983), "Mawdudi and the Islamic State," in John L. Esposito (ed.), *Voices of Resurgent Islam.* New York: Oxford University Press, pp. 99–133.

Addison, Paul (2007), *Winston Churchill.* Oxford: Oxford University Press.

Afkhami, Mahnaz (1995), *Faith and Freedom: Women's Human Rights in the Muslim World.* London: I. B. Tauris.

Afshari, Reza (2003), *Egalitarian Islam and Misogynist Islamic Tradition: A Critique of the Feminist Reinterpretation of Islamic History and Heritage.* Amherst, New York: Center for Critical Enquiry, http://www.centerforinquiry.net/isis/islamic_viewpoints/egalitarian_islam_and_misogynist_islamic_tradition_a_critique_of_the_femini/, accessed February 1, 2010.

Āhameda, Sirājuddīna (1998), *Sheikh Hasina, Prime Minister of Bangladesh.* New Delhi: UBS Publishers' Distributors.

Ahmad, Khurshid (1999), *Islam: Its Meaning and Message.* Leicester: Islamic Foundation.

Ahmed, Akbar S. (1997), *Jinnah, Pakistan and Islamic Identity: The Search for Saladin.* London: Routledge.

Ahmed, Akbar (2002), *Islam Today: A Short Introduction to the Muslim World*. London: I. B. Taurus.

Ahmed, Leila (1992), *Women and Gender in Islam: Historical Roots of a Modern Debate*. New Haven: Yale University Press.

Ahmed, Leila (1999), *A Border Passage: From Cairo to America – a Woman's Journey*. New York: Farrar, Straus and Giroux.

Ali, Chowdhury Rahmat (1933), *Now or Never: Are We to Live or Perish for Ever*. Cambridge, UK: Founder of Pakistan National Movement.

Ali, Chowdhury Rahmat (1946), *India: The Continent of Dinia or the Country of Doom*. Cambridge, UK: Dinia Continental Movement.

Ali, Yusef (2001), *The Meaning of the Holy Qur'an*. Beltsville, MD: Amana.

Amin, Qasim (2002), "The Emancipation of Woman *and* the New Woman," in Charles Kurzman (ed.), *Modernist Islam 1840–1940: A Sourcebook*. New York: Oxford University Press, pp. 61–9.

Amin, Sonia Nishat (1996), *The World of Muslim Women in Colonial Bengal, 1876–1939* (Social, Economic and Political Studies of the Middle East and Asia, 55). Leiden: Brill.

Anderson, Benedict (1991), *Imagined Communities: Reflections on the Origin and Spread of Nationalism*. London: Virago; 1st edn 1983.

Anwar, Dewi Fortuna (2002), "Megawati: Search for an Effective Foreign Policy," in Soesastro *et al.* (eds), *Governance in Indonesia*, pp. 70–90.

Apostolov, Mario (2004), *The Christian–Muslim Frontier: A Zone of Contact, Conflict, or Cooperation*. London: RoutledgeCurzon

Arat, Yeşim (1989), *The Patriarchal Paradox: Women Politicians in Turkey*. Cranbury, New Jersey: Associated University Press.

Arat, Yeşim (2002), "Süleyman Demirel: National Will and Beyond," in Heper and Sayari (eds), *Political Leaders and Democracy in Turkey*, pp. 88–105.

Arat, Yeşim (2005), *Rethinking Islam and Liberal Democracy: Islamist Women in Turkish Politics*. Albany, New York: State University of New York Press.

Asian Development Bank (2001), *Women in Bangladesh: Country Briefing Paper: Bangladesh*. Manila, Philippines: Asian Development Bank, http://www.adb.org/documents/books/ country_briefing_papers/women_in_bangladesh/, accessed February 1, 2010.

Aspinall, Edward (2005), *Opposing Suharto: Compromise, Resistance, and Regime Change in Indonesia*. Stanford, CA: Stanford University Press, http://www.loc.gov/catdir/toc/ecip0416/2004008168.html.

Awami League (2009), *Biography of Sheikh Hasina*. Dhaka: Awami League, http://www.albd.org/autoalbd/index.php?option=com_content&task=view&id=120&Itemid=44, accessed February 1, 2010.

Awami League (2010), "60 Years of Struggle and Achievements: Bangladesh Awami League," p. 5, http://www.albd.org/autoalbd/index.php?option=com_content&task=view&id=32&Itemid=33&limit=1&limitstart=4.

Azra, Azyunmundi (2002), "The Megawati Presidency: The Challenge of Political Islam," in Soesastro et al. (eds), *Governance in Indonesia*, pp. 44–69.

Baaklini, Abdo I., Guilain Denoeux and Robert Springborg (1999), *Legislative Politics in the Arab World: The Resurgence of Democratic Institutions*. Boulder, CO: Lynne Rienner.

Badawi, Gemal A. (1999), "Woman in Islam," in Khurshid Ahmad (ed.), *Islam: Its Meaning and Message*. Leicester: The Islamic Foundation.

Ballington, Julie (2009), "Introduction," in Ballington and Karam (eds), *Women in Parliament*, pp. 23–30.

Ballington, Julie and Azza Karam (eds) (2009), *Women in Parliament: Beyond Numbers*. Stockholm: International IDEA.

Ban-ki Moon (2009), "Unite to End Violence against Women," http://www.un.org/en/women/endviolence/, accessed February 1, 2010.

Barton, Greg (2002), *Abdurrahman Wahid, Muslim Democrat, Indonesian President: A View from the Inside*. Honolulu, HI: UNSW Press.

Barzilai-Lumbroso, Ruth (2009), "Turkish Men and the History of Ottoman Women: Studying the History of the Ottoman Dynasty's Private Sphere through Women's Writings," *Journal of Middle East Women's Studies* 5 (2) (Spring), pp. 53–82.

Baxter, Craig (1998), *Bangladesh: From a Nation to a State* (Nations of the Modern World). Boulder, CO: Westview Press.

Begum, Anwara (2006), "Asian Women Leaders: A Comparative Study of the Images of Khaleda Zia and Sheikh Hasina of Bangladesh," *Asian Profile* 34 (3), pp. 265–80.

Bennett, Clinton (2005), *Muslims and Modernity: An Introduction to the Issues and Debates*. London: Continuum.

Bettencourt, Alice (2000), *Violence against Women in Pakistan*. Denver, CO: University of Denver International Human Rights Advocacy Center, http://www.du.edu/intl/humanrights/violencepkstn.pdf, accessed February 1, 2010.

Bhutto, Benazir (1989), *Daughter of Destiny: An Autobiography*. New York: Simon & Schuster.

Bhutto, Benazir (1998), "Politics and the Muslim Woman," in Kurzman (ed.), *Liberal Islam*, pp. 107–11.

Bhutto, Benazir (2008), *Reconciliation: Islam, Democracy, and the West*. New York: HarperCollins.

Blackburn, Susan (2004), *Women and the State in Modern Indonesia*, Cambridge, UK: Cambridge University Press.

Bukhārī, Muḥammad ibn Ismāīl and Muhammad Muhsin Khan (1987), *The Translation of the Meanings of Sahih al-Bukhari: Arabic–English*. New Delhi: Khitab Bhavan.

Burnell, Peter J. (2006), *Democratization through the Looking-glass* (Perspectives on Democratization). New Brunswick, NJ: Transaction Publishers.

Brendon, Piers (2008), *The Decline and Fall of the British Empire, 1781–1997*. New York: Alfred A. Knopf.

Bryce, Trevor (2005), *The Kingdom of the Hittites*. Oxford: Oxford University Press.

Carroll, Richard J. (1995), *An Economic Record of Presidential Performance: From Truman to Bush*. Westport, CT: Praeger.

Central Intelligence Agency (2009), *The World Factbook*. Washington, DC: CIA, https://www.cia.gov/library/publications/the-world-factbook/.

Chakrabarti, Sumon K. (2007), "Bangladesh, a Nation in Crisis," *World 360* CNN-IBN report, June 3rd, http://ibnlive.in.com/news/ bangladesh-a-nation-in-crisis/42058-2–single.html, accessed February 1, 2010.

Chatterji, Joya (1994), *Bengal Divided: Hindu Communalism and Partition, 1932–1947* (Cambridge South Asian Studies). Cambridge, UK: Cambridge University Press.

Cheema, Pervaz Iqbal (2004), "The Muslim League: Decline of a National Party," in Mitra *et al.* (eds), *Political Parties in South Asia*, pp. 130–55.

Chowdhury, Mahfuzul H. (2003), *Democratization in South Asia: Lessons from American Institutions*. Burlington, VT: Ashgate.

Chowdhury, Najma (1994), "Bangladesh: Gender Issues and Politics in a Patriarchy," in Nelson and Chowdhury (eds), *Women and Politics Worldwide*, pp. 94–113.

Chowdhury, Nazma and Barbara Nelson with Kathryn A. Carber, Nancy J. Johnson and Paula O'Loughlin (1994), "Redefining Politics: Patterns of Women's Political Engagement from a Global Perspective," in Nelson and Chowdhury (eds), *Women and Politics Worldwide*, pp. 3–24.

Chowdhury, Obaid (2009), "August 15, 1975: Coup or Killing? The Nation Must Learn the Truth" (*News from Bangladesh* report), Dhaka: Daily News Monitoring Service. September 8, http://newsfrom-bangladesh.net/view.php?hidRecord=283796, accessed February 1, 2010.

Çinar, Alev and Özudun, Ergun (2002), "Mesut Yilmaz: From Özal's Shadow to Mediator," in Heper and Sayari (eds), *Political Leaders and Democracy in Turkey*, pp. 181–98.

Cizre, Ümit (2002), "Tansu Çiller: Lusting For Power and Undermining Democracy," in Heper and Sayari (eds), *Political Leaders and Democracy in Turkey*, pp. 199–216.

Cohen, Stephen Philip (2004), *The Idea of Pakistan*. Washington, DC: Brookings Institution Press.

Commonwealth Secretariat (1999), *Women in Politics: Voices from the Commonwealth*. London: Commonwealth Secretariat.

Cromer, Lord Evelyn Baring (1916), *Modern Egypt*, Vol. 2. New York: Macmillan.

Dahlerup, Drude (2009), "Increasing Women's Political Representation: New Trends in Gender Quotas," in Ballington and Karam (eds), *Women in Parliament*, pp. 141–53.

Daily Star (2009), "Faruque Provoked All with Monarchy Story – Said in His Confession that Monarchy to be Declared Aug 15," Dhaka: *The Daily Star*, October 7, front page, http://www.thedailystar.net/story.php?nid=108630, accessed February 1, 2010.

Daniel, Norman (1966), *Islam, Europe and Empire*. Edinburgh: Edinburgh University Press.

Dar, Bashir Ahmad (1971), *Religious Thought of Sayyid Ahmad Khan*. Lahore: Institute of Islamic Culture.

Duran, Khalid (1995), "Bosnia: The Other Andalusia" in Abedin, Syeed Z. and Sarder, Ziaudin (eds), *Muslim Minorities in the West*. London: Grey Seal, pp. 25–36.

East, Roger and Richard Thomas (2003), *Profiles of People in Power: The World's Government Leaders*. London: Europa.

Eklöf Amirell, Stefan (2003), *Power and Political Culture in Suharto's Indonesia: The Indonesian Democratic Party (PDI) and Decline of the New Order (1986–98)*. Copenhagen: NIAS.

Esack, Farid (1997), *Qur'an, Liberation & Pluralism: An Islamic Perspective of Interreligious Solidarity against Oppression*. Oxford: Oneworld.

Esack, Farid (2005), *The Qur'an: A User's Guide – A Guide to Its Key Themes, History and Interpretation*. Oxford: Oneworld.

Esposito, John L. and John O. Voll (1996), *Islam and Democracy*. New York: Oxford University Press.

Evans, Eric J. (2004), *Thatcher and Thatcherism* (The Making of the Contemporary World series). London: Routledge.

Fic, Victor M. (2003), *From Majapahit and Sukuh to Megawati Sukarnoputri: Continuity and Change in Pluralism of Religion,*

Culture and Politics of Indonesia from the XV to the XXI Century. New Delhi: Abhinav Publications.

Forshee, Jill (2006), *Culture and Customs of Indonesia* (Culture and Customs of Asia series). Westport, CT: Greenwood Press.

Freedom in the World (2007), Washington, DC: Freedom House, http://www.freedomhouse.org/template.cfm?page=15, accessed February 1, 2010.

Fromkin, David (1989), *A Peace to End All Peace: The Fall of the Ottoman Empire and the Creation of the Modern Middle East.* New York: Avon.

Gandhi, Rajmohan (1986), *Eight Lives: A Study of the Hindu–Muslim Encounter.* Albany, NY: State University of New York Press.

Geertz, Clifford (1968), *Islam Observed: Religious Development in Morocco and Indonesia.* Chicago: Chicago University Press.

Gorjão, Paulo (2002), "Abdurrahman's Presidency: What Went Wrong?", in Soesastro *et al.* (eds), *Governance in Indonesia*, pp. 13–43.

Gouda, Frances (2002), "Militant Masculinity and Female Agency in Indonesia, 1945–1949," in Gregory Blue, Martin P. Bunton and Ralph C. Croizier (eds), *Colonialism and the Modern World: Selected Studies* (Sources and Studies in World History). Armonk, NY: M. E. Sharpe, pp. 200–18.

Gray, John (2007), *Black Mass: Apocalyptic Religion and the Death of Utopia.* New York: Farrar, Straus and Giroux.

Gultekin, Recep (2004), "Corruption in Turkey: An Overview," in Rick Sarre, Dilip K. Das and Hans-Jörg Albrecht (eds), *Policing Corruption: International Perspectives.* Lanham, MD: Lexington Books, pp. 189–206.

Gupta, Om (2006), *Encyclopaedia of India, Pakistan and Bangladesh.* Delhi: Isha Books.

Hadiwinata, Bob S. (2003), *The Politics of NGOs in Indonesia: Developing Democracy and Managing a Movement* (RoutledgeCurzon Research on Southeast Asia, 3). London: RoutledgeCurzon.

Hardy, Peter (1972), *The Muslims of British India.* Cambridge, UK: Cambridge University Press.

Harris, George (2002), "Celal Bayer: Conspiratorial Democrat," in Heper and Sayari (eds), *Political Leaders and Democracy in Turkey.* Lanham, MD: Lexington Books, pp. 45–64.

Hasan, Mushirul (1993), *India's Partition: Process, Strategy, and Mobilization* (Oxford in India readings). Delhi: Oxford University Press.

Hashmi, Taj ul-Islam (2000), *Women and Islam in Bangladesh: Beyond Subjection and Tyranny.* Basingstoke, Hampshire: Palgrave.

Hefner, Robert W. (2000), *Civil Islam: Muslims and Democratization in Indonesia* (Princeton Studies in Muslim Politics). Princeton, NJ: Princeton University Press.

Heitzman, James and Robert Worden (eds) (1989), *Bangladesh: A Country Study*. Washington: GPO for the Library of Congress, 1989; http://countrystudies.us/bangladesh/, accessed February 1, 2010.

Helsinger, Elizabeth K., Robin Lauterbach Sheets and William Veeder (1983), *The Woman Question: Society and Literature in Britain and America, 1837–1883*. Manchester: Manchester University Press.

Heper, Metin (2002), "Conclusion," in Metin Heper and Sabri Sayari (eds), *Political Leaders and Democracy in Turkey*, pp. 199–216.

Heper, Metin and Aylin Güney (2004), "Civil–Military Relations, Political Islam and Security: The Turkish Case," in Constantine P. Danopoulos, Dhirendra K. Vajpeyi and Amir Bar-Or (eds), *Civil–Military Relations, Nation Building, and National Identity: Comparative Perspectives*. Westport, CT: Praeger, pp. 183–96.

Heper, Metin and Sabri Sayari (2002), *Political Leaders and Democracy in Turkey*. Lanham, MD: Lexington Books.

Hershlag, Zvi Yehuda (1980), *Introduction to the Modern Economic History of the Middle East*. Leiden: Brill.

Horton, Rosalind and Sally Simmons (2007), *Women Who Changed the World*. London: Quercus.

Hossain, Golam (2004), "Bangladesh National Party: From Military Rule to the Champion of Democracy," in Mitra *et al.* (eds), *Political Parties in South Asia*, pp. 196–215.

Hossain, Kamrul (2003), "In Search of Equality: Marriage-related Laws for Muslim Women in Bangladesh," *Journal of International Women's Studies* 5 (1) (November), pp. 96–113.

House of Commons (2008), *Factsheet M4* (Members Series). London: House of Commons Information Office, http://www.parliament.uk/documents/upload/M04.pdf, accessed February 1, 2010.

Human Development Report (2007/2008), New York: UNDP.

Hunter, William Wilson (1871), *The Indian Musalmans: Are They Bound in Conscience to Rebel against the Queen?* London: Trübner and Co.

Hussain, Naseem A. and M. Salimullah Khan (1998), "Culture and Politics in Bangladesh: Some Reflections," in Bayes, Abdul and Muhammad, (eds), *Bangladesh at 25: An Analytical Discourse on Development*. Dhaka: The University Press, pp. 197–216.

Iqbal, Muhammad (1930), *The Reconstruction of Religious Thought in Islam*. Oxford: Oxford University Press.

Iqbal, Muhammad (1998), "The Principle of Movement in the Structure of Islam," in Kurzman (ed.), *Liberal Islam*, pp. 255–69.

Iqbal, Muhammad (2002), "Islam as a Moral and Political Idea," in Kurzman (ed.), *Modernist Islam*, pp. 304–13.

Jaffrelot, Christophe (2004), *A History of Pakistan and Its Origins*. London: Anthem Press.

Jalal, Ayesha (1985), *The Sole Spokesman: Jinnah, the Muslim League, and the Demand for Pakistan* (Cambridge South Asian Studies, 31). Cambridge, UK: Cambridge University Press.

Jayapalan, N. (2000), *India and Her Neighbours*. New Delhi: Atlantic Publishers.

Johari, J. C. (1993), *Voices of Indian Freedom Movement*. New Delhi, India: Akashdeep Publishing House.

Jones, Owen Bennett (2002), *Pakistan: Eye of the Storm*. New Haven, CT: Yale University Press.

Kahf, Mohja (1999), *Western Representations of the Muslim Woman: From Termagant to Odalisque*. Austin, TX: University of Texas Press.

Karlekar, Hiranmay (2005), *Bangladesh: The Next Afghanistan?* London: Sage.

Katz, Richard S. (1997), *Democracy and Elections*. New York: Oxford University Press.

Keddie, Nikki R. (2007), *Women in the Middle East: Past and Present*. Princeton, NJ: Princeton University Press.

Khan, Sayyid Ahmed (1871), "Review of W. W. Hunter's *The Indian Musalmans: Writings and Speeches of Sir Sayyid Ahmed Khan*," ed. Shan Mohammed. Bombay: Nachiketa Publications, pp. 66–82.

Khan, Sayyid Ahmed (2002), "Lecture on Islam," in Kurzman (ed.), *Modernist Islam 1840–1940*, pp. 291–303.

Kingsbury, Damien (2002), *The Politics of Indonesia*. South Melbourne, Victoria: Oxford University Press.

Kingsbury, Damien (2003), *Power Politics and the Indonesian Military*. London: Routledge.

Kinzer, Stephen (1999), "Back to the Center of Turkish Power," *New York Times*, January 15, http://www.nytimes.com/1999/01/15/ world/back-to-the-center-of-turkish-power.html.

Krämer, Heinz (2000), *A Changing Turkey: The Challenge to Europe and the United States*. Washington, DC: Brookings Inst. Press.

Krook, Mona Lena (2009), *Quotas for Women in Politics Gender and Candidate Selection Reform Worldwide*. Oxford: Oxford University Press.

Kukreja, Veena (2003), *Contemporary Pakistan: Political Processes, Conflicts, and Crises*. New Delhi: Sage Publications.

Kurzman, Charles (1998), *Liberal Islam: A Sourcebook*. New York: Oxford University Press.

Kurzman, Charles (2002), *Modernist Islam 1840–1940: A Sourcebook*. New York: Oxford University Press.

Lewis, Bernard (1984) *The Jews of Islam*. Princeton, NJ: Princeton Univesity Press.

Lewis, Reina (2004), *Rethinking Orientalism: Women, Travel and the Ottoman Harem*. New Brunswick, NJ: Rutgers University Press.

Lindholm, Cherry and Charles Lindholm (1993), "Life Behind the Veil," in David E. K. Hunter and Philip Whitten (eds), *Anthropology: Contemporary Perspectives*. New York: HarperCollins College Publishers.

Lindsey, Timothy (2008), *Indonesia: Law and Society*. Annandale, NSW: Federation.

Lubis, Tudung Mulya (2002), "Constitutional Reforms," in Soesastro *et al.* (eds), *Governance in Indonesia*, pp. 106–13.

Mahmutćehajić, Rusmir (2000), *Bosnia the Good: Tolerance and Tradition*. Budapest and New York: Central European University Press.

Mango, Andrew (2002), "Atatürk: Founding Father, Realist and Visionary," in Heper and Sayari (eds), *Political Leaders and Democracy in Turkey*, pp. 9–24.

Maranto, Robert, Tom Lansford and Jeremy Johnson (2009), *Judging Bush*. Stanford, CA: Stanford University Press.

Marcus, Rachel. 1993 *Violence against Women in Bangladesh, Pakistan, Egypt and Sudan*. Institute of Brighton: University of Sussex Institute Development Studies, http://www.bridge.ids.ac.uk//bridge/Reports/re10c.pdf, accessed February 1, 2010.

Matin, Abdul (1997), *Sheikh Hasina: The Making of a Prime Minister*. London: Radical Asia Publications.

Mawdudi, Abul A'la (1955), *Islamic Law and Constitution* (ed. Khurshid Ahmed). Karachi: Jamaat-e-Islami Publications.

Mawdudi, Abul A'la (1972), *Purdah and the Status of Women in Islam*, 2nd edn (1st edn 1939) Lahore: Islamic Publications Ltd.

Mawdudi, Abul A'la (1996), *Jihad in Islam*. Kuwait: International Islamic Federation of Student Organizations.

Mawdudi, Abul A'la (1999), "Political Theory of Islam," in Khurshid Ahmad (ed.), *Islam: Its Meaning and Message*. Leicester: The Islamic Foundation, pp. 147–71.

McIntyre, Angus (1997), *In Search of Megawati Sukarnoputri* (Working papers, Centre of Southeast Asian Studies, 103). Clayton: Monash University.

McIntyre, Angus (2005), *The Indonesian Presidency: The Shift from Personal toward Constitutional Rule*. Lanham, MD: Rowman & Littlefield.

Mernissi, Fatima (1991), *The Veil and the Male Elite: A Feminist Interpretation of Women's Rights in Islam*. Cambridge, MA: Perseus.

Mernissi, Fatima (1992), *Islam and Democracy: Fear of the Modern World*, trans. Mary Jo Lakeland. Cambridge, MA: Perseus.

Mernissi, Fatima (1998), "A Feminist Interpretation of Women's Rights in Islam," in Kurzman (ed.), *Liberal Islam*, pp. 112–26.

Mernissi, Fatima and Mary Jo Lakeland (1993), *The Forgotten Queens of Islam*. Minneapolis: University of Minnesota Press.

Metcalf, Barbara Daly and Thomas R. Metcalf (2002), *A Concise History of India* (Cambridge Concise Histories). Cambridge, UK: Cambridge University Press.

Metz, Helen Chapin (1995), *Turkey: A Country Study*. Washington, DC: GPO for the Library of Congress, Metz's Library of Congress Country Study http://countrystudies.us/turkey/.

The Mishkat-al-Masabih, trans. James Robson, 2 vols. Lahore: Muhammad Ashraf, 1990.

Mitra, Subrata Kumar, Mike Enskat and Clemens Spiess (eds) (2004), *Political Parties in South Asia: Political Parties in Context*. Westport, CT: Praeger.

Moghadam, Valentine M., *From Patriarchy to Empowerment: Women's Participation, Movements, and Rights in the Middle East, North Africa, and South Asia*. Ithaca, NY: Syracuse University Press, 2007.

Moghissi, Haideh (1999), *Feminism and Islamic Fundamentalism: The Limits of Postmodern Analysis*. London and New York: Zed Books.

Moghissi, Haideh (2005), *Women and Islam: Critical Concepts in Sociology* (Critical Concepts in Sociology series). London: Routledge.

Molla, Gyasuddin (2004), "The Awami League: From Charismatic Leadership to Political Party," in Mitra *et al.* (eds), *Political Parties in South Asia*, pp. 216–35.

Morin, Isobel V. (1994), *Women of the U.S. Congress*. Minneapolis: Oliver Press.

Müftüler-Bac, Meltem (1999), "Turkish Women's Predicament," *Women's Studies International Forum* 22 (3), pp. 303–15.

Muir, William (1915), *The Caliphate: Its Rise, Decline and Fall*. Edinburgh: John Grant.

Nafisi, Azar (2008), *Reading Lolita in Tehran: A Memoir in Books*. New York: Random House.

An-Na'im, Abdullah Ahmed (1998), "Shar'ia and Basic Human Rights Concerns," in Kurzman (ed.), *Liberal Islam*, pp. 222–38.

Naipaul, Vidiadhar Surajprasad (1998), *Among the Non-Believers: An Islamic Journey*. London: Peter Smith.

Nasr, Seyyed Vali Reza (2001), *Islamic Leviathan: Islam and the Making of State Power*. New York: Oxford University Press.

Nasrin, Taslima (2000), "They Wanted to Kill Me," *Middle East Quarterly* 7 (3) (September), pp. 67–74.

Nelson, Barbara J. and Najma Chowdhury (1994), *Women and Politics Worldwide*. New Haven: Yale University Press.

Novak, James J. (1993), *Bangladesh: Reflections on the Water* (The Essential Asia series). Bloomington, IN: Indiana University Press.

Nurbakhsh, Javad (1983), *Sufi Women*. New York: Khaniqah-Nimatullah Publications.

Office of the Law Commission, Government of Bangladesh (2005), *Report on a reference by the government towards the possibility of framing out a uniform family code for all the communities of Bangladesh relating to marriage, divorce, guardianship, inheritance, etc.* Dhaka: BDLC, http://www.commonlii.org/bd/other/BDLC/report/R69/69.pdf, accessed February 1, 2010.

O'Shea, Stephen (2006), *Sea of Faith: Islam and Christianity in the Medieval Mediterranean World*. New York: Walker & Co.

Özdalga, Elizabeth (2002), "Necmettin Erbakan: Democracy for the Sake of Power," in Heper and Sayari (eds), *Political Leaders and Democracy in Turkey*, pp. 127–46.

Parawansa, Khofifah Indar (2009), "Enhancing Women's Political Participation in Indonesia," in Ballington and Karam (eds), *Women in Parliament*, pp. 82–90.

Pipes, Daniel (1995), "Tansu Çiller: 'Secularism is an Indispensable Principle for Turkey'," *Middle East Quarterly* 2 (2) (June), pp. 73–80.

Prasetyawan, Wahyu (2005), "Indonesia Election 2004: A Political Economy Perspective," in *Kyoto Review of Southeast Asia 6*. Kyoto: Centre for Southeast Asiatudies, http://kyotoreview.cseas.kyoto-u.ac.jp/issue/issue5/article_479_p.html, accessed February 1, 2010.

Rai, Shirin M. (2009), "Reserved Seats in South Asia: A Regional Perspective," in Ballington and Karam (eds), *Women in Parliament*, pp. 174–84.

Raudvere, Catharina (2003), *The Book and the Roses: Sufi Women, Visibility, and Zikir in Contemporary Istanbul*. Istanbul: Swedish Research Institute in Istanbul.

Reynolds, David (2000), *One World Divisible: A Global History since 1945* (The Global Century series). New York: W. W. Norton.

Riaz, Ali (2004), *God Willing: The Politics of Islamism in Bangladesh*. Lanham, MD: Rowman & Littlefield.

Rinakit, Sukardi (2005), *The Indonesian Military after the New Order.* Copenhagen: NIAS Press.

Sabbagh, Amal (2009), "The Arab States: Enhancing Women's Political Participation," in Ballington and Karam (eds), *Women in Parliament,* pp. 52–71.

Saeed, Abdullah (2008), *The Qur'an: An Introduction.* London: Routledge.

Sayyid, Bobby (1988), *Fundamental Fear: Eurocentrism and the Emergence of Islamism.* London: Zed.

Schmetzer, Uli (2001), "Indonesia has Calm First Day under New Leader," *Chicago Tribune,* July 24, http://www.chicagotribune.com/topic/sns-indonesia,0,5981989.story, accessed February 1, 2010.

Senevirate, Kalinga (2003), "Megawati Snub Reflects Touchy Ties with Australia," Chinah Mai: *The Irrewaddy.* October 10, http://www.irrawaddy.org/article.php?art_id=74, accessed February 1, 2010.

Shah, Sayed Wiqar Ali (2004), "Pakistan People's Party: The Twin Legacies of Socialism and Dynastic Rule," in Mitra *et al.* (eds), *Political Parties in South Asia,* pp. 156–76.

Shehabuddin, Elora (2008), *Reshaping the Holy: Democracy, Development and Women in Bangladesh.* New York: Columbia University Press.

Shvedova, Nadezhda (2009), "Obstacles to Women's Participation in Parliament," in Julie Ballington and Azza Karam (eds), *Women in Parliament: Beyond Numbers,* pp. 33–50.

Siddiqa, Ayesha (2007), *Military Inc.: Inside Pakistan's Military Economy.* London: Pluto Press.

Smith, Anthony L. (2002), "Epilogue: The Bali Bombing and Responses to International Terrorism," in Soesastro *et al.* (eds), *Governance in Indonesia,* pp. 305–22.

Smith, Margaret (2001), *Muslim Women Mystics: The Life and Work of Rabika and other Women Mystics in Islam.* Oxford: Oneworld.

Sobhani, Rob S. (2005), "A Model for the Middle East: Qatar's Progressive Path," *World & I* (November–December), pp. 18–33.

Soesastro, Hadi (2002), "Introduction: Indonesia under Megawati," in Soesastro *et al.* (eds), *Governance in Indonesia,* pp. 1–12.

Soesastro, Hadi, Anthony L. Smith and Mui Ling Han (2002), *Governance in Indonesia: Challenges Facing the Megawati Presidency.* Singapore: Institute of Southeast Asian Studies.

Souroush, Abdolkarim (2000), *Reason, Freedom and Democracy in Islam.* Oxford: Oxford University Press.

Sow, Fatoumata (1989), "Le Harem Politique," *Fippu, Journal de Yewwu Yewwi pour a la liberation des femmes,* No. 2. Dakar: Senegal, p. 33.

Sudarsono, Juwono (2007), "The Military's Dual Function," in John H. McGlynn and Hermawan Sulistyo (eds), *Indonesia in the Soeharto Years: Issues, Incidents, and Images*. Jakarta, Indonesia: Lontar (in association with Ridge Books), pp. 151–7.

Suryadinata, Leo (2002), *Elections and Politics in Indonesia*. Singapore: Institute of Southeast Asian Studies.

Tachau, Frank (2002) "Bülent Ecevit: From Idealist to Pragmatist," in Heper and Sayari (eds), *Political Leaders and Democracy in Turkey*. Lanham, MD: Lexington Books, pp 107–26.

Ṭāhā, Maḥmūd Muḥammad (1987), *The Second Message of Islam* (Contemporary Issues in the Middle East). Syracuse, NY: Syracuse University Press.

Ṭāhā, Maḥmūd Muḥammad (1998), "The Second Message of Islam," in Kurzman (ed.), *Liberal Islam*, pp. 270–83.

Thompson, Mark R. (2003), "Female Leadership of Democratic Transitions in Asia," *Pacific Affairs Journal* 75 (4), pp. 535–55.

Thompson, Mark R. (2004), *Democratic Revolutions: Asia and Eastern Europe* (Routledge Research in Comparative Politics, 5). London: Routledge.

Tibi, Bassam (1988), *The Challenge of Fundamentalism: Political Islam and the New World Disorder*. Berkeley, CA: University of California Press.

Turner, Bryan S. (2003), *Islam, State and Politics*. London: Routledge.

Vaswani, Karishma (2010), "Indonesia's Army 'Retains Business Empire'." London: BBC News report, January 12, http://news.bbc.co.uk/2/hi/asia-pacific/8452829.stm, accessed February 1, 2010.

Vatikiotis, Michael R. J. (1992), *Indonesia under Suharto: Order, Development, and Pressure for Change* (Routledge Politics in Asia series). London: Routledge.

Wadud, Aminah (1998), "Qur'an and Women," in Kurzman (ed.), *Liberal Islam*, pp. 127–38.

Wadud, Aminah (1999), *Qur'an and Women: Rereading the Sacred Text from a Woman's Perspective*. New York: Oxford University Press.

Wanandi, Jusuf (2002), "Challenge of the TNI and Its Role in Indonesia's Future," in Soesastro *et al.* (eds), *Governance in Indonesia*, pp. 91–105.

Women in Congress. Washington, DC: Office of the Clerk, US House of Representatives. http://womenincongress.house.gov/, accessed February 1, 2010.

World Bank (2009), *GDP 2008*. Washington, DC. World Bank.

Index